1983

Gogol's
Dead Souls

James B. Woodward

Gogol's
Dead
Souls

PRINCETON UNIVERSITY PRESS

Princeton, New Jersey

Published by Princeton University Press,
Princeton, New Jersey
In the United Kingdom: Princeton University Press,
Guildford, Surrey

Library of Congress Cataloging in Publication Data will
be found on the last printed page of this book

Publication of this book has been aided by a grant from
the Paul Mellon Fund of Princeton University Press

This book has been composed in VIP Bembo

Printed in the United States of America
by Princeton University Press, Princeton, New Jersey

Contents

	Preface	vii
	Introduction	ix
1	Sobakevich	3
2	Nozdryov	33
3	Manilov	52
4	Korobochka	70
5	Plyushkin	106
6	The Masters and the Slaves	138
7	The Masters and the Ladies	171
8	Forgeries of Fact and Counterfeit Truths	192
9	The "Paternal" Theme	215
10	Chichikov and Russia	230
	Conclusion	252
	Notes	257

Preface

Alone of the great Russian novels of the nineteenth century Gogol's *Dead Souls (Myortvyye dushi)* remains nearly as profound a mystery today as when it first appeared. With the possible exception of some of its author's shorter narratives, it is the most perplexing work of fiction in the Russian language—a work that appears to owe no significant debt to any literary tradition, to elude every attempt at an all-embracing interpretation, and to be explicable only as the bizarre creation of a bizarre personality. Virtually every important aspect of the novel is still subject to sharply contrasting judgments, and even the term *novel* is applied to it with some hesitation, as Gogol emphatically called it an "epic poem [*poema*]."

In the present book an attempt is made to dispel some of the confusion by examining the fundamental question of how the first part of the projected three-part "epic"—the only part completed—functions as a work of art. The premise here, quite simply, is that the traditional view of the novel as a sprawling mass of loosely connected episodes, details, and digressions which often bear little perceptible relation to the plot (i.e. the story of the hero's adventures) is entirely misconceived and attributable to a failure to determine the nature of Gogol's creative method. The purpose of the book is to provide a new interpretation of the novel's meaning by tracing the essential features of this method and to show thereby that its structure is not only far more taut and disciplined than it appears, but also highly expressive. It is hoped that these conclusions will lay a sound foundation for future debate.

References to the novel are to the definitive version and early drafts contained in volume VI of the fourteen-volume edition of Gogol's works published by the Soviet Academy of Sciences,[1] and page numbers are entered in the text. In references to the edition in footnotes the abbreviation *PSS* is used. Unless otherwise indicated, all translations from the Russian are my own and all dates are in "Old Style."

J.B.W.
Swansea
November 1977

Introduction

Art instills harmony and order into the soul, not confusion and disorder. —N. V. Gogol[1]

Strangely enough, the central theme of *Dead Souls* is one of the few aspects of the novel about which no serious dispute exists. The title of the work expresses it succinctly. It is true that the ambiguity of the noun *dushi* (which means "serfs" as well as "souls") raises the question of the importance to be attached in the novel to the social theme of serfdom and its evils, and that Western and Soviet critics differ sharply in their attitudes to this question, but no one presumably would disagree that from beginning to end the novel is primarily an exposé of mortified souls.

The major dispute concerns the manner in which this theme is developed, and the two extreme views on this subject associated with the names of Belinsky and Nabokov are sufficiently well known to obviate the need for further lengthy summaries. It will suffice to reiterate that according to Belinsky, from whom Soviet critics have almost unanimously taken their cue, the exposé is achieved by means of a satirical portrayal of Russian life and society that is basically realistic in character, and Nabokov contends that the world of *Dead Souls* is essentially a creation of the author's fantasy designed to provide glimpses of the *realiora*—in his own phrase, "the shadows of other worlds"[2]—behind the façade of contingent *realia*.

The view most commonly held by Western critics is that the truth probably lies somewhere between these two extremes—that while Nabokov's view is the more convincing, it cannot be held to the complete exclusion of the opposite view. Hence the kind of compromise that may be illustrated by Victor Erlich's following comments on the novel:

> If . . . the sloth, the greed, the stupidity of the freakish squires in *Dead Souls* are not *the* point, these are graphic illustrations of the point, a telling mode of symbolization. The social institutions which were part of Gogol's immediate environment provided here the appropriate set of images, or to use T. S. Eliot's phrase, the "objective correlative" for an idiosyncratic moral vision of reality.[3]

Thus Erlich replaces Nabokov's "shadows" with "an idiosyncratic moral vision" and implies that while Gogol is prepared to distort reality for the purpose of projecting this vision, he nevertheless presents a recognizable picture of contemporary Russian institutions and character-types which may justly be regarded as a social satire.

This view is as acceptable to the present writer as it probably is to most Western readers, but it clearly casts no more light on the mysteries of Gogol's art than the two extreme views. Restricting the term "mode of symbolization" to mean little more than "fictional material," Erlich, like most of his predecessors, confines his scrutiny to the surface of the text and simply repeats the conventional arguments about its "centrifugal impulse," its "lateral darts," and its "upward flights," i.e. its alleged digressive character, which he makes no attempt to explain. As before, Gogol is accredited with creating a magnificent work of art while seemingly ignoring one of the fundamental requirements of art—coherence.

From the critics let us turn briefly for illumination to Gogol himself—in particular, to two of his statements that at least provide a certain indication of the manner in which the text should be approached. The first, from *An Author's Confession (Avtorskaya ispoved')* (1847), has often been quoted and describes the early stages of writing the novel:

> I began to write without drawing up a detailed plan for myself and even without any clear idea of the kind of character the hero should be. I simply thought that the comic scheme which Chichikov was engaged in carrying out would itself lead me to a variety of characters and that my personal desire to laugh would itself create a large number of comic episodes which I intended to combine with episodes of an affective character. But at each step I was halted by the questions: Why? What is the purpose of this? What should be expressed through this character? What should this phenomenon express? . . . I saw plainly that I could no longer write without a clearly defined plan and that I must first of all clarify to myself the purpose of my work.[4]

The second statement is taken from the novel itself. It is an apostrophe to the reader interpolated into the description of Chichikov's approach to Manilov's estate in chapter two:

> Here you must strain your attention with great effort before you can make all the subtle, almost invisible features disclose themselves to you, and in general you must penetrate deeply with your eye which has already become expert in the art of eliciting truth. (24)

The first passage informs us not only that the novel was written according to a clearly defined plan and purpose, but, in effect, that the choice of every character and "phenomenon" was dictated by this purpose. The second tells us implicitly that in order to discern this purpose we must penetrate beneath the narrative and descriptive façade. Gogol is telling us, in short, that his novel has a distinct intellectual and aesthetic coherence and that its sources are deeply immersed in the text and therefore not immediately apparent.[5]

The two critics whose studies of the novel have shown the clearest awareness of this fact are Andrey Belyy[6] and Carl R. Proffer,[7] both of whom have appreciated that in relation to the central theme of the work the plot (understood as the story of Chichikov's adventures) is of relatively minor importance and that the theme is chiefly developed by means of inconspicuous patterns of scattered details. With his celebrated observations on the recurrent references in the novel to the various types of "sideways movement" executed by Chichikov, Belyy has come closer than any other critic to illuminating the essential features of Gogol's creative method, and one can only regret that he was seduced from his inquiries into Gogol's "plot of details" and his "symbolism of trivialities"[8] by the euphonic attractions of his prose. He leaves us with merely a few random samples of unrelated patterns. In his admirable study of the similes of the novel, Proffer offers a number of similar insights. Inevitably compelled to look beyond the similes to their connections with the rest of the text, he is led to conclude not only that "seemingly inapposite detail may actually be important and germane to a given simile,"[9] but that the novel as a whole "is a maze of these interrelated details and repetitions."[10] For obvious reasons he is able to attempt only a limited substantiation of this truth.

The studies of Belyy and Proffer illustrate the only approach to the novel that can lead to a proper understanding of how it functions as a work of art. At the same time their interpretations of the patterns and connections that they establish are often deficient or questionable, simply because plausible conclusions can be reached only on the basis of an examination of all the major patterns in their development and interaction. Only against this wider background is it possible to discern the sources of the novel's coherence, of which the individual patterns of details detected by Belyy and Proffer are merely signals. It is precisely this kind of comprehensive examination that has prompted the conclusions of the present study.

The basic argument of this study is that *Dead Souls* is no less an allegory than the work by which it was probably more profoundly influenced than by any other—*The Divine Comedy* of Dante. It is contended that the central theme of the novel ("dead souls") is developed not only by means of the "bureaucratic, manorial imagery" to which Erlich refers,[11] but primarily with the aid of interrelated symbolic themes conveyed by elusive patterns of details which in combination with one another comprise the most complex and aesthetically compelling moral allegory in the Russian language—an allegory that is related to no Russian literary tradition, but rather harks back to the tradition of the medieval moral allegory and, beyond that, to the tradition of the allegorical journey through the underworld, which was a staple ingredient of the classical epic. Hence, perhaps, the genre-designation *poema*. It is suggested further that it was precisely to the structure and elusive elements of this allegory that Gogol was alluding when he spoke of a "clearly defined plan," urged us to strain our attention, and remarked, in another of his oft-quoted statements about the novel, that he wrote it "as a consequence not of imagination, but of consideration."[12]

The point has repeatedly been labored that Gogol's knowledge of Russian provincial life was extremely limited, and his own acknowledgment of his ignorance[13] is in itself, of course, an indication that a scrupulously accurate reproduction of the essential features of this life was far from his intentions. Yet he clearly knew enough about it to create an illusion capable of deceiving a Belinsky, if not a Nabokov. The important point is that Gogol took from Russian provincial life merely the details that enabled him to express the symbolic themes that were his point of departure in the creative process and that constitute the true source of the novel's unity. The factual aspect of Russian provincial life is consequently reflected, but the reflection is continually distorted by the process of adaptation whereby the concrete details are translated into symbolic motifs that signal the presence of the underlying themes. And there are strong grounds for believing that Gogol's term "consideration" denotes precisely this process. Herein lies the source of the oddities, discords, and apparent absurdities that produce most of

Gogol's comic effects. Yet it must be stressed that these symbolic motifs are by no means peepholes into eternity, as Nabokov would have us believe. They are peepholes simply into the symbolic themes that are the means by which the artist projects his central theme. The motifs are symbolic, not symbolistic.

Therefore, the general view of the novel advanced in this study is that it is an intricate labyrinth of details derived from various aspects of Russian provincial life, which are integrated on the basis of the symbolic themes that comprise the allegory. The distinction traditionally made between the central narrative and the so-called "digressions" is completely rejected. For it is here held that the content of the "digressions" is equally dictated by the allegory, and that they may justly be termed "digressions" only as part of the fictional façade. In reality, they are simply threads, like the narrative and descriptive sections of the text and the exchanges of dialogue, in the masterfully woven veil that is cast over the sources of the novel's aesthetic unity by an artist whose powers of deception far exceed those of his chameleonlike hero. Digressiveness is merely one of the rhetorical procedures with which Gogol conceals the real relations between words and the coordinative presence of the symbolic motifs.

At the same time, it would be patently implausible to argue that the uniquely variegated character of the façade can be attributed solely to the tendency to beguile, mystify, or deceive that Gogol continually displayed as both man and artist. The relationship between the façade and its symbolic substratum is certainly more complex than this, and it is necessary to remind ourselves in this connection of one self-evident fact that tends to be obscured—that although the universal implications of Gogol's character portraits were presumably apparent to him from the outset, his primary concern was to portray characters, in his own words, "in whom the mark of our fundamental, truly Russian characteristics is most clearly and deeply imprinted."[14] In other words, Gogol's theme is not simply the mortification of the soul, but the mortification of the Russian soul, and the symptoms of this mortification are explored at all levels and in every facet of a society that, despite all the distortions and hyperbole, remains unequivocally Russian. Gogol's object was clearly to extend his indictment to as many aspects of Russian life as possible, "to show," as he put it in one of his earliest comments on the novel, "the whole of Russia, at least from one side."[15] The so-called "digressions" were obviously his principal means of achieving this breadth.

It must be reemphasized, however, that they are digressions only in relation to the superficial narrative level of the novel. In relation to the allegory they are as relevant as any other part of the text, and it is one of the main aims of this study to provide convincing evidence for the conclusion that every "digression" in the work, large or small, is contextually apt by virtue of its relation to the symbolic theme or themes expressed through the motifs which dominate the context concerned. Contrary to Nabokov's contention,[16] Gogol's "guns" do not hang in midair, and they *do* go off.[17] Even the most digressive details retain their link with the allegorical basis, serving as conductors by which the allegory is extended to encompass material that reflects "the whole of Russia".

The final introductory point concerns the method of analysis that has been employed as the most appropriate means of substantiating the arguments presented. In theory, the choice would seem to lie between two methods, one based on an examination of each chapter in turn, and the other on a consideration of the development and function of each motif individually in the novel as a whole. In reality, however, there is no choice. The dominant motifs of the novel are so closely interwoven and interdependent that it is impossible to consider the significance of one without constant reference to the others with which it is combined in each successive context. With certain modifications, therefore, the first method has duly been adopted. But there is an additional, more cogent reason for selecting this method—Gogol's treatment of each chapter as a distinct context dominated by motifs that are in some cases confined to the chapter in question. It is true that some of the more important motifs are found in all eleven chapters, and others recur in the majority of them. They include not only those woven into the portrait of Chichikov, e.g. the references to his nose, his rotundity, his proneness to hopping and skipping, and the "sideways movements" noted by Belyy, but also such immense conglomerations of details as those one might generically refer to as the "military motif." Yet it is noticeable that their prominence is by no means uniform. Their role in some chapters is appreciably greater than in others, and it will be seen that in each case their return to prominence is explained by the context of the chapter concerned or, more precisely, by the symbolic themes that establish the context. Thus it is no accident, as the analysis shows, that the "military motif" is most prominent in chapter four of the novel, the "Nozdryov chapter," or that Gogol chooses to reveal the structure and contents of Chichikov's box and provide the first major glimpse of "the second—acquisitive—layer of Chichikov's character"[18] in the chapter that is chiefly devoted to the portrayal of the pathologically acquisitive Korobochka. These examples will suffice for the present to indicate that the primary relationship of a given motif each time it appears is with the other motifs that express the dominant symbolic themes of the chapter concerned, and that its presence in that chapter is explained precisely by that relationship.

The only chapter not examined individually is chapter one, owing to its primarily introductory character. It introduces the hero, his valet and driver, three of the five landowners, the wife of Sobakevich, the senior officials of the town, and a number of its formidable female inhabitants; it also introduces all the principal motifs of the chapters that follow. Viewed as a whole, the novel can be divided into two main sections: the five chapters (two through six) that record Chichikov's meetings with the five landowners, and the four chapters (seven through ten) in which the scene reverts to the town of N. Chapters one and eleven form the frame in which Gogol pulls together and knots the strands that wind their way individually and in clusters through the intervening chapters, combining them, in chapter one, in the portrayal of the town and its inhabitants and, in chapter eleven, in the biography of Chichikov. It is thereby implied that the town and Chichikov uniquely display all the various forms of spiritual mortification represented separately in chapters two through ten. The difficulty for the reader is that the implications of the various motifs, like the personality and background of Chichikov and the scheme that has brought him to the town, are disclosed only in the later chapters. The effect of chapter one, in other words, is to pose a succession of questions, the answers to which are provided at different stages in the subsequent development of the novel. It has been decided, therefore, to examine its content in the light of the "answers" as they successively reveal themselves.

Although, however, a whole chapter is devoted to each of the other ten chapters of the novel, Gogol's habit of furnishing the most revealing indications of the meaning of his motifs after they have already been used extensively has necessitated two deviations from a strictly chronological study, as a result of which chapters five and four (the portraits of Sobakevich and Nozdryov) are considered, in that order, before chapter two (the portrait of Manilov). The decision to begin with an examination of chapter five is explained by the fact that in this chapter Gogol introduces the criterion by which the condition of every soul in the novel is measured, the only substantial symbol in the novel of a soul which is not dead, moribund, or captive. This symbol is the key to the novel's most important symbolic themes to which the most recurrent motifs in the work are directly related. It may be argued, therefore, that an understanding of the symbolism in chapter five is a prerequisite for due appreciation of vitally important elements in every other chapter. The "premature" consideration of chapter four is similarly dictated by the need for early clarification of the "military motif." At the same time, these departures from chronology should not be taken to imply that no logic is perceptible in Gogol's arrangement of the five "portrait chapters." On the contrary, it is hoped that paradoxically the disruptions of chronology will shed new light on this "logic," and in chapter five of this study an attempt is made to interpret it.

Gogol's
Dead Souls

1

Sobakevich

In the second of his four letters on *Dead Souls* Gogol informs us that "the last half of the book is less finished than the first half" and that in the later chapters "the inner spirit of the whole work" is less striking than "the motley diversity of the parts."[1] By the first half he plainly meant, above all, the five "portrait chapters," and it is clear that in one respect at least he experienced rather less difficulty with them than with the chapters that follow. The distinctive feature of these chapters is that each is dominated by symbolic themes related to the psychological attributes of a single personality—that of the landowner concerned. In effect, the salient characteristics of this personality provide the entire contextual basis on which the development and interaction of motifs in the given chapter take place. In the later chapters, in which individual characters, except Chichikov, are less prominent than social groups, a comparable contextual cohesion was not so easily achieved.

Even so, a first reading of chapter five would certainly convey the impression that cohesion is perhaps the last quality which might appropriately be ascribed to it, for no other "portrait chapter" is so rich in apparent digressions or in incidents that seem totally unrelated to the central figure and his dialogues with Chichikov. To check the validity of this impression, we must begin by identifying the principal features that Gogol combines in the personality of Sobakevich.

Most conspicuous of all, of course, are the bearlike attributes denoted by his name, Mikhail Semyonovich—his immense, rough-hewn frame, his lumbering gait, his gargantuan appetite, his guile, and his misanthropy. Critical comment on

Sobakevich has generally not proceeded far beyond the enu-
meration and illustration of these features. Yet each of them is
merely the center of a whole constellation of details, which add
progressively to its significance and implications. Moreover,
the details comprising each individual constellation are not
only brought into repeated contact with those of the other
constellations; they also extend outward from their center to
the furthest limits of the chapter, i.e., to those parts that precede
the appearance of Sobakevich and follow his exit.

The misanthropy of Sobakevich, for example, which is high-
lighted on his first appearance in chapter one,[2] expresses itself
most blatantly in his reactions to Chichikov's complimentary
references, reminiscent of the earlier exchanges with Manilov,
to the senior officials of the town. Unlike Manilov, he responds
with a succession of "strong expressions": "fool" (*durak*),
"brigand" (*razboynik*), "scoundrel" (*moshennik*), and the term
moshennik rapidly develops into one of his main lexical
emblems. He concludes: "They are all scoundrels. The whole
town there is the same: one scoundrel sits on another and drives
him on with another scoundrel" (97). It is true that he compli-
ments the public prosecutor as "the only decent man among
them" (97), but in the same breath he calls him "a swine," from
which we may deduce that the compliment is prompted solely
by the prosecutor's profession, of which the misanthropist
could hardly disapprove; as a man, he is as contemptible as the
rest.

The significance, however, of Sobakevich's hostility to the
officials cannot be appreciated without due regard for the fact
that they are by no means the sole beneficiaries of his summary
judgments. Thus Chichikov's remarks on the quality of the
governor's cuisine immediately prompt a verbal assault on the
governor's chef—"the one who was taught by a Frenchman"
(98)—which culminates in a remarkable outburst on the merits
of the saddle of mutton, replete with buckwheat stuffing, that
adorns his own table:

> This is not one of those fricassees which are made in the
> kitchens of gentlemen out of mutton which has been lying

about for four days or so in the market. That's all been
invented by German and French doctors. I'd hang them
for it! They are the ones who thought up dieting and the
starvation cure! Just because they've got feeble German
constitutions, they imagine they can cope even with a
Russian stomach! (98–99)

Here we perceive perhaps the most important aspect of Sobakevich's misanthropy—its powerful nationalistic or chauvinistic
overtones. The "strong expressions" of Sobakevich are chiefly
motivated by a profound hostility to every manifestation of
foreign influence on Russian life—above all, to the Gallic customs of St. Petersburg. And since these customs are studiously
aped by the officials of the town of N., they may be plausibly
identified as the principal cause of Sobakevich's contempt for
these men. In an earlier version of the chapter the link with St.
Petersburg was established quite explicitly. Sobakevich's remark on the measures that he would personally take to eradicate the French and German doctors was followed by the
statement: "Just look at the eating habits of all these people
who have visited that Petersburg" (747).

It seems hardly coincidental, therefore, that the connection
between "strong expressions" and the Russian national character is not only introduced, *en passant,* in the first paragraph of
the chapter, but also forms the basis of the famous paean to the
Russian language in its last two paragraphs, the wholly personal, "literal," and digressive character of which has never
been questioned. Indeed, Belinsky criticized Gogol for giving
expression to such chauvinistic attitudes.[3] Reflecting, in the
opening paragraph, on his timely escape from Nozdryov,
Chichikov "promised Nozdryov all kinds of grievous and
fearful misfortunes; even a few strong words were said." And
the narrator adds: "What can one do? He is a Russian and,
what's more, a Russian in a rage" (89).[4] The immediate pretext
for the "digression" at the end of the chapter is the "strong
word" applied to Plyushkin by one of Sobakevich's peasants,
whose capacity for summary judgments duly reveals him to
be, like everyone and everything else on Sobakevich's estate, a

mirror of some aspect of his master. While Chichikov quietly chuckles to himself in his carriage, the narrator launches into his eulogy:

> The Russian people express themselves strongly! . . . How apt are all the sayings that have emerged from the depths of Russia where there are neither German nor Finnish nor any other tribes, but everything is indigenous, lively and ready Russian wit, which does not grope for a word or hatch it out like a broody hen, but sticks it on at once like a passport to be carried around for ever. (108–109)

And in the final paragraph the chauvinistic note rises swiftly to a crescendo as the English, French, and German "words" are successively declared inferior to the "aptly uttered Russian word."

Thus the interrelated motifs of "strong words" and the indigenous Russian element are employed as a kind of frame to the chapter, and it may reasonably be concluded even from the few statements quoted thus far that this frame is dictated less by the personal attitudes of Gogol than by a cardinal feature of the personality of the chapter's central figure. Even without additional evidence, the development of these two motifs alone would confirm that the "presence" of Sobakevich is felt even in those parts of the chapter where he does not appear.[5] It is already apparent, therefore, that considerable caution must be exercised before any statement in *Dead Souls* is interpreted as an expression of Gogol's personal sentiments. It is true, of course, that the whole novel is punctuated with reflections on various aspects of Russian life and the Russian character, and it obviously cannot be argued that they are all connected in some way with Sobakevich. But the important point is that in chapter five they greatly exceed similar reflections in other chapters in both number and prominence, and the recurrently evident chauvinism of the chapter's protagonist is the only plausible explanation.

It is significant in this connection that one such reflection is prompted immediately by Sobakevich's entry in chapter one as a guest at the governor's party, where Chichikov first meets him. We read:

> Sobakevich said somewhat laconically: "I invite you to visit me too," shuffling a foot which was shod in a boot of such gigantic dimensions that it would hardly be possible to find anywhere a foot of the corresponding size, especially at the present time when even in Russia men of Herculean stature [*bogatyri*] are becoming extinct. (17)

Thus when the *zakuska* at Sobakevich's becomes a pretext for contemplating the national character of this custom[6] and when Chichikov decides to preface his request for his host's dead serfs with a verbose panegyric to the vastness of the Russian empire,[7] there can be little doubt that Gogol is intent, as in the concluding "digression" of the chapter, on further amplification of one of Sobakevich's most distinctive characteristics. And it is noteworthy that the preparation for this process at the beginning of the chapter is by no means confined to the reference to Chichikov's "strong words." Do we not perceive, for example, an allusion to the same characteristic in Selifan's lament in the second paragraph on Nozdryov's spiteful substitution of hay for oats as the feed for Chichikov's horses? He says: ". . . a horse likes oats. They're his victuals. Oats are the same to him as maintenance, for example, is to us. They're his victuals" (89). Does this not anticipate Sobakevich's later insistence on the importance of Russian food for Russian stomachs and even, obliquely, the insistence at the end of the chapter on the superiority of the "Russian word"? As though to confirm the point, almost immediately afterwards in the wake of the collision between the carriages, Gogol reintroduces the "national motif" explicitly in the description of Selifan's reaction: "Selifan was conscious of his error, but since a Russian does not like to admit before others that the fault is his, he at once retorted with a dignified air" (90). Equally striking is the verbal reaction of the other coachman: "Oh, you scoundrel [*moshennik*]!" (90)—a summary judgment using Sobakevich's favorite term from which we may deduce, even without explicit notification of the fact, that we have already entered the domain of

the "bear." On the territory of Sobakevich even those, like the
eloquent coachman, who have nothing at all to do with him
and are probably unaware of his existence, are obliged to
express themselves in an appropriate manner. The implications
of this linguistic uniformity merit particular attention.

It has long been the practice, of course, in studies of Gogol's
technique in the novel to refer to the harmony he establishes in
chapters two through six between the personalities of the five
landowners and their surroundings, but it has not been observed that in this respect also the portrait of Sobakevich is
exceptional. In none of the other four "portrait chapters" is this
harmony so pronounced or all-embracing. The props that
surround Manilov, Korobochka, Nozdryov, and Plyushkin
certainly provide the most revealing insights into their personalities, but they are never actually cast in their image like the
table, chairs, and armchairs of Sobakevich, which even seem to
say: "I'm also a Sobakevich! . . . I, too, am very like Sobakevich!" (96). Similarly, every other physical object in his
domain (the asymmetrical house, for example, the sturdily
constructed well, the portraits of the Greek generals and
Bobelina, and even his pet thrush) reflects one or more of his
most distinctive qualities—above all, bulk, strength, crudity,
durability. There can be little doubt that this enhanced degree
of harmony between the protagonist of the chapter and the
array of props Gogol assembles around him is quite as meaningful as the qualities themselves. Like the "strong words" of
Chichikov and the coachman, it expresses a degree of control
over his surroundings that is as comprehensive as his "control"
over the chapter. Everything in the realm of Sobakevich bears
the mark of his personality; everything is held tightly in his fist,
and it is primarily in relation to this central feature of his
portrait that we should understand both the term *kulak* ("fist"),
which Chichikov contemptuously applies to him, and also his
surname (derived from the noun *sobaka*, "dog"), which alludes
to the canine habit of imposing rigid territorial boundaries and
repelling all invaders.[8] Certainly, as Proffer observes, the name
"sometimes gives rise to odd and humorous effects,"[9] but the

desire for such effects may hardly be considered the major reason for its selection. The name "Sobakevich" illustrates the general point that the names of Gogol's landowners allude to the fundamental symbolic themes which are developed in their portraits.

In connection with this "canine" aspect of Sobakevich we should note the symbolic associations of physical bulk that emerge from the contrast in chapter one between the fat men and the thin men at the governor's party. Of the former, the narrator observes:

> Their faces were plump and rounded. . . . The fat men . . . never occupy ancillary posts but always the main ones, and if they sit down anywhere, they sit squarely and securely, so that the seat is more likely to start creaking and bending beneath them than they are to be dislodged from it. (15)

The imposing physique of Sobakevich denotes the same canine tenacity. Moreover, it is already apparent that his control is by no means limited to his inanimate surroundings; far more significantly, it extends, as the reproach of the coachman and the "strong words" of Chichikov testify, to the people who enter and inhabit his domain.

Gogol's chief method of conveying this point is to endow them with the physical attributes of Sobakevich himself, with the result that they present themselves, like the peasant who so "aptly" summarizes the character of Plyushkin, as extensions of their master's personality. Hence the immense size and crude physical strength of the dead serfs whose praises Sobakevich sings in such emotional terms. Still more revealing, however, are their names: Mikheyev (which suggests "belonging to Mikhail"); Stepan Probka ("Stephen the Cork", i.e. a "light-weight" despite his "enormous strength"); Milushkin ("dear fellow"); Maksim Telyatnikov ("Maksim the Calf"); and Yeremey Sorokoplyokhin ("Jeremiah of the Forty Slaps").[10] The names clearly suggest passivity, a degree of subservience to the lord and master, which contrasts ironically with the serfs' physical might.[11] The five hundred roubles provided by Yeremey Sorokoplyokhin in labor-exemption tax (*obrok*) were plainly not accumulated without Sobakevich's vigorous encouragement. It might be objected, of course, that the sturdy structure of his serfs' huts is evidence of a concern for their well-being, and this concern undeniably exists, but it would be an error to assume that it is motivated by anything other than a desire to maximize their productive capacity. Proffer's contention that he "respects the serfs as human souls"[12] is conclusively invalidated, as we shall see, by the main symbolic theme of the chapter, and it will become apparent that his lack of respect is in no way contradicted by the posthumous praise that he bestows on them. These former subjects of Sobakevich were held in the vicelike grip of his fist, and it is entirely appropriate that his list of their names should include notes on their conduct and sobriety. His control, we may deduce, had extended to every aspect of their lives.

Similarly, the living Uncle Minyay bears both nominal and physical imprints of his master's authority,[13] sporting a name that is a diminutive of Mikhail, the same broad shoulders (which inflict such a punishing burden on Chichikov's shaft-horse and which seem to allude to the shoulders of his master, whose back is later described as "as broad as that of a sturdy Vyatka horse" [106]), and a stomach that resembles the national utensil for boiling water (a samovar) (91),[14] just as the face of Sobakevich resembles the kind of pumpkin that may allegedly be adapted to form a variant of the national instrument (the balalaika) (94). Here, too, the "national motif" is detectable, and as the complex pattern of details is slowly unfurled, it becomes increasingly clear that between the chauvinism of Sobakevich, his authoritarian control of his realm, and his rhapsodic delight in the qualities of physical might and crudity, which Shevyryov found irreconcilable with the dominant traits of his character,[15] Gogol is intent on establishing a subtle correlation, in the light of which the name "Mikhail Semyonovich" acquires a hitherto unnoticed significance.

Before we consider this question, however, it is necessary to take account of a more obvious aspect of the connection between the "canine" trait of Sobakevich's character and his admiration of physical might—an aspect that answers the simple question which, curiously enough, does not seem to have been asked before: why does Gogol choose to endow Sobakevich and his estate specifically with the qualities of bulk, strength, crudity, etc.? The question, as we shall see, admits of more than one answer, but the one most immediately apparent is clearly suggested by his chauvinism and tenacious authoritarianism. It has already been indicated that for Sobakevich the resolute preservation of his domain from every manifestation of non-Russian or nonindigenous influence is an *idée fixe*. Only two subjects move him to eloquence—his uncompromising hostility to insidious French and German customs and his pride in the animate and inanimate embodiments of his personal, i.e. indigenous or Russian, "virtues," and it is solely as reflections of this pride that we should regard his unexpected lyrical eulogies of his dead serfs in whom these "virtues," he alleges, were spectacularly reproduced. More important than these lyrical outbursts, however, is the siege-mentality which is the corollary of his xenophobia and the resultant conviction that the survival of his realm is threatened by plots, subversive sects, and the forces of chaos. In an earlier version of the chapter his attack on the insubstantial nature of French and German food was preceded by the remark: "It's a plot, I tell you; it's a sect. They have deliberately plotted to starve us to death" (747), and his description of the governor and vice-governor in the final version as Gog and Magog (97) betrays the same apprehension. Herein we perceive the main explanation for the esteem in which he holds the "virtues" of strength, solidity, durability, etc. This siege-mentality explains why his estate, on which everything is characterized by these "virtues," so markedly resembles a fortress.

Significantly, the martial note is struck at the very beginning of the description of the house by the remark that it "was of the kind that are built in Russia for military settlements" (93), and thereafter it gains progressively, though unobtrusively, in volume. We are informed, for example, that the courtyard "was enclosed by a strong and inordinately thick wooden fence" (94) (which casts some light, incidentally, on Chichikov's choice of proverb at the height of his negotiations with Sobakevich: "A dead body is good only for propping up fences" [103]). In addition, the reference to the imposing structure of the well conceivably alludes to the master's fears about possible threats to his water supply. Everything observed by Chichikov, we read, "was firm, unshakable and of a sturdy and clumsy character" (94). The impression of military preparedness is further reinforced by the disclosure that the windows on one side of the house had been boarded up and replaced by one small window—a stratagem manifestly designed to provide the master not with a "dark store-room," as Gogol with typical mock ingenuousness suggests (94), but with an inconspicuous vantage point from which to spy the land. Thus it is not by chance that Chichikov's first sight of Sobakevich and his wife is the spectacle of their strikingly dissimilar faces peering down at him precisely from this window as he drives up to the steps, and it is appropriate that the same motif of surveillance should be reintroduced on his departure by Sobakevich's irritating attempts to ascertain his route. Perhaps even the customary laconic nature or curtness of Sobakevich's utterances, to which, as we have seen, attention is also drawn in chapter one, should be regarded primarily as a military attribute, and it is interesting to note that in an earlier draft of the chapter the livery of his footman was adorned with a "light blue military collar" (743) rather than the "stand-up collar" of the final version (94).

But the most eloquent testimony to Sobakevich's military cast of mind and preoccupation with defence against "nonindigenous" invaders is provided by the portraits on the walls of his drawing room of warriors renowned for their exploits in the Greek war of independence and, not coincidentally, one of the victorious Russian generals in the war against the French, the puny Bagration. Each of them was dedicated to the expulsion from his land of an alien foe, and we must conclude that it is precisely this common commitment that explains their presence in the Sobakevich household. In the portraits of the Greeks, who were obliged to combat the formidable Turk, the physical characteristics of Sobakevich himself are again vividly reproduced. For the defeat of the French, conversely, fed on their pitiful fricassees, the skinny Bagration was more than adequate. Far from being "out of place" with his lack of muscle, as Proffer asserts,[16] Bargration is a comment incarante on the prowess of his adversaries—a comment which may be linked not only with the narrator's remark immediately afterwards that one leg of Bobelina "seemed larger than the entire Torso of one of those dandies [*shchegoley*] who fill present-day drawing rooms" (95) (i.e. the drawing rooms of St. Petersburg, synonymous in the novel with the alien, "nonindigenous" elements in Russian life[17]), but also, perhaps, with the definition of French sayings in the final paragraph of the chapter: "The ephemeral word of the Frenchman will flash and fly away like a light-headed dandy [*shchegolem*]" (109). Again we obtain a glimpse of the elusive connections between disparate details that appear to be incorporated at random or, as the narrator puts it in reference to the juxtaposition of Bagration and the Greeks, "goodness knows why or for what reason" (95).

From these connections between the patterns of details that are woven around the figure of Sobakevich we may deduce why Gogol chose to give preeminence in his portrait, as in his Christian name and patronymic, to his ursine, as distinct from his canine, attributes. Sobakevich is not simply a bear; he is the Russian bear par excellence, an incarnation of the principal attributes with which Russia has traditionally been invested by the non-Russian imagination—immensity, totalitarianism, xenophobia, suspiciousness, intolerance of individuality, cunning, and, above all, a crude reliance on physical power and an unshakable belief in its efficacy. More precisely, he embodies those attributes of "indigenous," pre-Petrine, Muscovite *Rus'* that more than a century of sustained foreign influence had signally failed to undermine and that to the Ukrainian Cossack Gogol, who was contemplating Russia from the "wondrous,

beautiful afar" (220) of Rome, and whose subsequent glorifica-
tion of the political structure of the Russian state should be
weighed against his frequently attested nostalgia for the demo-
cratic traditions of the *Zaporozhskaya sech'*, [18] were as unappeal-
ing as to any other "alien." It is noteworthy in this connection
that when Chichikov enters the office of the president of the
court in chapter seven, Sobakevich is sitting there completely
screened by one of the traditional triangular pieces of glass
(*zertsala*) on which the edicts of Peter the Great were inscribed
(144). It is difficult to conceive of any other plausible explanation for this detail than that it alludes to the essentially "pre-
Petrine" character of Sobakevich's attitudes, and it is probably
to his consciousness of having been "superseded" that we
should primarily ascribe his nostalgia for the past and sorrow-
ful acknowledgments that the strength of his father was much
greater than his own (145).

Equally noteworthy is the "digression" in which it is asserted that even if Sobakevich had been born and reared in St.
Petersburg, he would have been essentially the same; the only
difference, we are told, would have been the greater severity
with which, as the head, conceivably, of some civil service
department, he would have treated nominally free subordinates tainted by the non-Russian air of the capital. And here
again we may perceive how relevant to the preceding content
of the chapter is the concluding hymn to Russian verbal dexterity, for one of the "verses" of the hymn contains the following
comment on the Russian people:

> And if they reward someone with a nickname, it will pass
> to his kin and descendants; he will carry it with him to his
> work and into retirement and to St. Petersburg and to the
> ends of the earth. (108–109)

There is clearly good reason to assume that far from being a
generalization suspended in a void, this is an oblique allusion to
Sobakevich, that it implicitly reiterates the contention that the
ursine qualities of the Russian are ineradicable, and that its
meaning, quite simply, is: once a bear, always a bear. We might

observe the care with which Gogol paves the way for the introduction of this idea in the opening paragraph—in the context of Chichikov's reflections on the fate that might have befallen him, had Nozdryov not been deterred from his assault by the arrival of the captain of police. "I should have vanished," he remarks, "like a bubble on the water, without a trace, leaving no descendants and providing my future children with neither property nor an honorable name" (89). At the end of the chapter it is precisely to this question of inherited names that Gogol returns, relating it now to the character traits of the Russian bear, which even the pernicious influence of the capital is powerless to change.

The domain of Sobakevich, however, is located not in St. Petersburg, but at a point roughly equidistant from the two capitals, and there he rules with the authority of a Tsar—Sobakevich the Fist, a parody of Nicholas the Rod. The revealing details with which Gogol contrives to invest him with an aura of imperial grandeur, and thus to reinforce the symbolism of his position as the quintessential Russian sovereign of a quintessential Russian realm, have been consistently ignored by criticism. Like many other important motifs in the novel, the "imperial motif" is first introduced, in a typically oblique manner, in the vehicles of seemingly unrelated similes. The two forests, for example, that flank Sobakevich's estate are likened to a pair of wings (93), and it seems hardly conceivable at this stage in the narrative that the simile may allude to the imperial eagle. But when Sobakevich's complexion is described on the next page as being "of the fiery red color which one finds on a copper five-copeck coin" (94), i.e. on a coin bearing the imperial crest, the suspicion no longer seems so fanciful, particularly when it is discovered that in an early draft the following sentence read: "And in general his whole face bore a certain resemblance to this coin. . . . The only difference was that instead of the two-headed eagle there were lips and a nose" (743). This excision may be additional evidence of Gogol's preference for less overt indications of his meaning—a preference that on this occasion predictable reactions to the

parody make fully intelligible and that explains why, in the final version, the most overt exposure of the parody is postponed to chapter seven, in which Sobakevich remarks in reference to his deceased coach-builder Mikheyev: "In reality, he should be working only for the Emperor" (147).

Quite apart, however, from these oblique indications of Gogol's purpose, we should also take account of the curious air of formality prevailing in the Sobakevich household: the highly formal attire, for example, of the footman; the brevity and long silences that characterize Chichikov's initial exchanges with his hosts; Sobakevich's invariable "Please" (*proshu*) and repeated attempts to veil his clumsiness with decorous or apologetic inquiries about his guest's well-being; the formal, albeit farcical, kissing of Feoduliya Ivanovna's hand; and her fastidiousness at table. Indeed, despite the obvious elements of farce in the portrait of Sobakevich's wife, which highlight, as we shall see, the main symbolic theme of the chapter, her words, gestures, and movements are the principal means by which the house of Sobakevich is parodically imbued with its atmosphere of a royal or imperial court. We read, for example: "She entered in a dignified manner, holding her head erect like a palm tree" (95),[19] and with the instinctive gesture of a monarch demanding due obeisance she thrusts her hand into Chichikov's face, after which, the author continues, she "asked him to sit down, also saying: 'Please!,' and motioned her head like an actress playing the part of a queen" (96). Once more the most explicit revelation of Gogol's meaning is unobtrusively inserted into the vehicle of a simile, and he appropriately completes the description of Feoduliya Ivanovna's entrance by depicting the regal posture, suggestive of a royal portrait, into which she finally settles: "She then sat down on the divan, draped her merino shawl about her and thereafter moved neither eye nor eyebrow" (96).[20]

There is ample evidence, therefore, to suggest that in the figures of Sobakevich and his wife Gogol aimed to create the parodic emperor and empress of a parodic Russian empire. The parody, however, is not the only symbolic level of meaning in

the chapter. We must now consider its meaning and implications as conveyed by the main symbolic theme of the chapter
and, indeed, of the novel as a whole—the relationship between
man and woman. The usual contention, of course, is that the
females of *Dead Souls* are little more than mirror images of their
partners,[21] but their role, in reality, is vastly more complex and
important; chapter five provides the most revealing clues to it.

Given the authority that Sobakevich wields over his domain,
it follows that the position of woman in it is one of complete
subservience. It is aptly defined by the name "Feoduliya",
which means literally "servant of God." The pervasive crudity
of the realm, which is reflected in the crudity of its "emperor's"
language (his "strong expressions") and most vividly symbolized by the rough-and-ready manner in which nature has
allegedly fashioned him,[22] should be seen primarily as a mark
of its essential "masculinity." It is devoid of feminine frills and
refinement. Its values and ideals are exclusively physical and
earthbound; hence Sobakevich's habit of keeping his eyes
firmly rivetted to the ground. Everything is huge, rough, and
functional, and the complete anonymity to which woman is
condemned by such surroundings is most graphically illustrated by the description of the mute occupant of the fourth
place at dinner who is probably Sobakevich's daughter. This
hypothesis is by no means irreconcilable with the narrator's
reference to her as "someone who could not be definitely
identified as a mature woman or a girl, a relative, a housekeeper, or simply someone residing in the house" (98). Indeed,
a correct understanding of the symbolism makes it quite clear
that the reduction of even his own daughter to a state of such
indeterminacy is entirely in harmony with his character. The
appearance of this "thing without a cap, about thirty years of
age, in a parti-colored kerchief" (98) prompts the narrator to
reflect:

There are persons who exist in the world not as objects,
but as extraneous specks or spots on an object. They sit in
the same place, they hold their heads in the same way, you

are almost ready to take them for pieces of furniture, and
you think that in all their born days a word has never yet
emerged from such lips. (98)

Such, we are led to assume, is the customary fate of the female
in the "masculine" realm of Sobakevich—reduction to a speck
devoid of identity and even of a cap to mark her sex. She
is subjected to a process of remorseless "masculinization."
Herein lies the less obvious explanation (as distinct from the
explanation provided by the plot) of Sobakevich's "defeminization" of his dead serf Yelizaveta Vorobey, whose name, as
we learn in chapter seven, appears in the list supplied to
Chichikov in the "masculinized" form "Yelizavet," and it is in
relation to the development of this same symbolic theme that
we should also consider the masculine dimensions of the heroic
Bobelina.

But how should we interpret the ambivalent figure of
Feoduliya Ivanovna? As Sobakevich's queen, she obviously
occupies a special position among the females of his realm, and
her ambivalence is undoubtedly connected with this fact. An
emperor must have an empress who is at least partially recognizable as such, and this would seem to explain her retention of
at least some feminine characteristics. Thus unlike her silent
companion at dinner, she is adorned with a beribboned cap,
and it may be noted that husband and wife, when first introduced in the chapter, are emphatically contrasted as man and
woman: "As he [Chichikov] drove up to the porch, he noticed
two faces looking out of the window almost simultaneously: a
woman's face in a bonnet . . . and a man's . . ." (94).

The feature that most obviously distinguishes Feoduliya
Ivanovna both from her husband and from almost everything
else in his domain is her thinness. She is conspicuously devoid
of Bobelina's awesome muscles, and it has been suggested by
Proffer that we might regard her thinness simply as a reflection
of Gogol's long-standing habit of presenting pairs "as types
which are polar opposites".[23] Even if we discount the fact,
however, that no other married couple in *Dead Souls* is por-

trayed in such physically contrasting forms, it is already apparent that the physical attributes of Gogol's characters invariably have meaning beyond mere comic effects. Thinness, no less than fatness, has distinct symbolic associations in the novel, and it is a mark of their importance that Gogol attempts to clarify them in chapter one—in the contrast between the fat and thin men at the governor's party, to which reference has already been made. Certainly not all the connotations of thinness that emerge from this contrast are relevant to Feoduliya Ivanovna. But the statement that the existence of thin men "is somehow too light and airy and completely insecure" (15)—a feature of their "existence" conveyed by forms of the verb "to fly" (*letet'*), which are repeatedly applied to them—seems to allude directly to Feoduliya's total subservience to her "fat" husband, as symbolized by her name.

Far more expressive, however, of this subservience is the concrete evidence that even Feoduliya Ivanovna is by no means exempt from the process of coarsening or "defeminization" that is the common lot of Sobakevich's female subjects. She likewise bears the indelible imprint of her husband's "masculinity," and again an indication of the general importance Gogol attached to this symbolic theme is that he introduces it in chapter one, in the penultimate paragraph of which she responds to Sobakevich's announcement of his meeting with Chichikov by giving him a shove with her foot (18)—a patent variation of her husband's habit of treading on people's toes. Although the face of Feoduliya Ivanovna is still recognizably that of a woman and is sharply distinguished from her husband's by its thinness, it likewise evokes comparison to a vegetable. The consort of the bear with a face like a pumpkin is a goose with a face like a cucumber. Moreover, the solemnity of her entrance is immediately dissipated by the odor of cucumber brine emanating from her hands, while the homemade dye that colors the ribbons of her bonnet instantly deprives them of their pretensions to refinement.

But the main symbol of her sexual ambivalence is introduced in the narrative before the reader even makes her acquain-

tance—Uncle Mityay. The parallel between Sobakevich and
Uncle Minyay has already been noted. The common name and
similar physique combine to identify the serf with the samovar-
like stomach as essentially an extension of his master's mighty
arm. The contrasting thinness of Uncle Mityay indicates his
comparable relation to Feoduliya Ivanovna, and again the
name is informative, enhancing the impression of duality. The
name "Mityay" is a diminutive of "Dmitriy," which is derived
in its turn from "Demeter," the name of the Greek *goddess* of
fertility, and Gogol makes it quite clear that he has this derivation in mind by comparing Uncle Mityay, as he sits astride the
shaft-horse, to "a crane with which water is drawn from wells"
(91).[24] This, in fact, is the second of two similes that Gogol
employs to convey Uncle Mityay's appearance at this moment.
In the first he is compared to a belfry—the image which Gogol
had used as a symbol of a wife eleven years earlier in his story
*Ivan Fyodorovich Shpon'ka and His Aunt (Ivan Fyodorovich
Shpon'ka i yego tyotushka)* (1831). By such means the masculinity of Uncle Mityay is rendered as questionable as the femininity of Feoduliya Ivanovna, and there can be little doubt that just
as Uncle Minyay is a "double" of his master, so Uncle Mityay
is a "double" of his mistress. Perhaps an additional minor
reinforcement of the parallel is observable in the fact that just as
the "cucumber" is mentioned before the "pumpkin" when
Chichikov spots them at the window, so Uncle Mityay is
named before Uncle Minyay. In both cases the sexually ambivalent thin partner precedes.

The term *masculinity* in this context has already been defined.
It is expressive, as stated, of a purely physical approach to life
with distinct animal or bestial ("ursine") connotations. It is not
unreasonable, therefore, to suppose that "femininity" is expressive of the opposite, spiritual principle. And since everyone
and everything in Sobakevich's domain, including its female
inhabitants, has been wholly or partly "masculinized", it follows that we must look elsewhere for direct confirmation of
this hypothesis—specifically, to the only other detailed female
portrait in the chapter, that of the governor's daughter which,

according to Setchkarev, justifies its presence in the chapter solely by the funniness of its details and "could be left out."[25]

The purely symbolic role in the fiction of the governor's daughter is immediately apparent from her description, in which similes again play the dominant role:

> The pretty oval of her face was rounded like a small fresh egg, and it shone with the same transparent whiteness as when a fresh, new-laid egg is held up to the light in the dark-skinned hands of a housekeeper who is testing it and the rays of the radiant sun pass through it. (90)

The simile plainly alludes to the quality of innocence, but for a conclusive explanation of the choice of image we must turn to the author's comments eleven pages later on the soul of Sobakevich:

> It seemed as if there was no soul at all in this body, or rather that there was a soul there, but it was not at all where it should have been; like that of the immortal Koshchey, it was somewhere beyond the mountains and enclosed by such a thick shell that whatever moved at the bottom of it produced no movement at all on the surface. (101)

Collation of the two passages finally clarifies both the true nature of the young girl's role and the precise meaning that we should attach in this context to the principle of "femininity." It suggests that the projected three-part etructure of the allegory is not the only reflection of the confirmed influence on Gogol's conception of Dante's "comedy," for the governor's daughter may justly be viewed as the direct counterpart in the novel of the symbol of spiritual purity which in the allegory of Dante likewise assumes female form—the etherial Beatrice, to whose dazzling radiance corresponds the whiteness and translucence of the "shell" of the young girl's face. The soul, conversely, of Sobakevich, the embodiment of the "masculine" principle, is enveloped in a shell of impenetrable thickness. In the scene of Chichikov's second meeting with the governor's daughter in

chapter eight, the contrast is restated. There she is described as
"a young, sixteen-year-old girl with fair hair, a fresh complexion, delicate and graceful features, a little pointed chin and a
charmingly rounded oval face, such as a painter would take as a
model for a Madonna and such as is rarely found in Russia [*na
Rusi*], where everything that exists likes to assume large dimensions: mountains, forests, steppes, faces, lips, and feet"
(166). We may infer that just as the reference to large faces, lips,
and feet is an allusion to Sobakevich, so *Rus'* here alludes to his
"indigenous" Russian realm. The passage plainly lends support to our interpretation.

   In the light of this interpretation, all else in the chapter
becomes immediately intelligible. We are now in a position to
appreciate the reason not only for Gogol's decision to introduce the governor's daughter in this chapter, but also for the
representation of Sobakevich as a creation not of God, but of
nature. This insight in its turn suggests the main reason for
Gogol's decision to accredit him with an admiration of the
Greeks which extends so far that he even chooses a wife with a
Greek name. The Greek names are not testimony, as Nabokov
claims, to the existence of a "thin, wispy little poet" in
Sobakevich's "burly breast";[26] they allude to the pre-Christian
era, to deification of the body, to ignorance of the soul, and we
may conclude that in this symbolic context the terms "Greek"
and "masculine" are virtually synonymous.

   The implications of the "masculinization" of Sobakevich's
female subjects are now clear. The destruction of pure "femininity" in his domain, foreshadowed by the disdain with which
the fat men treat the ladies at the governor's party in chapter
one (14–15), is symbolic of rigorous mortification of the soul.
In the person of its overlord with his perpetual downward
gaze, "indigenous" Russia is exposed in its ignorance of the
very concept of a soul, as a realm in which the soul is condemned to be transformed from a "sweet morsel" (*lakomyy
kusochek*), as Chichikov describes the governor's daughter (93),
into the sour brine of Feoduliya Ivanovna and the radish jam
with which she replaces at dinner the anticipated sweet of pears

and plums (100).[27] Losing its translucence, the perfect oval of the egg ("such as is rarely found in Russia") is stretched and bent into the elongated contours of a cucumber. In the gargantuan feast that Chichikov enjoys at Sobakevich's table, and indeed in all the other remarkable acts of consumption that punctuate the hero's travels, we should see not, as the Freudians would assert, a substitute for woman as a sexual object,[28] but evidence of the "masculine" body's triumph over the "feminine" soul. Not for nothing, we may assume, are salted cucumbers included in the meal served to Chichikov in his hotel in chapter one (9).

But this is not the only detail in chapter one that now appears in a new light, for it is evident that the famous Homeric simile in that chapter, in which the dancers at the governor's party are compared to flies swarming over a loaf of sugar, has implications extending far beyond those identified by Proffer.[29] The simile reads:

> Here and there black frock coats flitted and sped by, singly or in clusters, like flies skimming over a gleaming white sugar loaf on a hot summer's day in July when an old housekeeper hacks it and divides it up into glittering lumps in front of an open window; all the children gather round and look on, following with curiosity the movements of her coarse hands as they raise the hammer, while the aerial squadrons of flies, borne on the buoyant air, fly in boldly as if they own the place and, taking advantage of the old woman's weak eyesight and of the sun that troubles her eyes, bestrew the sweet morsels [*lakomyye kuski*], in some places singly, in others in thick clusters. Sated with the riches of summer, which even without such bounty as this lays out sweet dishes [*lakomyye blyuda*] for them at every step, they fly in not at all in order to eat, but simply to display themselves, to stroll to and fro over the heap of sugar, to rub their hind legs or their forelegs together, or to scratch with them under their wings, or, stretching out both their forelegs, to rub them over their heads, and then to turn round and fly

away again, and once more come flying back with new
tiresome squadrons. (14)

We can certainly agree with Proffer that the actions performed by the flies in the last sentence of the simile parallel "the
dandies clicking their heels, rubbing their hands together,
touching their foppishly combed hair to keep it in place, brush-
ing pieces of fluff from their black frockcoats, flipping the tails
of their coats up in the air, hopping around nimbly to please
their superiors and the ladies, rushing in and out of the main
ballroom."[30] We can also agree that "the brightness of the
ladies' dresses is comparable to the whiteness of the gleaming
sugar."[31] But although Proffer is aware that women in the
novel "are often referred to metaphorically as 'sugar,' "[32] he
shows no appreciation of the symbolic theme that is reflected in
this motif—the theme revealed by the echoes of this simile in
the simile which describes the face of the governor's daughter.
Thus the whiteness of the sugar not only alludes to the brightness of the dresses; it also resembles the whiteness of the egg. In
both similes the scene is suffused with the radiance of a bright,
summer day. The sugar gleams; the egg is translucent. And
lastly, both the sugar and the egg are gripped by a housekeeper
(klyuchnitsa) whose identity, we may infer from the epithets
applied to her hands, is the same in both cases. On the symbolic
level, the "dark-skinned" hands that hold the white egg are the
same as the "coarse" hands that hack the gleaming sugar loaf.
Their connection is with the coarse, brine-covered hands of
Feoduliya Ivanovna, the "masculinized" spouse of the Russian
bear. The two pairs of hands symbolize the forces inimical to
the soul in the town of N. and the domain of Sobakevich. In the
former it is violently smashed; in the latter it is brutally "defeminized."[33]

Sobakevich's misanthropy, therefore, may now be seen in a
significantly different light. His "masculinization" of females
denotes his contempt for the human soul, and this explains his
contempt for people, his inability to recognize a human personality behind the façades of flesh and muscle, which is
foreshadowed in chapter four by Nozdryov's riposte to

Chichikov: "It is quite impossible to speak to you as one would to a friend. . . . No straightforwardness, no sincerity! A veritable Sobakevich . . ." (81–82). This insensitivity is not only conveyed by his delight in physical or "masculine" attributes alone and by the silent anonymity of the female who is probably his daughter; it is also reflected, for example, in the curtness that on a less profound symbolic level may be related, as we have seen, to the martial element in his portrait and to the "imperial motif,"[34] and in his total indifference when Chichikov attempts to broach the subject of private family circumstances in the course of their heated negotiations.[35] An additional indication of it is the nostalgia, prompted by memories of the prowess of his dead serfs, which induces him to betray for a fleeting instant his true attitude to his surviving subjects: "What kind of people are they? They are flies, not people" (103). The irony of the remark lies in the fact that, shortly before, he employs the image of the fly to convey to Chichikov the mortality rate of the serfs of Plyushkin, adding: "It would be difficult to imagine such a miser. Convicts in prison live better than he. He has starved all his serfs" (99). The criticism of Plyushkin is certainly apt, but the characteristically summary judgment is equally relevant to Sobakevich's treatment of his own subjects. Controlled by the heavy hand of their "emperor," confined behind his thick wooden fences, and maintained under constant surveillance, they are equally convicts in a prison. The only major difference is that whereas Plyushkin starves body and soul alike, Sobakevich starves only the latter. In both realms the status of the human being is no higher than that of an insect. Thus the peasant whom Chichikov meets on his departure is compared to an ant (108), and there is the comment in an earlier version of the chapter, regarding the type of people with whom the speechless female at dinner is compared, that the eye rests on them for the same incomprehensible reason as it does "on a fly climbing up the wall" (746).

It is not surprising, therefore, that Gogol should play more extensively in this chapter with the noun *dusha* ("soul") than in any other, and in consequence extreme circumspection is demanded of the translator. Thus appropriate translations must obviously be devised for the terms of endearment *dusha* and *dushen'ka* with which Sobakevich and his wife commonly address one another; while if we were to follow Magarshack and translate Sobakevich's remark:

«Лучше я съем двух блюд, да съем в меру, как душа требует»

(99) as "I'd rather eat only two dishes, but have a good helping of each, just as much as I like,"[36] the important irony of the final clause, which resides in Sobakevich's inability to conceive of food for the soul except in terms of buckwheat stuffing and half a saddle of mutton, would be completely lost.[37]

But Gogol does not restrict his verbal games to the noun *dusha* alone. Far more elusive are the various images related to that of the egg, and here again is evidence of the close connection between the concluding "digression" and the major symbolic themes of the chapter. Thus when Gogol informs us that Russian wit "does not grope for a word or hatch it out like a broody hen", is he not alluding once more to Russia's intolerance of the soul (i.e. the egg)? The allusions, however, are not always so direct.

After Chichikov's verbose and circuitous approach, for example, to the "main business," the text continues: " 'You want dead souls?' asked Sobakevich very simply, without the slightest surprise, as if the subject of discusson were wheat" (101). The simile is plainly another indication of his inability to conceive of a soul except in concrete, physical terms. But, more significantly, it alludes to Sobakevich's success in inflicting upon his serfs the same mortification of the soul that he has wrought upon himself. The Greek source of Uncle Mityay's name, which was not uncommonly used in ancient Greek with the meaning "bread," while its Latin equivalent *Ceres* could actually be used to mean "wheat,"[38] confirms that the oblique comparison of Sobakevich's serfs to grains of wheat is entirely apt, and as such, of course, their souls are implicitly endued with husks, in which we may perceive a direct parallel to the "thick shell" that stifles his own.

A further development of this motif is discernible in his later

remark about his serfs: "Mine are like juicy nuts" (102).
Magarshack renders the phrase *chto yadryonyy orekh:* "as sound
as a bell,"[39] and this translation captures the normal force of the
expression, but its inadequacy in the present instance is self-
evident. Like Gogol's proverbs, the popular sayings that he
employs, can rarely be replaced by foreign equivalents without
loss of revealing allusions. The image of "juicy nuts," like the
image of wheat, alludes to the coexistence in Sobakevich's serfs
of physical health and infirmity of the soul; and we may
confidently assume that the same allusion applies as Chichikov
muses during the negotiations:

«. . . по полтине ему прибавлю, собаке, на орехи!»

(104), which Magarshack, seemingly unaware that the colloquial phrase *na orekhi* is simply a mask, translates as: ". . . I'll
offer him another half rouble, the cur, and I hope it chokes
him."[40] The allusion demands the translation: ". . . I'll offer
him another half rouble, the cur, for his nuts."

Just as Sobakevich himself is presented as a creation of nature, so the "Sobakevichan" soul, in both senses of the term, is
presented in the form of natural produce—as a grain of wheat, a
nut, a cucumber, a pumpkin, and a radish. At the ticklish point
in the negotiations when Chichikov declares two and a half
roubles to be his limit and Sobakevich promptly responds by
treading on his toes, Gogol contrives to add two more vegetables to the list. Muttering his usual apology, Sobakevich "sat
him down in an armchair displaying even a certain dexterity,
like a bear which has already been trained and can turn somer-
saults and perform a variety of tricks when asked: 'Show us,
Misha, how women steam themselves [*paryatsya*],' or 'How do
little children steal peas, Misha?' " (105). When it is understood
that "peas" in this context are a symbol of mortified souls, the
implications of Sobakevich's alleged dexterity immediately
suggest themselves: he is an authority on the purloinment of
souls and, as well, on the steaming of women, i.e. the "masculinization" of souls. The key to this metaphor is provided a
few lines later when he remarks to Chichikov: "Truly, your
soul is just like a stewed turnip [*parenaya repa*]" (105). Thus are

the pea and the turnip added to the list of metaphors that define the soul's condition in the realm of the Russian bear.

But what about Chichikov? Is Sobakevich's reproach deserved? Does his soul really merit comparison to a stewed turnip? Appropriately enough, the answers to these questions are in the first sentence of the novel, which contains the first of numerous references to Chichikov's carriage as "the kind of carriage in which bachelors usually drive" (7). But for the more complex metaphorical answer provided by chapter five we must turn to the collision between the carriages. It is now clear that the import of this episode is entirely symbolic, that it represents a dramatic confrontation between Chichikov and the human soul in its pristine purity. It is also clear that the typically "neutral," generalized principal "digression" from this episode effectively masks Gogol's intent to extend the relevance of the confrontation from Chichikov to the entire "indigenous" Russian nation, i.e. the subjects of Sobakevich. The "digression" reads:

> Everywhere, wherever it may be in life, whether among its stale, rough, poor, and untidily mildewed lower orders or among its monotonously cold and boringly tidy higher orders, everywhere a man's path will be crossed at least once by some phenomenon which is unlike anything he has happened to see before and which for once will arouse in him a feeling unlike any that he is fated to experience for the rest of his life. Everywhere, across whatever sorrows of which our life is woven, some resplendent joy will merrily race by, just as sometimes a gleaming carriage with golden harness, picturesque horses, and brightly shining windows will suddenly speed past some poor village which has run wild and which has never seen anything but a country cart, and for a long time the peasants stand bare-headed and gaping open-mouthed, though the wondrous carriage has long since whirled away and disappeared from view. (92)

By implication the "digression" highlights the revelatory

character of this spectacle of the pure, "feminine" human soul both to Chichikov and the gaping representatives of the Russian *narod,* and its effect is totally captivating. But in the domain of the Russian bear it cannot but be a shortlived effect. Uncle Mityay and Uncle Minyay, the emissaries or "doubles" of the cucumber and the pumpkin, promptly supervene to sever the bond and break the spell, and the intrusion of hostile "masculinity" is immediately apparent in the crudity of their language and the violence of their methods: "Give it to him hot, give it to him hot! Give that light bay a taste of the lash! What's he squatting there for like a daddy-longlegs?" (91). The horses are duly subjected to the weight of Uncle Minyay, just as the toes of Chichikov are flattened by the feet of Sobakevich, and the violence ultimately has the anticipated result: ". . . such a steam [*par*]," we read, "rose from the horses as if they had rapidly covered the distance of a stage without stopping for breath"— an entirely predictable effect of the attentions of experts on the bathing habits of women[41]—and after a moment's rest they "set off of their own free will" (92). The scene symbolically represents Russia's expulsion of the pure, living soul. The enthralling vision evaporates as rapidly as it materialized, and with it the exalted contemplation of Chichikov, giving way to reflections on both the thoroughly distasteful character of the feminine milieu to which the girl with the egglike face is being speedily transported, and the purely materialistic benefits of a possible match. The principle of "femininity" is as alien to the "fat" Chichikov[42] as it is to the "fat" host who awaits him. As though to reinforce this identity of position, Gogol introduces, in two of the chapter's most imaginative passages, the figure of the twenty-year-old youth.

Very different, we are told, from the reaction of the middle-aged Chichikov to the confrontation would have been that of a twenty-year-old-youth—"a hussar, a student, or one who had simply just begun his career in life"—and the narrator adds:

> For a long time he would have stood insensibly on the same spot, peering vacantly into the distance, oblivious of the road and of all the reproofs and scoldings that awaited

him for his delay, oblivious of himself, his work, the
world and everything in it. (92)

Two pages later we encounter the famous simile (regarded by
Proffer as light relief for the depressed Russian reader[43] and by
Setchkarev simply as a means of "retarding the flow of the
narrative"[44]) in which the face of Sobakevich is compared to
the pumpkin from which balalaikas are made—balalaikas that
are described in the further reaches of the simile as "the pride
and joy of a dashing twenty-year-old youth, a lady's man and
dandy, who both winks and whistles at the white-breasted and
white-necked maidens who have gathered to listen to his gentle
strumming" (94). In both passages the youth is clearly of an
image of contrasting purity, wholly responsive to the purity of
soul symbolized first by the governor's daughter and, in the
simile, by her white-breasted, white-necked sisters. The youth
reappears in the same role in an equally famous simile at the end
of chapter six (131). The two contrasts in effect offset the
complete estrangement of the two central figures' souls from
the principle of pure "femininity"—the turnip of Chichikov
and the pumpkin of Sobakevich, which is fit only for the
manufacture of a physical object. To extract from this object, it
is implied, music appealing to the uncorrupted soul, a comparable purity is required, and Gogol clearly indicates what treatment threatens this image of purity in the realm of the Russian
bear, reminding us, by referring to the "reproofs and scoldings"
the youth will receive for his absorption in the spectacle of
purity, of the "harsh rebukes" (106) with which Sobakevich, as
the head of a Civil Service department in the capital, would
unfailingly have belabored his hapless subordinates. Here again
is evidence of the invisible threads that bind the seemingly
disparate parts of the chapter together.

We can also now perceive the symbolic, as distinct from the
social, significance both of the price at which Sobakevich offers
his dead female serfs (a rouble apiece) and of Chichikov's terse
rejection of the offer. Chichikov's reply—"I have no need of
the female sex" (107)—succinctly summarizes the main symbolic theme of the chapter; in chapter seven his subsequent

deletion from Sobakevich's list of the cunningly inserted name "Yelizavet Vorobey" is clearly an extension of this theme. This name also introduces us to another motif inseparably related to the same symbolic theme. Its constituent elements are the novel's many references to birds. The combination in the name "Yelizavet Vorobey" (Elizabeth Sparrow) of the bird motif with a symbolic expression of "masculinized" femininity (the truncated form "Yelizavet") suggests that it is employed not simply as a conventional symbol of the craving for freedom, but as an additional symbol of the soul, and its obvious connection with the image of the egg plainly reinforces this conclusion. Thus it does not seem coincidental that the caged thrush, which, we are told, "also bore a close resemblance to Sobakevich," is placed not only "right by the window"—an evident allusion to the craving for release—but also next to another prominent symbol of "masculinized" feminity: the portrait of Bobelina (95). And just as the egg is debased into a cucumber in the figure of Feoduliya Ivanovna, so the comparison of her to a "lightly stepping goose" as she leads the way into the dining room (97) suggests a similar debasement of the bird image.

Viewed against the background of these details, the statement in the chapter's first paragraph that the heart of Chichikov, as he reflects on his escape from Nozdryov, "was fluttering like a female quail in a cage" (89) manifestly acquires a new significance. There can be little doubt that the caged quail of Chichikov and the caged thrush of Sobakevich are parallel symbols of souls in thrall. But like the soul of Chichikov, which is fated to succumb for a second time to the lure of the young "Madonna," so even the soul of Sobakevich was evidently destined to be purified in the "Purgatory" and "Paradise" that were ultimately to follow the "Inferno" of volume one. The pumpkin's thick skin was to be refined into the egg's translucent shell and in the statement that the thrush "was of a dark color with white specks" (95) we may detect an indication of this future development.

Like every other major revelation in the chapter, this important prediction is conveyed by symbolic physical detail, and the examination of the entire chapter should have served at least to illuminate the generally symbolic character of Gogol's alleged realism and to clarify the point of his remark in his article *Concerning "The Contemporary" (O "Sovremennike")* (1846): "I have never aspired to be an echo of everything or to reflect reality as it exists around us."[45] Having ascertained that the central theme of the chapter is the mortification of the "indigenous" Russian soul, we have seen that the theme is developed by a plurality of symbolic motifs that constantly intersect one another from the first paragraph, which appears deceptively to relate solely to the events of the preceding chapter, until the equally deceptive concluding eulogy. We have also seen that even the apparently most digressive details, and in particular the seemingly random details inserted into the vehicles of similes and those that fill the passages of ostensibly "personal" comment, are in each case directly or obliquely connected with at least one of these motifs; sufficient evidence has been adduced to contend that it is these connections which chiefly explain their presence. The "second lover of art" declares in Gogol's *Departure from the Theatre after a Performance of a New Comedy (Teatral'nyy raz'yezd posle predstavleniya novoy komedii)* (1842): ". . . the parts of a comedy in all its massiveness must be tied together to form a single, huge, common knot."[46] Our analysis thus far has indicated that at least in chapter five the same principle of composition was adopted in his "epic poem."

2

Nozdryov

The charge that Nozdryov hurls at Chichikov in chapter four when the latter refuses to join him in a game of cards—"A veritable Sobakevich!"—would suggest that he sees himself and the "bear" as polar opposites, and indeed there seem to be no points in common between the two landowners. The circumspection of Sobakevich, his tightfistedness, his sparing use of words, his consistency of manner and conduct, his secure entrenchment in his formidable lair—all these characteristics are matched by diametrically contrasting features in the portrait of Nozdryov, who is reckless, profligate, loquacious, unpredictable, nomadic, and apparently indifferent to the efficient administration of his estate. Of all the landowners, as Richard Freeborn has observed, he is "the one least firmly related to a particular setting,"[1] and it seems entirely appropriate both that Chichikov should meet him in a wayside inn and that one of Nozdryov's most treasured possessions, his tobacco pouch, should have been embroidered by "some countess who had fallen head over heels in love with him somewhere at a posting station" (75).

In two respects, however, Nozdryov bears a significant resemblance to Sobakevich. His attitude toward women, for example, is plainly one of equal contempt—a feature that is first adumbrated by his contradictory comments on his associate Lieutenant Kuvshinnikov. Scarcely more than a page after describing him as "a most delightful man" (65) because of his prowess as a reveller, he refers to him as "a beastly fellow" (66) on recalling his weakness for the fair sex. Far more scathing, however, is the abuse that he pours on the head of his unfortu-

nate brother-in-law Mizhuyev when the latter insists on being
allowed to return to his long-suffering wife. The arpeggio
finally culminates in Nozdryov's most extreme term of
abuse—the untranslatable *fetyuk* which, according to Gogol's
footnote, is derived from the "indecent letter" θ (*theta*) (77) and
presumably alludes to the female genitalia. We are not unduly
surprised, therefore, to learn that although Nozdryov had once
been married, his wife had soon died, and that the experience
had left him completely unchanged. And it seems fitting that
the author should illustrate the contradictory nature of his
behavior with the remark that "he would upset a wedding . . . without at all considering himself your enemy" (71).[2]

The second respect in which Nozdryov resembles
Sobakevich is indirectly suggested by the first: he is likewise
the possessor of a powerful, "masculine" physique. At the
same time, however, his physical portrait displays significant
differences of emphasis and nuance. When he first appears, for
example, the author draws our attention to his "thick black
hair", his "jet-black side whiskers" and his "snow-white
teeth" (64), and he later informs us that his chest is covered by
"a kind of beard" (83). One of the penalties, we are told, that he
suffers for cheating at cards is the indignity of having "his
excellent, thick side whiskers juggled, so that he sometimes
returned home with whiskers on only one side and those, too,
rather straggly" (70). Such, indeed, is the state of his whiskers
when Chichikov meets him in the inn. But the narrator adds:
". . . his healthy, plump cheeks were so well created and possessed such vegetative powers that his whiskers soon grew
again even better than the old ones" (70). Thus the visual image
of Nozdryov that Gogol maintains is that of an individual
virtually covered in thick black hair, which serves to offset his
gleaming white teeth. These two details provide the key to his
entire personality and to the primary symbolic theme that
Gogol develops in chapter four.

The two affinities noted between Nozdryov and Sobakevich
indicate clearly that in chapter four Gogol again uses the symbolic theme which in chapter five is his principal means of

expressing the novel's central theme. Again the condition of "soullessness" assumes the symbolic form of crude "masculinity." The "masculinity" of Nozdryov, however, though indicative of the same spiritual affliction, expresses itself in an entirely different psychological condition, which is conveyed by means of quite distinct symbolic motifs. Hence the coexistence of the affinities between the two landowners with the striking differences in their physical portraits.

Although the particular form of "masculinity" that identifies Sobakevich is characterized by the animal or bestial attitudes signified by his name, comparison to an animal is plainly even more appropriate in the case of the hirsute Nozdryov. In an earlier draft of chapter four Gogol actually introduced the comparison, though in a typically indirect manner:

> As soon as there was a fair somewhere or a fashionable gathering, a party or a ball, it was impossible to tell whether his nose was so sensitive or whether fate decreed it in accordance with the proverbial truth that "the beast chases after the hunter," but even before you could turn round and look, Nozdryov was already there. (728)

Not for the first time a proverb was used to disclose a significant feature of a character, and we may probably conclude from its later excision that the disclosure, though far from explicit, was nevertheless too explicit for Gogol's liking. In the final version the most explicit indications of Nozdryov's "bestiality" are his ostentatious pride in the wolf cub that he feeds on raw meat, exclaiming: "I want him to be a genuine wild animal" (73), and his love for his dogs among whom, we read, he "was just like a father among his family" (73).

Despite this passion for dogs, however, Proffer's statement that "the name Sobakevich would seem to be more fitting for Nozdryov"[3] is misleading, for the implications of the "canine motif" as it is employed in the portrait of Sobakevich (and in that of Korobochka) are totally irrelevant to the nomadic lover of fairs who is seemingly incapable of retaining a single possession for more than a few hours. Nozdryov's dogs are not symbols of their master's tenacity or territorial omnipotence; they are hounds, the beloved "children" of a passionate hunter. It is not the implied meaning of their relationship with Nozdryov, but simply the nature of this relationship that finds a parallel in chapter five, for they are related to him in much the same way as Uncle Minyay is related to Sobakevich. Their "radiant health," the repetition of the color "black" in the list of their colors, and their cohabitation with a blind Crimean bitch on the point of death, in which we may recognize an allusion to Nozdryov's rapidly achieved deliverance from his own female encumbrance—these details indicate that the dogs are similarly an extension of their master's personality. But this personality is neither "canine" nor "ursine" in the sense in which these terms may be applied to Sobakevich. Its driving force is the primitive hunting instinct. Hence the name "Nozdryov" (derived from the noun *nozdrya*, "nostril"), which alludes to the sensitivity of his nose, to the keen sense of smell that enables him to detect infallibly the proximity of a fair before it has even been announced, and we may assume that when Chichikov is compelled to pay tribute to the "good scent" of one of Nozdryov's pups (68), the compliment was meant by the author to apply as much to the "father" as to the "child." Indeed, Chichikov himself seems to confirm the point later when he responds to Nozdryov's persistent inquiries about his reason for wishing to acquire dead souls with the comment: "Oh, how inquisitive he is! He would like to feel every bit of trash with his hands and smell it too!" (78). We may now comprehend, therefore, the intrusion into Chichikov's language of the noun *okhotnik*, which he uses not only in the literal sense of "hunter," but also with the figurative meaning "enthusiast." Thus when Nozdryov tries to sell him a pair of hounds, Chichikov replies: "I'm no hunter [*okhotnik*]" (80), and when Nozdryov then suggests that they play cards, he responds: "I am not at all an enthusiast [*okhotnik*] of games" (81). The figurative meaning, of course, like that of the phrase *na orekhi* in chapter five, is simply a mask Gogol uses to conceal the allusive force of the literal meaning. No less than the latter, the figurative meaning alludes to the central feature of Chichikov's host.

Almost every detail in chapter four relates directly or indirectly to this central feature of Nozdryov's character. Indeed, although the focal point of a fixed setting is less in evidence here than in any of the other four "portrait chapters," with the result that it conveys an impression of even greater diffuseness than chapter five, it is perhaps the most concentrated and tightly knit of them all in the sense that virtually every detail and episode reflects a single psychological condition—the instinctive hunter's state of mind. No other chapter illustrates more vividly Gogol's unique capacity for masking coherence with a veil of seemingly chaotic variety by substituting allusive concrete details, verbal play, figurative jargon, and deceptive asides for direct statement. Every word, in consequence, demands the reader's full attention, and the task of the translator is again exceptionally difficult. Thus when Nozdryov remarks: ". . . I have long been eager to acquire a mastiff" (68), it should be noted that the Russian means literally ". . . I have long been sharpening my teeth [*ostril zuby*] for a mastiff." And when Gogol informs us, in his characteristic throwaway manner, that Nozdryov would offer "to exchange anything at all for anything you like. A gun, a dog, a horse—everything was available for barter" (71), we should not assume that the three named items are merely chosen at random from a much longer list of possibilities.

The psychology of the hunter is the symbolic theme which invests the entire content of the chapter and the conduct of its hero with the "logic" that has consistently been denied them.[4] In order, however, to recognize this "logic," we must understand the manner in which psychology is translated into word and action. It expresses itself in a single, unchanging impulse—the impulse to challenge and destroy. For Nozdryov everything that exists and every truth that is asserted is a pretext for a challenge. It is something to be pursued, provoked, contradicted, and, if possible, transformed, broken down, and vanquished. He is an instinctive foe of stasis in whatever form it might manifest itself, of all that is ossified, crystallized, and seemingly immutable, and we may deduce that it was his instinctive hostility to the stasis of domestic life[5] which hastened his wife to a premature grave.

Contradiction, paradoxically, is the essence of Nozdryov's consistency. He is possessed of an irresistible compulsion to shatter every preconceived notion, to thwart every expectation, and to disrupt every arrangement,[6] and it is precisely this compulsion, this instinctive inability to concur or yield or let matters take their course that explains both his refusal simply to sell his dead serfs without complicating the issue and his subsequent disclosure of Chichikov's purpose at the governor's ball in chapter eight. In an earlier version of the chapter the author commented:

> He did not do this kind of thing because he was some kind of demon and looked on everything with evil eyes. Not at all. He looked on the world with rather gay eyes, and the dirty tricks that he played by no means gave him pleasure; it was simply something as necessary to him as bread without which he could not live. (729)

It is plainly not enough, therefore, merely to accredit Nozdryov with "careless immaturity"[7] or to charge him with being a "brazen bully and braggart."[8] His "immaturity," "bullying," and "bragging" are simply the superficial manifestations of the profoundly consistent attitude to life that represents the distinctive "Nozdryovian" form of "masculinity." Like his passion for gambling and fairs, they merely reflect the hunter's psychology, the conception of life as an endless succession of challenges and quarries.

Nozdryov's grotesque exaggerations and falsehoods are instinctive assaults on the immutability of truth and fact. Their lack of subtlety exposes them as naked challenges or provocations designed to incite the kind of verbal or physical battle that the hunter relishes. Another example of Gogolian demetaphorization discloses their essential nature:

> Suddenly he would tell a tale that he had a horse with a
> light blue coat or a pink coat, and similar nonsense, so that
> his audience would finally depart saying: "Well, my lad, it
> seems you've started telling lies already." (71)

Again the English language is incapable of providing a fitting
translation, for the phrase "to tell lies" conveys only the
metaphorical force of the Russian phrase *puli lit'*, which means
literally "to mould bullets."[9] Thus his "lies," in effect, are
bullets aimed at the breasts of his adversaries, and Gogol loses
no time in introducing us, by means of Nozdryov's verbal
jousts with Mizhuyev, to a typical battle sequence.

Mizhuyev owes his presence in the fiction to the single fact
that he is the perfect foil for Nozdryov's provocations. His fair
hair, which contrasts so sharply with the black "coat" of Nozdryov, denotes the "antagonistic" role in which he is cast. In a
very real sense he symbolizes reality itself as Nozdryov sees
it—as a foe to be relentlessly engaged in conflict. Hence the
succession of baits, in the form of outrageous boasts, with
which Nozdryov mercilessly taunts him, and on each occasion
the victim is predictably hooked, responding at first with resolute indignation and then yielding before the explosive outbursts of his exultant tormentor. The author comments on this
foil incarnate:

> The fair-haired man was one of those people whose
> characters display at first glance a certain stubbornness.
> You have no time to open your mouth before they are
> ready to argue, and it seems they will never agree to that
> which plainly conflicts with their way of thinking . . . ;
> but it always turns out in the end that there is a softness in
> their character and that they agree to the very thing which
> they rejected. (69)

Nozdryov's reluctance to release Mizhuyev to his wife is
explained precisely by the gratification of instinctive need that
he derives from his brother-in-law's invariable skepticism and
predictable obstinacy, from the incessant conflicts that his presence guarantees.

At the same time it should not be deduced from Mizhuyev's repeated submissions that Nozdryov is primarily motivated by a need to conquer. Compared with the exhilaration of the fight itself, the issue is of relatively minor importance to him. Hence his tendency to boast even of his disasters and the facility with which he shrugs off his losses and drubbings. Although Nozdryov is notorious for his cheating, his tricks are by no means designed to bring success; like his lies (e.g. his claim that one of his daggers signed "Made by Saveliy Sibiryakov" is Turkish [75]), they are exposed by their sheer blatancy as simply another form of provocation, as a challenge to the "stasis" of rules and regulations. Their purpose is revealed by another expressive proverb which, like the proverb quoted earlier, was excluded from the final redaction for the apparent reason that it alluded too explicitly to the dominant symbolic theme of Nozdryov's portrait: ". . . the more stupid and senseless the game [*dich'*], the more marksmen it attracts" (729). For Nozdryov a "juggling" of the whiskers is not only a small price to pay for a chance of indulging his seemingly congenital iconoclasm; it is the ultimate proof of the only kind of success that he recognizes—the success of disruption.

Equally expressive of his success are the remarkable conglomerations of heterogeneous, often tattered or defective objects that litter the backcloth to his portrait. The long, rambling inventories in which they are jumbled together constitute a distinctive syntactic feature of chapter four that is quite as meaningful as their lexical content. They epitomize the dislocated, splintered world the destructive hunter strives to create around himself—a world in which the normal relations between phenomena are gleefully shattered and nothing performs the role for which it was designed. Thus we learn that in Nozdryov's study "no traces were noticeable of what is usually to be found in studies" (74), that his horses are stabled with a goat, and that his cook (another obvious extension of his own personality) is given to pitching into his concoctions "whatever came to hand" (75). Moreover, Gogol does not confine his evocations of this disrupted world to those parts of the chapter in which Nozdryov is actually present. The manifestations of

"Nozdryovian masculinity," like those of the "canine" and "ursine" forms of the malaise in chapter five, extend to the furthest limits of the chapter. Hence the chaotic inventory of props at the inn in the third paragraph and the inclusion among them of two objects that appear to have undergone "Nozdryovian" transformations: "a mirror which showed four eyes instead of two and instead of a face a kind of flat cake" and "a salt-cellar which it was completely impossible to stand up straight on the table" (62). It is noteworthy that the inventory ends with the first olfactory reference in the chapter: ". . . finally, sweet-scented herbs and pinks stuck in bunches by the icons and so dried that anyone who conceived the desire to smell them would simply sneeze and nothing more" (62).

Like Sobakevich, Nozdryov also has his distinctive lexical emblems, the most resonant of which is the challenging monosyllable *vryosh'* ("you're lying"), his predictable trumpeting response to every claim made in his presence. It is a mechanical, instinctive response, an expression not so much of skepticism as of an uncontrollable urge to transform passivity into indignation, a friend into an adversary. Thus given his indifference to making a loss, we may assume that the monosyllable is hurled at the old woman in the inn not because her charge of twenty copecks for a glass of vodka is blatantly exorbitant, but because the twenty copecks represent a fact to be undermined and destroyed, a challenge to be gratefully accepted. And for the same reason the same response is directed both against Chichikov's specious explanations of his wish to acquire dead serfs (78–79) and, at the end of the chapter, against the captain of police's accusation (87). For Nozdryov statements are neither true nor false; they are quarries to be hounded with all the resources at his disposal.

Undoubtedly the most effective of these resources are his total disregard for social convention and his violent swings from presumptuous familiarity and endearments to completely uninhibited abuse. The unsettling effect of this tactic on Chichikov is indicated on their first meeting in chapter one when Nozdryov "began to use a familiar form of address after the first three or four words" (17), and in chapter four he affects at once the same provocative manner. Moreover, the manner of the "father" is appropriately aped by his "family." During the conducted tour of the "very handsomely built little house" constructed by Nozdryov for his hounds, one of the inmates displays his affection for Chichikov by "raising himself on his hind legs and licking him right on the lips" (73). By the time, however, the subject of the "main business" is finally broached, simple familiarity and even the hectoring *vryosh'* have given way to the devastating final phase of the tactic, wherein amiability and insult follow one another in rapid, bewildering succession:

> You're a great rascal, you know. Allow me to tell you this as a friend. If I were your superior, I would hang you from the nearest tree. . . . I swear I'd hang you. . . . I tell you this frankly not to insult you, but simply as a friend. (79)

He expresses himself in this manner, of course, fully aware of Chichikov's acute sensitivity to modes of address and social conventions, displaying for the "rules" of society the same challenging disdain as for the rules of whist and checkers.

These rapidly alternating modes of address provide some indication of the harmony between Nozdryov's language and the world he surrounds himself with. Language, like everything else, represents for him an entity to be transformed and dismembered, a challenge to his powers of disruption, and his jubilant acceptance of the challenge produces the bizarre mixture of hunting, gambling, and military terms which, with his impressive range of abuse and obscenities, comprise his inimitable personal vocabulary.

The prominence of military terminology in Nozdryov's language is not surprising once it is appreciated that his lies and distortions are essentially verbal "bullets." It reflects his fundamental view of life as an inexhaustible source of opportunities for conflict. Even when his speech is not actually laced with military terms, it is still characterized by that "military" disregard for the social graces, which prompts Chichikov to remark: "If you want to flaunt such speeches, then be off to the

barracks!" (79). The monosyllable *vryosh'* is merely an extreme
example of the martial brevity and pungency that distinguish
all his utterances and which are perhaps most conspicuously
reflected in the list of eloquent imperatives he has used to
christen his hounds: Shoot, Curse, Flit, Obliterate, Plague,
Harass (73).

In general, the "military motif" is the most prominent and
extensive of all motifs in the chapter that express the dominant
symbolic theme of the hunter's destructive psychology.
Among its more obvious components are the details that testify to the pleasure Nozdryov derives from the company of
soldiers, i.e. fellow "hunters," and to his passionate love of
weapons—a love that explains not only the array of guns,
swords, and daggers on the walls of his study, but also his
indicated readiness to exchange anything for a gun and his
insistence that Mizhuyev bet his gun when the latter challenges
his claim to have drunk seventeen bottles of champagne at one
sitting (66). Even his barrel organ, apparently designed to play
mazurkas and waltzes, has been subjected to an authentic
"Nozdryovian" challenge and partly converted into an instrument of war:

> The barrel organ played quite pleasantly, but something
> seemed to happen in the middle, for the mazurka ended
> with the song "Marlborough has gone to war," and
> "Marlborough has gone to war" finished unexpectedly
> with an old familiar waltz. (75)

If we turn, however, to the sentence immediately succeeding
this one, we will see that not all the forms of the "military
motif" are so readily discernible:

> Nozdryov had long since stopped turning the handle, but
> there was one pipe [*dudka*] in the barrel organ which was
> very lively [*boykaya*] and reluctant to calm down, and for a
> long time afterwards it continued to whistle by itself. (75)

The first point to note here is the use of the epithet "lively" to
identify the pipe with its owner, for the author has already

drawn our attention four pages earlier, in one of his more
explicit comments on Nozdryov, to his "restless energy and
liveliness [*boykost'*] of character" (71). But it is the "military"
allusion contained in the image of the pipe that merits particular attention, and to recognize it, we must go back even further
to one of the author's remarks about the type of person
Mizhuyev allegedly exemplifies: ". . . they will never call a
stupid man intelligent and, in particular, will never agree to
dance to someone else's pipe [*plyasat' po chuzhoy dudke*]" (69).
Not only does "someone else" here refer patently to Nozdryov, but we are also well aware that Mizhuyev can be relied
on to "dance" to very "pipe" that Nozdryov plays. The significant point, however, is that when the effects on him of this
experience are first disclosed by the author, the allusion is not
to the pipe that Nozdryov plays but to the pipes that he
smokes. The whole development, in fact, of the "military
motif" in the chapter begins with the comment on Mizhuyev:
"It was possible to conclude from his tanned face that he knew
what smoke was—if not the smoke of gunpowder, then at least
the smoke of tobacco" (63), and it is noteworthy that his
moustache is ginger (i.e. singed). We may now understand
why Nozdryov, after demonstrating the pipes of the barrel
organ, proceeds immediately to show Chichikov his varied
assortment of pipes for smoking. The noun *dudka* is an allusion
to Nozdryov's most bizarre weapon—his riflelike "chibouk"
(defined by Dal' in his dictionary as a *derevyannaya dudka* ["a
wooden pipe"][10]), the smoke of which is indirectly compared
to that of gunpowder. To dance to Nozdryov's *dudka* is to feel
the force of his chibouk, as Chichikov learns later to his cost.
His exposure to the "lively" *dudka* of the barrel organ is merely
a subtle foretaste of the attack by chibouk to which he is
subjected in the chapter's violent conclusion:

> "Give him a thrashing!" cried Nozdryov as he rushed
> forward with the cherrywood chibouk, hot and sweating
> all over, as if he were attacking an impregnable for-

tress. . . . Screwing up his eyes and petrified, the fortress was already preparing himself for a taste of his host's Circassian chibouk. (86–87)

This connection between the *dudka* and the chibouk not only presents us with another glimpse of the unity of idea underlying the diversity of the chapter's content; it also highlights the essentially "military" character of the entire operation that Nozdryov mounts against Chichikov and Mizhuyev from the moment of their arrival at his estate. After the conducted tour, their visit rapidly assumes the character of a series of tests, as weapons of increasing potency are brought to bear against them in swift succession. Predictably, Mizhuyev quickly succumbs—a victim of the ordeal by falsehood and wine. Much to Chichikov's disquiet, Nozdryov appears to have little interest in food, but he clearly sets great store by his wines, and although, as Chichikov shrewdly observes, he partakes of only limited quantities himself, the glasses of his guests are filled even before the arrival of the soup. The wines are described as follows:

Then Nozdryov ordered a bottle of Madeira to be brought which was better than any drunk even by a field marshal. Indeed, the Madeira even burnt their mouths, for the merchants, knowing well the tastes of landowners who liked a good Madeira, seasoned it mercilessly with rum and sometimes poured even aqua regia into it in the hope that Russian stomachs would be capable of standing anything. Then Nozdryov ordered a special bottle to be brought which, he claimed, was a mixture of burgundy and champagne. . . . Shortly afterwards a rowanberry liqueur was brought to the table which, according to Nozdryov, tasted just like cream, but in which a strong taste of raw vodka was surprisingly detectable. Then they drank a kind of balsam with a name which was even difficult to remember and, indeed, the host himself later called it by a different name. (75–76)

Like every other possession of Nozdryov, each of the wines has been "challenged" and subjected to a process of radical transformation, the object of which requires little comment. Just as a song of war is added to the mazurkas and waltzes of the barrel organ, so debilitating spirit is added to his mild liqueurs. Like Marlborough marching to war, the field marshal who would have appreciated the "enriched" Madeira is plainly an allusion to "lieutenant" Nozdryov,[11] engaged in battle with his guests, and for victory over Mizhuyev the wines suffice. With his will to fight undermined and the obscenity *fetyuk* ringing in his ears, he leaves the novel in haste.

In Chichikov, however, Nozdryov discovers a more resilient foe. Seeing that he has survived the test of the wines, he promptly unsheathes his next weapon—a pack of cards. But the next phase of the battle is briefly postponed, for finding himself alone with his host, Chichikov now proceeds to the "main business," and he begins by demanding from Nozdryov in advance a promise that he will not divulge its nature. The demand, of course, is not only ludicrous; as an indication of Chichikov's failure to appreciate the character of his host, it indirectly preannounces the total collapse of his scheme. For Nozdryov the sole reason for giving a promise is to break it, and in chapter eight he duly demonstrates his consistency. For the moment, however, he confines himself to transforming the deal proposed by Chichikov into a pretext for further hostilities. His initial tactic is to offer his dead souls on terms that Chichikov will never accept—on condition that he will also purchase one, or perhaps even two, of his three horses. He knows that Chichikov will decline the offer not only because of the outrageous sums that he demands for the horses, but also because the horses are virtually identical to the three that Chichikov already possesses. Nozdryov's dapple-gray (*seraya v yablokakh*), his bay stallion, and his chestnut mare parallel almost exactly Chichikov's dapple-gray (*chubaryy*) side-horse, his bay shaft-horse, and the light chestnut named "Assessor"; this parallel was progressively reinforced in successive drafts of the chapter.[12] By such means Gogol makes clear that Nozdryov is less interested in Chichikov's money than in provoking his indignation.

The "hunter's" response to the anticipated rejection of the horses is to offer instead a pair of his hounds, and it is this offer, as stated, that elicits from Chichikov the revealing allusion: "I'm no hunter." Although, however, the intervention of the hounds is highly informative for the reader, it reveals nothing at all, it seems, to Chichikov, who regards them less as a threat than as an absurdity. With a cry of astonishment he immediately rejects them only to incur a new provocation in the form of Nozdryov's offer of his barrel organ, and here for the first time since their encounter in the inn, when Nozdryov had helped him to obtain a good view of his horses standing outside by bending his head down "so that he almost knocked it against the window frame" (64), the "hunter" gives notice of his readiness, if necessary, to resort to physical violence:

> Here Nozdryov seized Chichikov by the hand and began to drag him into the next room, and however much Chichikov dug his feet into the floor and assured him that he was already familiar with the nature of the barrel organ, he was obliged to hear once more how Marlborough went to war. (80)

The exasperation of the guest increases in direct proportion to his host's exhilaration. Rejecting first the barrel organ and then the offer of "another carriage," he is again confronted with the pack of cards, and as though in obedience to a telepathically communicated command, Nozdryov's servant Porfiriy, the ever-present steward of his arsenal, silently materializes with a bottle of wine. When the cards are also declined, Nozdryov deals a swift blow with his most powerful verbal weapon (fetyuk), orders hay to be substituted for oats as the feed for Chichikov's horses (thereby, presumably, seeking to weaken his quarry's capacity for escape), and treats Chichikov at dinner to the worst wine in his cellar.

The night brings Chichikov no respite. The cards, the "lively" pipe, and the "lively" hounds are merely replaced by

"some small and very lively [*preboykiye*] insects," which
"inflicted intolerable pain with their bites" (82). Continuing to
demonstrate his complete failure to understand Nozdryov, he
is astonished to find his host the next morning in the best of
spirits, and his surprise is all the greater when he learns that
Nozdryov, too, has had some difficulty sleeping. The insomnia
of Nozdryov, however, is attributable to very different causes,
which provide an even surer indication than this characteristic
"challenge" to Chichikov's expectations that for the "hunter"
the battle has hardly begun. Apparently alluding to the wine
consumed at dinner, he remarks: ". . . after yesterday's experiences my mouth feels as if a troop of horses had spent the night
there" (83). In reality, the allusion is to the excitement and
presentiments of the warrior on the eve of the battle's most
crucial phase. He continues:

> Just imagine! I dreamt that I was being flogged. Truly!
> And imagine who was doing it! You'll never guess. Cap-
> tain Potseluyev together with Kuvshinnikov. (83)

In other words, the possibility of defeat is clearly envisaged, yet
its effect is negligible. Suspended from his mouth is the
chibouk that has "tanned" the face of Mizhuyev, and his dressing gown reveals the "beard" on his chest. He is stripped for
battle, and on the pretext of wishing to reprimand his agent he
departs to give his final instructions.

Once more he attacks with the pack of cards, and when the
blow is again predictably parried, he switches menacingly to
checkers, the Russian word for which (*shashki*) also means
"swords" or "sabers." The switch has a telling effect, forcing
Chichikov into yet another serious error of judgment. Recalling his former competence at checkers, he finally lowers his
defenses and Nozdryov joyfully hurtles into the breach. Two
moves are enough for him to commit a flagrant violation of the
rules which, to his delight, prompts an indignant reaction, and
each of the succeeding moves is obliquely equated, by repetition of the noun *shashki,* with the lunges of a blade. The final
lunge is Nozdryov's unconcealed attempt to move three checkers simultaneously, which duly propels the conflict into its

final, physical stage conveyed by the Homeric simile, from which Chichikov is opportunely rescued by the arrival of the captain of police in appropriate semimilitary attire.

To the end, therefore, Nozdryov acts in total obedience to the single imperative that dictates his entire behavior. The account of the conflict with Chichikov is merely a consummate expression of the symbolic theme, which the actions prompted by this imperative dramatize, confirming that the portrait of "Nozdryovian masculinity" is quite as coherent as that of the "ursine" variety in chapter five. Nozdryov, no less than Sobakevich, is all of a piece. They differ only in the forms of soulless "masculinity" of which they are the novel's principal embodiments. The symbolic theme of the "canine bear" implies a defensive mentality, a centripetal outlook, and the imposition of inflexible limits; the theme of the "hunter" implies relentless aggression, the destruction of all boundaries. Hence the barely visible boundary-markers on Nozdryov's estate. They consist only of "a small wooden post and a narrow little ditch" (74), and not unexpectedly he claims that even the lands beyond really belong to him. As we have seen, however, Nozdryov's hostility extends to boundaries of every conceivable kind—to the "boundaries" of truth, fact, games, social conduct, and even language. His weakness for Gallicisms, therefore, which is reflected in his phrases *en gros* (66) and *subtilement superflues* (75),[13] is entirely apt. Just as the defensive attitude of the "bear" expresses itself in xenophobia, so the iconoclasm of the "hunter" is mirrored in Francophilia, in the destruction of "indigenous" boundaries, and it is fitting that when he reappears in chapter eight, he is surrounded by the female francophiles of N.

Again, however, it must be stressed that the physical presence of Nozdryov is not a prerequisite for the "presence" in the novel of the affliction that he personifies. Its symptoms are perceptible in almost every chapter, and its principal signal is the "military motif" in all the multiplicity of its forms— officers, weapons, games, military phraseology, uniforms, paintings of battle scenes, etc. The "military motif" is at once the dominant motif of chapter four and one of the most sus-

tained motifs in the whole work, and on almost every occasion
on which it appears it connotes the aggressive, destructive
instincts of the "bestial Nozdryovian hunter," which form one
of the most distinctive features of the "soulless" world that the
allegory evokes. Not for nothing is it introduced on the very
first page of the novel, where it appears in the form of the pin
with which the shirt-front of the itinerant young man is
fastened—"a pin with a bronze pistol" manufactured in Tula,
the Russian armaments center (7). The young man's function is
not, as Belyy weakly argues, merely to "distract attention from
the newcomer,"[14] but rather to signal at the very outset the
existence of the "Nozdryovian" element in the town's com-
pound personality and to foreshadow the appearance of its two
main types of male inhabitant. While his cap, which "almost
flew away [*sletevshiy*] in the wind" and his "pretensions to
fashion" (7) identify him as a "thin man," his pin anticipates the
appearance of the "fat men" who at the governor's party prefer
whist to women and at the end of their game "argued, as is the
custom, rather loudly" (16), thereby presenting conclusive
evidence of their common "Nozdryovian" streak. The reaction of Chichikov, ironically, is to offer them a pinch of snuff
(*tabak*), the "Nozdryovian" substitute for gunpowder.

Yet although Chichikov contrives continually to misjudge
Nozdryov and his motives and differs from him in many
obvious respects, it should not be concluded that they have
nothing in common. We may confidently assume that Gogol
would not have given them almost identical horses merely to
enable Nozdryov to propose an impossible bargain. In addition, we might note the similarity between their entrances into
the novel, their common preference for a nomadic kind of
existence, their common partiality for whist and the comparison of Chichikov's carriage, in the first sentence of the novel, to
the kind in which retired colonels and staff-captains usually
drive (7), while in Nozdryov's tirades against his enemies we
may detect distinct echoes of Chichikov's references to his
"many enemies who had even made attempts on his life" (13).
Each of these details alludes to the "Nozdryovian" element

that is an integral part of Chichikov's personality. The difference between them is solely one of complexity. Nozdryov is Nozdryov and only Nozdryov; the chameleonlike Chichikov, conversely, combines in himself symptoms of all the five forms of spiritual mortification that are embodied individually in the figures of his five curious hosts.

3

Manilov

In our study of chapter five we have seen that the part of the text preceding the description of Chichikov's arrival at Sobakevich's estate forms in a very real sense an introduction to the portrait that follows. The same two-part structural scheme is perhaps not so evident in chapter four simply because Nozdryov is detached from his estate and appears much earlier than the other landowners. As a result, his portrait begins on the third page of the chapter. But in each of the other three "portrait chapters" the scheme of chapter five is essentially reproduced, and they accordingly confront the reader with the same recurrent problem. The difficulty once more is that the introductory function of their opening sections, like that of chapter one in the structure of the novel as a whole, is recognizable only retrospectively. In each case the reader is faced with a mass of details that disclose their raison d'être only in the light of the symbolic themes developed in the following portraits.

The first major component of the introductory section in chapter two is the comically fragmentary portrait of Chichikov's valet Petrushka ("Parsley") whose name may be related to the motif of "natural produce," which plays such a notable part in chapter five. The restriction of the portrait to two main features (despite the narrator's statement that he likes to be "circumstantial in everything" [19]) is a clear indication of the constraints to which it is subject. Both features— Petrushka's curious reading habits and his disquieting smell— prepare the way for the entrance of Manilov, and it is precisely this introductory function of the portrait that explains both its brevity and its inclusion at this point in the narrative. The

portrait of Petrushka is an introduction to the portrait of Manilov, just as the portrait of Selifan in chapter three introduces
that of Korobochka.

It is true, of course, that Petrushka's primary relationship in
the novel, like that of Selifan, is with Chichikov, and that the
second of the two main features which comprising his portrait
alludes directly to the nature of this relationship. Petrushka, in
Belyy's phrase, is "the bearer of Chichikov's stench,"[1] a mirror
in which Chichikov is unwittingly confronted with the corruption of his own soul. He is a "human" counterpart of the
sinister lower compartment of Chichikov's box, a personification of the decomposing vegetable behind the immaculate
exterior that his master soaps so energetically before embarking on the journey to Manilov's estate. Hence the castoff coat of
Chichikov, which he is given to wearing. At the same time it
will become evident that in the context of chapter two even this
primary symbolic role of Petrushka is as relevant to Manilov as
to his guest. But more immediately obvious is the relevance to
Manilov of the author's comments on Petrushka's reading
habits:

> He was of a taciturn rather than talkative disposition; he
> even felt a noble urge to educate himself, that is, to read
> books, bothering little about their contents. It was com-
> pletely immaterial to him whether it was the adventure of
> a hero in love, a primer, or a prayer-book—he read every-
> thing with equal attention. Even if a book on chemistry
> had been slipped to him, he would not have refused it. It
> was not what he read that gave him pleasure, but the
> reading itself, or rather the process of reading, the fact that
> the letters, as he put it, always formed a word, which
> sometimes meant the devil only knew what. (20)

Although Petrushka's appetite for reading is clearly not
shared by Manilov, who in two years has not progressed
beyond the fourteenth page of the book in his study, the
limitation of his interest solely to the "process" of reading is
indirectly definitive of Manilov's entire approach to life. It

alludes to the preoccupation with form at the expense of content that is the dominant trait of Manilov's character. Like the contradiction between the fragmentary nature of Petrushka's portrait and the narrator's avowed preference for being "circumstantial in everything," the valet's method of reading foreshadows the landowner's unique and inexhaustible capacity for disembodied language, for refined phraseology devoid of all significant meaning.

The vacuity of Manilov's language, of course, implies the vacuity of his entire personality. His inability to articulate, in the narrator's phrase, "a single living or even arrogant word" (24) betrays a state of complete emotional, intellectual, and spiritual paralysis. Like his language, he is an empty shell. His life is merely a sustained display of decorous, but lifeless, gestures. Hence the brevity of the initially favorable impression he makes. When introduced to him at the governor's party in chapter one, Chichikov finds him "a most pleasant and courteous landowner" (15–16), and this impression is reinforced by the greeting that he receives in chapter two, but their first conversation prompts a rather different reaction. Only a few words are required to puncture the shell. The author remarks:

> During the first minute of a conversation with him you could not help saying: "What a pleasant and kind man!" During the following minute you would say nothing, and during the third you would say: "The devil only knows what kind of a fellow he is!" and you would step a little further away from him. If you did not, you would be bored to death. (24)

And after a brief excursus on the subject of allegedly normal human "passions [zadory]", he concludes: ". . . everyone has his own passion, but Manilov had nothing." (24)

The remaining sections of the "introduction" and almost the entire portrait of Manilov comprise an oblique exposé of the void behind the charming exterior and the state of complete detachment from the reality of life to which it testifies. Thus,

the narrator's apology for dwelling so long on Petrushka and
his pretext for prematurely cutting short the portrait of Selifan
clearly prefigure the later evidence of Manilov's class consciousness, which is merely one reflection of his exclusive
concern with formal proprieties. The author writes:

> Knowing from experience how loath his readers are to
> acquaint themselves with the lower orders [*nizkimi sos-
> loviyami*], the author is very ashamed of taking up so much
> of their time with persons of the lower class [*nizkogo
> klassa*]. Such is the nature of the Russian: he is passionately
> fond of feeding his conceit by making the acquaintance of
> anyone who is at least one rank above him, and a nodding
> acquaintance with a count or a prince is more important to
> him than any close, friendly relationship. (20–21)

The opening words anticipate the narrator's feigned apology
for later dwelling on the evidenced incompetence of Manilov's
"well-educated" wife as a housekeeper ("But these were all
squalid matters [*predmety nizkiye*], and Manilova was well
brought up" [26]); the alleged national characteristic foreshadows the daydream to which Manilov succumbs at the end
of the chapter after Chichikov's departure:

> Then he imagined that he and Chichikov arrived in fine
> carriages at some social gathering where they charmed
> everyone with the pleasantness of their manner, and that
> the Emperor, learning of their great friendship, made
> them generals. (39)

Manilov's aspiration to the social heights is yet another manifestation of his flight from life's realities, which is "introduced" by the narrator's comments on Chichikov's servants.

Perhaps more obvious an introduction, however, is the description of Chichikov's journey to the estate:

> As soon as the town had been left behind, all kinds of
> nonsense and rubbish, as is usual in Russia, began to
> appear on both sides of the road: hummocks, fir-woods,

low, sparse bushes of young pine, charred trunks of old
pine trees, wild heather, and nonsense of that sort. (21)

Here a generalization about Russia masks a symbolic revelation
of Manilov's detachment from life. Once more a significant
allusion is presented in the guise of a statement that seems
deceptively to reflect the author's personal attitudes. In reality,
the passage is a comment not on the Russian landscape but on
the symbolic environs of Manilov's domain, characterized by
the same infertile earth and sparse vegetation:

On the lawn two or three flower beds with lilac bushes and
yellow acacia were scattered in the English fashion. Here
and there five or six birch trees in small clumps raised their
sparse, fine-leaved tops. . . . Nowhere among the huts
was there a growing sapling or any vegetation. (22–23)

Like the contemptuously described landscape of the environs,
the land of Manilovka itself is as devoid of substance or vitality
as its fastidious master, who even under the gray skies, which
similarly allude to his colorless character, is obliged to shield
his eyes in order to descry the approaching carriage. The sun,
symbol of nature's regenerative powers, is alien to Manilov
and Manilovka alike. On its symbolic height far above the
peasant huts, the house is exposed solely to the force of the
symbolic winds that threaten to sever its few remaining ties
with life on earth and to blow it appropriately into the same
airless, supraterrestrial void in which the sterile thought of its
master senselessly revolves during the long hours of reflection
in his "Temple of Solitary Meditation."

This tenuous contact between the house and its "earthly"
foundations is doubtless intended to explain, in part,
Chichikov's difficulty in finding it. Not that Manilovka, of
course, is the only estate to pose this problem, for the arrival at
Korobochka's estate and the encounter with Nozdryov are
both unforeseen results of the difficulty in locating the domain
of the "bear." But although these locational problems, which
Belyy has linked with the motif of "sideways movements,"[2]
may be regarded collectively as preparatory allusions to the

collapse of Chichikov's scheme, each of them must be assessed in relation to its own immediate context. Thus it is not only fitting that Manilovka should prove to be twice as far from the town as its master indicated at the governor's party; it is equally apt that Chichikov should aggravate the problem of finding it by referring to it as Zamanilovka ("Trans-Manilovka") when asking the way. The announcement of the peasant with the wedge-shaped beard to whom he turns for directions that "there's no such place as Zamanilovka" (22) succinctly summarizes the entire character of Manilov's realm. It suggests that beyond Manilovka there is nothing, that the estate is located on the edge of a void, and since it is precisely to this void "beyond Manilovka" that Manilov's thought is irresistibly drawn, we may conclude that "Zamanilovka" is indeed the most accurate designation of his true home, while Manilovka itself is merely the lodging of his hollow frame. Hence the narrator's remarks that "at home he said very little" (24) and that "in his house there was always something lacking" (25).[3]

The two armchairs in the drawing room that are still covered only in bast matting and the completely unfurnished state of some of the other rooms confirm that Manilov's attachment to the house is as tenuous as the house's attachment to earth. The deficiencies of the house parallel the "deficiencies" of the vegetation. And it is plainly the aversion to the mundane implied by these details that explains Manilov's complete indifference to the efficient management of his estate, evidenced by the wayward habits of his house-serfs and steward and by his ignorance of how many dead serfs he has available for sale. Even to discuss these matters, as Chichikov quickly discovers, is a bewildering experience for him, a disorientating descent to earth. His speech suddenly becomes fractured and incoherent and, at the mention of the verb "died," (*umerli*), suffers a momentary seizure. Describing his reaction to this "very curious word," the narrator notes: "Manilov was utterly perplexed" (35), to which was added in an earlier draft the phrase "as if someone had sat him in mud" (710). The verb represents a violent intrusion of physical reality into Manilovka's rarefied atmos-

phere, and on recovering his composure Manilov swiftly replaces it with the less direct and more decorous "ended their
existence," (*okonchili svoyo sushchestvovaniye*) (36).

To suggest, however, that the portrait of Manilov is limited
to such illustrations of his detachment from the physical reality
of life would be to minimize its complexity and to ignore its
significant dramatic element. In this connection, we should
consider the implications of Manilov's name, which is no less
informative than "Nozdryov" and "Mikhail Semyonovich
Sobakevich." Derived from the verb *manit'* ("to beckon, attract, lure"), it alludes to an aspect of Manilov's character that
ostensibly contradicts his aspiration to sever every earthly
connection—to a craving for friendship or companionship that
his inner void has rendered him incapable of ever gratifying.
"In his gestures and turns of phrase," we read, "there was
something that seemed to be asking ingratiatingly for sympathy and friendship. He smiled alluringly [*zamanchivo*[4]]" (24).
Moreover, it is this compelling need for friendship that apparently inspires one of his most recurrent visions:

> Sometimes as he looked out from the porch on to the
> courtyard and the pond, he used to say how good it would
> be if an underground passage could be built from the
> house or a stone bridge constructed over the pond with
> shops on both sides of it and merchants sitting in them
> selling the various small articles needed by the peasants.
> (25)

In his daydream after Chichikov's departure his thoughts re-
vert to the same subject:

> He thought of the happiness of a life with friends, of the
> pleasure of living with a friend on the bank of some river,
> and then in his thoughts a bridge began to be built over
> this river followed by a huge house with a belvedere so
> high that even Moscow could be seen from it, and he
> pictured himself drinking tea there in the evenings in the
> open air and discussing agreeable subjects. (38–39)

The dream ends logically with the Emperor's gracious reaction to the spectacle of Manilov's moving friendship with Chichikov. Reality, however, presents a very different picture. "The village of Manilovka," observes the narrator "could attract [*zamanit'*] few people with its location" (22). Similarly its master attracts few people with his superficial charms. At the very outset, as we have seen, Chichikov feels obliged to "step a little further away from him," and after the completion of the "main business" he is quick to take his leave. " 'What? You wish to go already?' said Manilov, suddenly coming to himself and *almost frightened*[5]" (37).

The dreams of Manilov reflect an inner conflict, which criticism has thus far ignored. It is conveyed by the contrasting directions in which his thought moves—downward in the first dream, upward in the second. Manilov is torn between the belvedere and the underground passage, which respectively symbolize his aversion and lingering attachment to the earth and its inhabitants. The implications of this conflict can be appreciated only in the light of its background as reflected in the fragments of his biography.

Plyushkin is not, as critics have claimed, the only character in the novel besides Chichikov with a biography. Manilov's is certainly less detailed, but it certainly exists, and it is equally revealing, for it tells us that he had not always been the same. Gogol communicates this point once more by the expressive "military motif." We are told that before settling in, Manilovka Manilov was in the army and, in addition, that it was there he contracted the habit of smoking the pipe. It is true that he was considered in the army "a most modest, tactful, and educated officer" (25), and that even as a soldier he must have had the fair hair, which suggests a closer affinity with Mizhuyev than with Nozdryov, but it may be assumed that neither his service in the army nor his addiction to the pipe it apparently inspired would have merited the repeated references made to them, had they not been intended as signals of a vitality and residual "hunting instinct" which were subsequently lost. And it is appropriate to recall in this connection the figures of Manilov's two sons, aged eight and six, who confirm by their very existence that their father's disdain for the life of the body was not always so profound.

Even as the master of Manilovka, of course, Manilov retains his liking for his pipe and even commends the habit to Chichikov (32), but it is now a very different pipe from that of a "hunter," having degenerated into a mere stimulant of sterile thought. Instead of a "very handsomely built little house" designed to accommodate hounds, he has erected his "Temple of Solitary Meditation," surrendering the role of "hunter" to the two peasant women with the torn net noticed by Chichikov on his arrival, who are more interested in their quarrel than in their pitiful catch. No longer a weapon capable of tanning faces and singeing moustaches, Manilov's chibouk has become an instrument for the production of neat piles of ash. In response to Chichikov's determined "assault," it falls weakly from his hand to the floor and thereafter "only wheezed and nothing more" (35). The pipe, like its owner, has lost its vitality.

Reverting, therefore, to the scene of Chichikov's arrival at the estate, we may now appreciate the force of the seemingly digressive simile with which Gogol conveys the state of the weather:

> The day was neither clear nor gloomy, but of a light-gray color such as one finds only on the old uniforms of garrison soldiers, that army which is peaceful, but not completely sober on Sundays. (23)

The reference to "Sundays," which must allude to the day of Chichikov's visit,[6] simply confirms what is already evident —that the simile is a symbolic description of Manilov's condition. From a professional officer he has degenerated into the master of Manilovka, into a "garrison soldier" drunk on the wine of sterile thought. The inebriated state of Selifan at the beginning of chapter three is merely additional evidence of Manilovka's heady atmosphere.

To establish the reason for Manilov's transformation, we must first consider the question of when it occurred. In other words, we must ascertain when he retired from the army. Our first reaction is perhaps to assume, based on the length of his marriage, that he has served eight years as a "garrison soldier," but there are grounds for believing that another detail is the vital clue—namely, the age of Manilov's younger son, Alcides. To support this, there is a detail in an earlier description of the furniture in Manilov's drawing room that was omitted from the final version—a reference to a broken armchair to which "an arm and leg had been fixed simply for the sake of appearance" (706). The important point is that whereas Manilov, according to the final version, has been warning people not to sit on the chairs with the bast covers "for several years" (25), his warning about the state of the broken chair in the early version, in the narrator's words, "had been issued for six years, i.e. since the time when the chair broke" (706). Thus the chair was broken at approximately the same time that Alcides was born. This coincidence would seem a rather insubstantial basis for important hypotheses were it not for the evidence already presented that such coincidences repeatedly provide the main insights into Gogol's meaning. The coincidence between the day of the week on which Chichikov is given to rubbing himself down from head to foot with a wet sponge and the day on which garrison soldiers are prone to be "not completely sober" is merely the most recent example to be noted of a procedure that is fundamental to Gogol's artistic method. Nor should we necessarily attach any particular significance to the replacement of "six" with "several," for collation of every chapter with its earlier drafts, as individual observations on points arising in chapters four and five have already suggested, also confirms that Gogol was consistently disposed to make his meaning ever more obscure and thus impose increasingly heavy demands on his readers. In composing the final version, he evidently decided that for the perceptive reader to whom he addressed the work the age of Alcides would alone suffice to indicate the turning point in his father's life. With the aid of this detail, the reference to the length of his marriage, and the description of the furnishings, he conveys the vital information that Manilov married while still in the army, that he resigned his commission about two years later, and that his transformation was completed almost immediately afterwards before the furnishing of Manilovka could be concluded. A more condensed biography could hardly be conceived of.

With this information we can now consider the question of cause, the answer to which is suggested by the same sequence of events: the transformation of Manilov was set in motion by his marriage. The age of Alcides and the partly completed state of the furnishings indicate that in the first two years of married life he still retained some measure of the vitality denoted by his military career, but the abruptness of the transformation, as reflected in his failure to complete the furnishing, presupposes a degenerative process of some duration, the inception of which can only be related to his marriage or, more precisely, to his surrender to a woman's influence. Once more, therefore, the relationship between the sexes assumes a major importance.

Sobakevich and Nozdryov, as we have seen, hold essentially identical attitudes toward women, and the implications of these attitudes have been considered at some length. Manilov's attitude to his wife is plainly quite different. His general behavior in her presence and, in particular, his propensity for occasionally dropping tasty morsels into her "little mouth" reflect a slavish adoration and total subservience; there can be little doubt that this attitude is intended to explain the mystery of his personality. It is indicative of the "emasculation" that has transformed him from a serving officer into a "garrison soldier," divesting him of the few "masculine" attributes he once possessed. Whereas the wife of Sobakevich has been "masculinized," the husband of Manilova has been "feminized." Far from being a mirror image of her husband, Manilova has created in him a mirror image of herself. If it is true, therefore, as we have claimed, that "femininity" is Gogol's main symbol of spiritual purity, are we to infer that with the soul of Manilov all is well? The suggestion, of course, is contradicted by almost

every detail in his portrait. It presupposes the equally absurd
conclusion that the "femininity" of the "palely attired" (27)
Manilova, who is so lacking in presence that at first Chichikov
fails to notice her, is of essentially the same order as that of the
governor's daughter. Manilova is not another female symbol
of the uncorrupted human soul, but simply a personification of
"femininity" in its outward forms alone. She embodies the
attributes of the symbolic condition that might be termed
"superficial femininity," and Manilov's fate on marrying her
was to be subjected to a process of "superficial feminization."
For the soul itself, we may deduce, this "modest, tactful, and
educated officer," whose "masculinity" had never expressed
itself in extreme forms, mistook the "shell" of a soul. Like the
flies in the Homeric simile in chapter one, he was drawn to the
sugar, but it turned out to be shallow, a superficial sweetness
concealing a gaping void. Such is the "sweetness" of Manilov
himself after eight years of exposure to his wife's influence—
"sickly," in the narrator's words, "like the medicine which a
clever society doctor has sweetened unmercifully in the belief
that it will please his patient" (29).

Among the various images that reflect this stunting of Manilov's "masculinity," two deserve special note—the "plain
brass cripple of a candlestick, lame, lopsided, and covered in
tallow," which is placed in the evenings on the drawing-room
table alongside a "very ostentatious candlestick of dark bronze
with the three Graces of antiquity" (25); and the cock heard by
Chichikov on his arrival, in whose portrait we may recognize
another "debasement" of the symbolic bird image:

> To complete the picture there was no lack of a cock, that
> harbinger of changeable weather, who, despite the fact
> that his head had been pecked through right to the brain by
> the beaks of other cocks as a result of certain instances of
> philandering, was bawling very loudly and even flapping
> his wings, which were as bedraggled as old bast mats. (23)

The cock's wings are thus linked with the bast covers on the
two neglected armchairs. The indicator of the "hunter's"

transformation is appropriately linked with the symbol of the
transformed "hunter" himself, who has lost the ability to
"philander" with success and is now fit only for "garrison
duty," for announcing, as Manilov duly demonstrates on
Chichikov's departure, imminent changes in the weather.[7] In
chapter eight the narrator informs us: ". . . staid gentlemen
who occupy important posts are somehow a little ponderous in
their conversations with ladies; it is lieutenants and those below
the rank of captain who are experts at this" (169). Excellence at
"philandering" is an attribute of the "masculine hunter" that
Manilov himself had clearly been capable of displaying some
eight years earlier as a young officer; but now, as his "bedrag-
gled" ornithological symbol testifies, it has been sacrificed on
the altar of the three Graces, which allude not, as we would
normally expect, to the "feminine" attribute of fertility, but
ironically to its opposite, sterility—to the three sterile ingredients of Manilova's education[8]: "the French language, which
is essential for the happiness of family life; the pianoforte to
provide husbands with pleasant moments; and finally, household management proper: the knitting of purses and other
surprises" (26). Such are the "superficially feminine" attributes
that seduced the "hunter" from his former "masculine" preoccupations, transforming him into the same kind of "esmascu-
lated" cripple as the governor, of whom Chichikov says:

> . . . how clever he is! I would never have thought it. How
> beautifully he embroiders all kinds of domestic patterns.
> He showed me a purse that he had made: few ladies could
> have embroidered it so skillfully. (28)

The skill of the governor, which is first indicated in chapter one
by the reference to his partiality for "embroidering on tulle"
(12), identifies him as the comparable victim of a "superficially
feminine" wife.

The symbolic theme of "superficial femininity" plays the
same dominant role in chapter two as the theme of "masculinity" does (in its two contrasting forms) in chapters four and
five. It is the theme that similarly ties every detail and "digres-

sion" of the chapter into a "single, huge, common knot,"
denoting the first of the five basic types of spiritual mortification which are allegorically represented as deviations from the
ideal of "pure femininity." At the same time, as we have seen,
the "condition" denoted by the theme contrasts diametrically
with the "conditions" of Sobakevich and Nozdryov. Its most
distinctive symptom—an exclusive concern with externals, with the superficial "sweetening" of objects,[9] words,
thoughts, and gestures—implies an attitude of fastidious contempt for the crude, physical preoccupations that are the primary symptom of "masculinity." Hence the numerous
juxtapositions of Manilov and Sobakevich in the course of the
novel.[10] The contrast is perhaps most striking apparent in their
differing attitudes to food. Thus, while in the domain of the
"bear" the cabbage soup served at dinner is accompanied by
"the well-known dish which . . . consists of a sheep's stomach
filled with buckwheat stuffing, brains, and trotters" (98), followed by saddles of mutton and more stuffing, the cabbage
soup at Manilovka is unaccompanied, badly made, and the
only course. The diet of Manilov and his wife is conspicuously
lacking in meat, and Manilova's appetite seems to demand little
more than the pieces of apple, the sweets, and the nuts with
which her husband spasmodically regales her. A beaded
toothpick-case, as distinct from a toothpick, is thus a fitting
present for her birthday (26). Very different, however, are the
appetites of the two younger Manilovs.

The portrait of Manilov's children serves two main functions in the chapter. On the one hand, it complements the
references to Manilov's army life and to the state of the furnishings in the house by indirectly confirming that his personality
was once quite different. On the other, it provides new information by casting additional light on the "process" that transformed him. In effect, it highlights the initial stages of the
"emasculating process," which in Manilov himself has been
completed, and we may therefore appreciate why the two
children are male. They embody the "masculine" attributes
their father has given up, and so it is fitting that, like the heroes

of Sobakevich, they should bear Greek names—Themistoclus
(the Latin suffix of which is merely another reflection of Manilov's intellectual limitations) and Alcides. Moreover, the
names are not only Greek and therefore intrinsically expressive
of the physical element; they are also taken from pre-Christian
figures renowned for their "physical" accomplishments—the
Athenian general at the battle of Salamis and Hercules.[11]

The passion for meat, therefore, of these two infants, whom
Chichikov addresses as "little souls" (30, 38), is entirely in
harmony with their names. Alcides "gnawing at a bone of
mutton which made both his cheeks shine with grease" (31) is
the direct precursor in the novel of Sobakevich gnawing and
sucking half a saddle of mutton "down to the last little bone"
(99). And in Themistoclus the atrophied "hunting instinct" of
his father is reborn in all its primitive, "Nozdryovian" sharp-
ness. Displaying, perhaps, a hint of nostalgia for his past,
Manilov says of him: ". . . if he comes across anything, a small
insect or a beetle, his little eyes suddenly begin to dart. He races
after it and immediately becomes absorbed in it" (30–31). It is
no surprise, therefore, to encounter a few pages later the
"military motif." As Chichikov takes his leave, he "caught
sight," we read, "of Alcides and Themistoclus, who were busy
with a wooden hussar which had already lost its nose and an
arm" (38), and he promptly undertakes to reward them on his
next visit with the gift of a sword and a drum.

The contrast between parents and children is yet another
important element in Manilov's portrait that is anticipated in
the chapter's introductory section. Among the sights that catch
Chichikov's eye as he drives in search of Manilovka is some
wayside cottages, from the upper windows of which "peasant
women with fat faces and tightly bound bosoms were looking
out; from the lower windows a calf was staring or a pig was
thrusting its blind snout" (21–22). While the "tightly bound
bosoms" may allude to Manilova's sterility, the animals on the
lower floor foreshadow the appearance of her children.
Themistoclus and Alcides are the "pigs" of Manilovka, whose
dripping snouts require periodic wipes from the footman's

handkerchief, "for otherwise a rather large, superfluous drop would have fallen into the soup" (31). Their role in the portrait of Manilov is directly comparable to that of Petrushka in the portrait of Chichikov. They are the "bearers" of Manilov's "stench," personifications of the crude "masculinity" he has suppressed behind a façade of "superficially feminine" gestures.

The children, however, are plainly destined for the fate of their father. The suppression of their "masculinity" has already commenced. It is conveyed by Themistoclus's vigorous attempts to liberate his chin from the napkin that the servant has fastened around it (30), and by the testing of his knowledge of the French and Russian capitals. The implications of this exercise become apparent in the light of the contrasting details in chapter five, in which Gogol, as we have noted, establishes a correlation between "maculinity" and xenophobia (especially Francophobia) and represents the "masculine" attributes of physical might and crudity as "indigenous" Russian attributes, as the traditional attributes of the Russian bear. It seems logical, therefore, that a principal emblem of "superficial femininity" should be the addiction to non-Russian (especially French) customs, an eagerness to replace the "masculine" Russian element with a "superficially feminine" Gallic veneer. Thus follows the elevation of the French language, in the description of Manilova's intellectual attainments, to the status of one of the three Graces and the sequence of the questions put to Themistoclus (he is asked to name the French capital before the Russian capitals, and to name the Gallicised St. Petersburg before the "indigenous" Moscow).

Similar implications are also perceptible in Manilov's decision to have Themistoclus trained for a career that will take him beyond Russia's boundaries—diplomatist. We react to this announcement, of course, with considerable mirth. A less suitable candidate for diplomatic service could scarcely be imagined, and Gogol makes it quite clear that Themistoclus is not enthralled by the idea. Though obliged to answer affirmatively when asked whether he would like to be an ambassador, he is wholly preoccupied with the piece of bread he is chewing, and he accompanies his answer with a vigorous shake of the head, thereby producing on the end of his nose the "rather large, superfluous drop," which prompts the footman's intervention. Yet despite the comedy, we must not overlook the implication here that by the time the suppression is complete, Themistoclus, like his father, will indeed be fit only for "garrison duty" in some remote outpost, that the "masculine hunter" will have been transformed into a "superficially feminine" or "superficially Gallicised" diplomat whose pipe has likewise degenerated into a stimulant of ineffectual thought and whose partiality for biting his brother's ear has given way to embroidery on tulle.

Detachment from physical reality, therefore, is equated with detachment from Russia, first directly alluded to in the chapter with the reference to Manilov's "English garden" (22). Thereafter the allusions tend to be more oblique and ironic. Thus Manilov is moved to excuse the insubstantiality of the meal his guest is served by remarking: ". . . we have simply cabbage soup, according to the Russian custom" (30). He also informs Chichikov that in the absence of congenial neighbors he occasionally reads *The Son of the Fatherland* (29) and displays concern for the "future prospects" of Russia when Chichikov introduces the "main business" (35). Finally, we might consider once more in this connection the contradiction on the chapter's first page between Petrushka's limited portrait of two main features and the author's comment that he likes to be "circumstantial in everything and in this respect, though a Russian, he wishes to be as thorough as a German" (19). The contradiction anticipates Manilov's vain attempts to conceal his inner emptiness behind a "luring" screen of non-Russian charms.

Chichikov's similar preoccupation with concealment has already been indicated. Like the two violets that he places at the bottom of his snuffbox "for the sake of the scent" (16), his energetic soaping of his person reflects a similar urge to "sweeten" the stench of the "Petrushka" within him.

Moreover, his weakness for "shirts of Dutch linen" betrays a similar preference for non-Russian "sugar." The same preference, as Sobakevich repeatedly informs us, is also displayed by the citizens of N., and in chapter one it is reflected in such apparently random details as the shop sign that reads "Vasiliy Fyodorov, Foreigner" (11) and the playbill advertizing a performance of Kotzebue's *Pizarro: The Spaniards in Peru, or the Death of Rolla,* "in which Rolla was to be played by Mr. Poplyovin and Cora by Miss Zyablova" (12). In both cases the foreign veil is comically rent by the emphatically Russian names. Like the "military motif," which radiates outward from the portrait of Nozdryov, the "foreign motif" expands beyond the portrait of Manilov to the most distant corners of the novel, alluding whenever it occurs to the same discord between form and content that is the primary symptom of "superficial femininity."

4

Korobochka

The first aspect of chapter three (the "Korobochka chapter") that should be stressed is its importance to the plot of the novel, for it provides the first unmistakable intimations of Chichikov's fallibility and thus indirectly preannounces the collapse of his fraudulent scheme. The opening sentence of this chapter depicts him sitting "in a contented frame of mind" in his carriage after his successful visit to Manilovka, but his mood is swiftly undermined—first by the violent change of weather accurately predicted by the cocklike "garrison soldier"; then by the waywardness of the inebriated Selifan, who loses the way and overturns the carriage, tipping him into the mud; and finally by the taxing confrontation with the exasperating Korobochka instead of the expected Sobakevich—and although by the end of the chapter Chichikov seems to have prevailed once more, his victory is wholly illusory, for Korobochka later returns to deal one of the two fatal blows that insure his failure. For Chichikov, therefore, the entire "Korobochka episode" is an unmitigated disaster, and it poses two basic questions: why is it specifically in this chapter that misfortunes suddenly begin to rain down on him? And why is Korobochka endowed with this decisive role in determining his fortunes? Her portrait provides the answers both to these two questions and to a third closely related question: why does Gogol make his second landowner (and only the second) a woman?

Chapter three is no more intelligible than any of the other three that have been examined without reference to the sexual symbolism of the novel. It is true, of course, that we do not need to be aware of this symbolism to recognize that the relationship between Manilov and Korobochka is one of sharp contrast; but without this knowledge it is impossible to appreciate the implications of the contrast, the highly disciplined structure of the two chapters, and the expressiveness of their imagery. Bidding farewell at the end of chapter two to the "superficially feminized" male Manilov, Chichikov is confronted in the figure of Korobochka with the opposite phenomenon—a thoroughly "masculinized" female who lacks, of all the major "masculine" attributes, only physical bulk. A male who is less "masculine" than "feminine" is directly followed by a female who is less "feminine" than "masculine," and it is *this* contrast that explains both the juxtaposition of the two portraits and this sole departure from the sequence of male landowners.

In almost every significant respect, Korobochka is a direct female counterpart of Sobakevich, and it is consequently fitting that Chichikov should be battling to find the way to Sobakevich's estate when he encounters her. The differences between them are explained solely by the difference of biological, as distinct from symbolic, sex. Whereas Sobakevich, for example, seems to have surrounded himself with male subjects in whom his own powerful "masculine" attributes are flamboyantly reembodied, Korobochka seems to have killed off virtually every male on her estate. Every chore is performed by a female—the greeting of Chichikov, his admission to the house, the preparation of his bed, the cleaning of his muddied clothes, and the task of guiding him to the right road on his departure. Also female are the two house-serfs whom Korobochka sells to Father Kiril. Except for the peasant who appears in the gateway as Chichikov takes his leave (58), all the male inhabitants of the estate who are mentioned are dead—Korobochka's husband, her blacksmith, and the eighteen serfs whose names she gives to Chichikov—and the references to her husband, who was regularly accustomed, we are told, to having his muddied clothes dried (47), leave little doubt about the cause of their deaths: exhaustion from extreme overwork.

Thus the fate of the male in Korobochka's domain is even less
enviable than that of the female in the realm of the "bear." But
this does not mean that her attitude to females is significantly
different. On the contrary, her capacity for the "masculinization" of females, as we shall see, is at least a match for that of
Sobakevich. The difference between them lies solely in their
attitude to males, and it is explained, as stated, by Korobochka's sexual ambiguity—more precisely, by her usurpation of
the male role as head of the household.

For Korobochka every male threatens the continuing pre-
dominance of her rampant "masculinity," and the premature
death of her husband, who has plainly suffered the misfortune
of a fate comparable to that of Nozdryov's wife, is merely the
most chilling illustration of how she deals with such threats.
His fate is allusively conveyed by a passage which, like so many
others, has been viewed hitherto as simply a digressive author-
ial interpolation—the well-known "digression" prompted by
the different manner Chichikov affects to address his host on
passing from the "refined" Manilov to the down-to-earth
Korobochka. To bolster his contention that Russian modes
of address are infinitely more varied and subtly graded than
French or German, the narrator bids the reader picture the
following situation:

> Let us suppose, for example, that there exists a certain
> government office—not here, but at the other end of the
> world—and let us also suppose that in this office there
> exists a director of the office. I ask you to look at him as he
> sits among his subordinates—why, simply out of awe you
> would be incapable of uttering a word! Pride and nobility
> and what else doesn't his face express? Just take a brush
> and paint away: a Prometheus, a veritable Prometheus! He
> has the gaze of an eagle and he paces with a smooth,
> measured step. But the same eagle, as soon as he has left
> the room and approaches the office of his superior, scur-
> ries along like a partridge with papers under his arm as fast
> as his legs will carry him. In society or at an evening party,

if everyone is of low rank, the Prometheus will remain a
Prometheus, but if they are even slightly above him, the
Prometheus will undergo a transformation such as even
Ovid could not have invented: a fly, even smaller than a
fly; he has been crushed into a grain of sand! "But this is
not Ivan Petrovich," you say as you look at him. "Ivan
Petrovich is taller, while this man is short and thin. Ivan
Petrovich speaks in a loud, deep voice and never laughs,
while this one speaks in the devil only knows what kind of
voice: cheeps like a bird and laughs incessantly." You
move closer and take a look—it is Ivan Petrovich after all.
(49–50)

The transposition of the scene to "the other end of the
world" may be compared, as an instance of ironic deception, to
Gogol's procedure of presenting specific allusions in the form
of digressive generalizations. Its function is plainly to obscure
the direct relevance of the scene to the relationship between
Korobochka and the deceased collegiate secretary who was her
husband. The identity of the "eagle" is disclosed most
explicitly toward the end of the passage when he is finally
invested with a name, for less than half a page later it is echoed
in Korobochka's own name, Nastas'ya Petrovna, which shows
the same patronymic. The proximity of the two names makes
it inconceivable that this is mere coincidence, and it may be
recalled that Gogol had similarly used a common patronymic
to link husband and wife in his story *The Old-World Landowners
(Starosvetskiye pomeshchiki)* (1835). There it alludes to the close-
ness of their relationship, to a state of mutual dependence so
complete that the wife's death is quickly followed by that of the
husband, who cannot sustain himself on being parted from her.
This connotation of the common patronymic in the story
highlights the ironic implications of the similar bond established between Nastas'ya Petrovna and Ivan Petrovich, and it
seems likely that Gogol had the story very much in mind when
creating this new picture of marital relations, conveyed almost
entirely by allusions. Now it is the husband who has died, and

the wife is certainly capable of surviving his death; she has even effected it, having reduced the tall, powerful eagle to a short, thin fly, whose sole compensation for his back-breaking toil in the mud was the nocturnal ritual of having his heels tickled. Hence the previously unknown propensity of the transformed Ivan Petrovich to laughter. And it is possible that Gogol is alluding directly to this transformation when, in feigned sympathy with Chichikov's later desperate struggles to break down Korobochka's resistance as he offers to buy her dead serfs, the narrator comments: "It sometimes happens that a respectable man, and even a civil servant [e.g. the "Promethean" director of some government office] turns out in practice to be a perfect Korobochka" (53). Ivan Petrovich does indeed become Korobochka, while Korobochka herself assumes the role of Ivan Petrovich. Like a female spider—an image evoked, as we shall see, by a number of details in her portrait—she has consumed her mate and usurped his position.

Among the more elusive indicators of these role changes is the flannel scarf that appears to be an invariable part of Korobochka's attire. Thus when Chichikov first meets her, she is described as "an elderly woman in a kind of nightcap which had been put on hurriedly and with a piece of flannel round her neck" (45), and on greeting her the next morning he notices that she "was better dressed than on the day before—in a dark dress and no longer in the nightcap, but something was still tied in the same manner round her neck" (48–49). The significance of this detail is indicated by the narrator's comments in chapter one on Chichikov's scarf:

> The gentleman threw off his cap and unwound from his neck a woolen, rainbow-colored scarf such as wives make with their own hands for their husbands, providing them with proper instructions on how they should wrap themselves up, but who makes them for bachelors I truly cannot say—God only knows—I have never worn such scarves myself. (9)

In the context of chapter one the detail seems to hang in a void, where it remains until drawn into the allegory's fabric by its connection with the similar detail in the portrait of Korobochka. Like Chichikov's carriage, the scarf is emblematic of "masculinity." It is an object that is usually made by wives for their husbands. Its appearance, therefore, around Korobochka's neck must be interpreted as yet another signal of her triumph over the hapless Ivan Petrovich, of her appropriation of the dominant male role, and it seems fitting that on no occasion should Chichikov see her without it. It is a mark of her defiant, challenging "masculinity," an indicator that she faces her visitor as an equal—male versus male.

We may now understand, therefore, why Chichikov's entry into the domain of Korobochka is fraught with hazard and why his misfortunes begin at this point. They are the predictable result of his encounter with a woman for whom the "masculinity" of every male represents a force she is instinctively impelled to compete with—a woman whose main purpose in life seems to be reducing males to the status of flies and eventually exterminating them before their threat to her position, as she sees it, can materialize. From Chichikov himself there is no sign that he is conscious of his predicament. On the contrary, he seriously misjudges his adversary from the start, adopting a totally inappropriate "Promethean" mode of address. The narrator comments: "The reader, I imagine, has already observed that Chichikov, despite his affable appearance, nevertheless spoke to her more freely than to Manilov and did not stand on ceremony at all" (49), and it is precisely at this point that he proceeds to illustrate how a Prometheus can be transformed into a grain of sand. But Chichikov is blissfully unaware that he himself is being measured for a similar Ovidian metamorphosis and has no compunction about addressing his hostess by the excessively familiar term *matushka* ("my dear lady", literally "mother"), which reflects his failure to perceive anything beneath the feminine exterior.[1] For Korobochka, who responds at once by addressing him as *batyushka* ("my dear fellow," literally "father")—a style that in this context has decidedly sinister overtones—the term is implicitly a challenge, and the continuing adherence of the two interlocutors to these terms in their ensuing dialogue is expressive of the struggle for "masculine" primacy that is fought below the surface of their heated dispute about the sale of dead serfs.

The alternating of *matushka* and *batyushka* exemplifies the oblique way Gogol conveys Korobochka's view of Chichikov as a threat to be silenced, but this is not the only evidence he provides. Equally revealing are the details that link Chichikov with the deceased Ivan Petrovich. From the moment Korobochka first appears, Gogol makes it plain that she sees him as a kind of double of her late husband. Following the latter's custom, for example, Chichikov presents himself in mud-bespattered clothes and immediately receives the same attentions of which Ivan Petrovich was apparently once the unfortunate beneficiary. Owing to the lateness of the hour, food is denied him; he is offered only grease for his back and a spell of heel-tickling, without which, Korobochka remarks, "my late husband could not get to sleep" (47). After comparing him in his muddied state to a hog (46), she then instructs the maid Fetin'ya in drying his clothes, adding: ". . . dry them in front of the fire as you used to do for your late master" (47). Moreover, the following morning Korobochka sees the half-conscious Chichikov as he lies in bed with the clothes pushed back, in the same state of nakedness in which presumably she had often seen her husband—a state that also alludes, of course, to his failure through ignorance to take proper precautions against the danger that threatens him. He exposes his naked body just as later in the chapter he exposes the contents and structure of his mysterious box, thereby conveying once more his total misjudgment of the "dear old lady" whom he addresses so informally. And finally, we might note the additional connection between deceased husband and guest in Chichikov's disclosure to Korobochka that a sister of his mother also bears the name Nastas'ya Petrovna (50). In other words, "Petrovna" is also the patronymic of Chichikov's mother. Since only paternal patronymics are normally bestowed on offspring, no significance would normally be attached to such a fact, but Gogol never includes such seemingly pointless details without reason. In this context of sexual conflict the situation is emphatically abnormal and the logic consistent. For the man-hating Korobochka the maternal patronymic is of greater importance, linking Chichikov with the husband whom she reduced to a fly.

In the scene that greets Chichikov as he looks through his bedroom window on arising, Gogol presents a symbolic picture of hostess and guest and of the relationship Korobochka seeks to impose:

> The window almost looked out on to the hen coop; at any rate the small, narrow yard that lay before it was filled with birds and all kinds of domestic animals. There were innumerable hens and turkey hens, and among them a cock was strutting about with measured steps, shaking his comb and turning his head to the side as if he were listening to something. There was also a sow there with her family; there and then, as she rummaged through a pile of rubbish, she gobbled up a chick in passing and, without noticing it, continued to devour the water-melon rinds one after another. (48)

Significantly, Chichikov sees the cock almost immediately after Korobochka has poked her head around the bedroom door, seen him naked, and promptly vanished, and, maintaining his unceremonious manner, he responds to the cock's gobbled greeting with the kind of abuse he later showers on the unyielding Korobochka. Considering the obvious indications that Gogol wishes to sharpen as much as possible the contrast between Korobochka and Manilov, whose sexual ambivalence is likewise symbolized by the state of his rooster, we can entertain few doubts that this imposing bird is likewise a symbol of its owner. While the cock of Manilov is a graphic sign of "emasculation," the proudly strutting turkey-cock of Korobochka loudly proclaims her triumphant "masculinity."

Like the estate as a whole, the pen seems to contain only one male—herself; and in her masculine ornithological guise she paces, in a manner reminiscent of the "masculinized," gooselike Feoduliya Ivanovna, with the "measured steps [*mernymi shagami*]" she has appropriated from Ivan Petrovich, who in his "Promethean" days was comparably given to walking with a "smooth, measured step [*plavno, merno*]", still turning her head to the side as she is accustomed to do in her feminine human form.[2] And beside her stands her new adversary, Chichikov, in the form she aspires to reduce him to. Having been compared by her in his muddied clothes to a hog, the luckless hero, whose luggage in chapter one included "a roast chicken wrapped in blue paper" (8),[3] is metamorphosed into a chick-devouring sow. Employing once more the "bird motif" later to be taken up in chapter five, Gogol portrays his hero as a "demasculinized" pig under the threatening surveillance of his "defeminized," cocklike hostess, whose habit of killing pigs is later disclosed by a reference to the pig fat she rubs into her aches and pains (49).

As informative as the inhabitants of the hen pen is the pen itself which, in effect, is a microcosm of Korobochka's entire estate—which, like the domain of Sobakevich, is essentially a prison governed with ruthless authority. Hence the recurrence of the motif of "fences," yet another link between chapters three and five and their closely related central figures. Just as the hen pen is "partitioned off by a fence made of planks" (48), so the estate as a whole is protected against intrusions from without by the fence that the shafts of Chichikov's carriage collide with on his arrival, making it impossible for Selifan "to drive any further" (43). It is a completely insulated realm for whose inhabitants, as Korobochka's ignorance of Manilov and Sobakevich testifies, the outside world is virtually nonexistent. Chichikov thus discovers it purely by chance after a painful journey across ploughed fields in impenetrable darkness. Even after entering the courtyard he still has difficulty seeing the house "because of the darkness" (44). Every effort seems to have been made by Korobochka to limit access as much as possible and to achieve the most complete isolation. It is not surprising, therefore, that she should find it so hard to tell Chichikov the way back to the main road: "How am I to do it?" she asks. "It's difficult to say, for there are many turnings. Perhaps I should give you a girl to guide you" (57).

Like Manilovka, the estate of Korobochka seems to be at the ends of the earth, but its isolation, of course, expresses a quite different meaning. It alludes not to transcendental aspirations and rejection of the mundane, but to the "canine" attributes of misanthropy and unyielding territorial domination. While the thought of Manilov soars into the shimmering heights, Korobochka digs her claws into the earth of her domain and even into the bones of her dead souls whom she finds such an intolerable financial burden. She is eventually prevailed on to release them only by the hope of subsequent gain and after Chichikov has assured her that "the bones and graves will all be left to you" (54). The collision of the carriage with the sturdy fence is a prefiguration of this later collision between the hero and his "canine" hostess, in the description of which Chichikov is indirectly compared to a rubber ball rebounding from a wall (53). It is wholly appropriate, therefore, that the first sound Chichikov should hear on his arrival at the estate is dogs barking and that at the height of his frustration in the later negotiations he should compare her to a "mongrel" (*dvornyazhka*) that "doesn't eat hay itself and allows no one else to eat it" (54). In the figure of Korobochka, Sobakevich has a precursor of equal "canine" tenacity, and we may consequently appreciate why Chichikov in chapter three, as both Selifan and Korobochka discover, is as prone to use "strong words" as he is in chapter five. Like the hounds of Nozdryov, the canine sentinels of Korobochka, which announce the intruder's arrival in such stentorian tones, are an extension of their owner's hostile personality.

The barking of the dogs is merely one of the deafening noises Chichikov is subjected to on the night he arrives. It is accompanied by thunder claps and the resonant hissing of Korobochka's clock. The association between Korobochka and noise has

frequently been indicated, but the possibility that this prominent element in her portrait might be meaningful has not been
seriously considered. As the image of the storm most obviously suggests, it may be interpreted, in one sense, to indicate
the dangerous situation into which Chichikov has trespassed
and thus as an allusion to the truth behind the appearance of his
welcome. He is battered by the noise just as the carriage is
battered by the fence and as he is later to be battered by the
"wall" from which he "rebounds." But there is no reason to
suppose that the noise is generated solely for Chichikov's
benefit. We may relate the noise of the thunder to his arrival,
but not the noise of the clock, which has presumably always
emitted the same stunning hiss. Chichikov is not alone in the
battering he receives; it is the daily lot of every inhabitant of the
estate. Noise, in other words, is an instrument of Korobochka's
authority. It is one of the scourges with which her subjects are
habitually lashed. Hence the connection between noise and
time.

The effect on Chichikov of the clock's striking is described
thus:

> The mistress's words were interrupted by a strange hiss-
> ing which caused the visitor almost to take fright. The
> noise was such that it seemed as if the room were full of
> snakes. But looking up he calmed down, for he realized
> that the clock on the wall had conceived the desire to
> strike. (45)

Although the knowledge that it is only the clock hissing reas-
sures Chichikov, we can be certain that it has the opposite effect
on Korobochka's serfs. For them the clock is indeed like a
snake, a symbol of the discipline that grips them in its coils and
fetters them to their life-devouring toil. The passage continues:

> The hissing was following at once by a hoarse wheezing,
> and finally, exerting all its strength, it struck two o'clock
> with such a sound that it seemed as if someone were
> banging with a stick on a broken pot. (45–46).

The simile graphically illustrates the function of time and noise in Korobochka's grim domain. They are just two of the various "sticks" that transform the souls in her charge with Ovidian (i.e. pagan) facility into "broken pots."

The "broken pot" image anticipates the disclosure ten pages later of the nicknames of three of Korobochka's dead souls —Pyotr Savel'yev Neuvazhay-Koryto ("Disrespectful-of-Troughs"), Koroviy kirpich ("Cow's Brick"), and Ivan Koleso ("Ivan the Wheel")—which similarly reflect the reduction of the soul (in both senses of the term) to the status of a tool, utensil, or implement, to an object of use. "Those who have died," remarks Korobochka, "were all such fine fellows, such good workers" (51). Their capacity for work is the sole criterion by which their value is measured. Accordingly, the two girls sold to Father Kiril merit the single comment: ". . . they've turned out to be such fine workers. They can even weave table napkins" (52), while the efficiency with which Chichikov's clothes are dried and with which his bed is made and then cleared testifies to a similar capacity for "fine work" on the part of the maid Fetin'ya, who "was obviously," the narrator observes, "an expert at shaking up featherbeds" (47). The discipline of the clock has transformed them all into productive automata doomed to toil with unstinting effort till, like Ivan Petrovich, they drop. Hence the statement that the first of the barking canine "sentinels" "brought forth his notes, with his head tossed back, in such a drawn-out manner and with such effort that it seemed as if he were receiving for it God knows what salary" (44); and even the shattering volume of the clock's hissing is perhaps intended to imply a comparable "over-fulfillment" of its norm.

For Selifan, of course, the brief exposure to this hive of productive activity swiftly dissipates the lingering effects of the visit to Manilovka. By the end of the chapter the chatty driver of the opening scenes has become decidedly surly:

Selifan was sullen the whole way and at the same time very attentive to his business, which always happened after he

had either done something wrong or been drunk. The
horses had been wonderfully groomed. The collar on one
of them, which hitherto had almost always been put on in
a torn condition, so that the oakum peeped out from under
the leather, had been skillfully sewn up. (59)

As later observations confirm, the reason suggested in the first
sentence for this remarkable "metamorphosis" is yet another
Gogolian red herring; the true reason has already been disclosed by the indicated pattern of allusive details.

Another curious detail that may likewise relate to the clock's
arresting noise is the intriguing proneness of Korobochka's
subjects to "hoarse wheezing." While the authoritarian control
of Sobakevich is denoted by the reproduction in his serfs of his
own physical dimensions, the control of Korobochka is conveyed by the echoes of the clock's sound in her subjects' voices.
For example, almost immediately on Chichikov's arrival, his
ears are twice assaulted by variations of the same symbolic
sound—the howling of the "heftily canine" fourth member of
Korobochka's choir of dogs who "wheezed," we are told "just
as a melodious basso profundo wheezes [*khripel, kak khripit
pevcheskiy kontrabas*] when a concert is at its height" (44), and,
more significantly, by the "hoarse female voice [*khriplyy babiy
golos*]" (44) of the "indeterminate figure [*kakaya-to figura*]" who
responds to Selifan's knocking at the gates. Although the motif
is clearly connected in the former example to the "canine"
character of Korobochka's control, in the latter it alludes to the
"masculinization" of her female serfs, to the blurring of their
sexual identity, which denotes the destruction of their souls.
This association of the motif with the sexual symbolism of the
novel is confirmed three chapters later by the description of
Plyushkin's housekeeper:

Near one of the buildings Chichikov soon noticed an
indeterminate figure [*kakuyu-to figuru*] who had started
squabbling with the peasant who had arrived in the cart.
For a long time he could not make out the figure's sex,
whether it was a man or a woman. Its dress gave no clear

indication; it bore a close resemblance to a woman's housecoat, and on its head was a cap such as is worn by female house-serfs in the country, but the voice seemed to him rather husky [*siplym*] for a woman's. (114)

Like the striped wallpaper, therefore, on the walls of Korobochka's sitting room, which suggests bars, the cacophonous noises on her estate, particularly those characterized by "hoarseness," are emblematic of the prison in which her female subjects are ruthlessly "masculinized." Equally expressive of this same symbolic idea is another prominent motif in the chapter—"mud." Reference has already been made to how this motif is used in linking Chichikov (as a "feminized" hog) with the deceased Ivan Petrovich and thus in highlighting the danger by which the unsuspecting hero is threatened. But its role is by no means confined to that of a signal. It has its own independent meaning—a meaning indirectly illuminated by the contrasting nature of the mud on Nozdryov's estate. When Nozdryov conducts his guests to the barely visible boundary of his lands, "they at first took care and walked slowly and cautiously, but afterwards, on seeing that this served no useful purpose, they ambled straight on without bothering to determine where there was more mud or less" (74). The mud of Nozdryov, therefore, has no inhibiting effect on movement at all; it can no more than any other obstacle arrest the progress of the "lively," reckless "hunter." The mud of Korobochka, however, has an entirely different character. When at the beginning of the chapter the rain predicted by Manilov begins to fall, the narrator notes: "The dust which lay on the road was quickly churned into mud, and with every minute it became more difficult for the horses to pull the carriage" (42); and at the end, when Chichikov takes his leave, the mud poses even greater problems:

Although it was a very fine day, the ground had become so muddy that the wheels of the carriage, as they threw it up, soon became covered with it, as if with felt, and this added considerably to the carriage's weight. Moreover, the soil was clayey and unusually sticky. For these two reasons they could not get away from the country roads before midday. (60)

The picture of Chichikov floundering in the mud at the beginning, after Selifan has overturned the carriage, foreshadows this one of them struggling to extricate themselves at the end. The mud is like a moat—an impediment, or rather deterrent, to both access and escape. Complementing the fences and the canine guards, it forms the outer defensive circle of Korobochka's prison, ensnaring like flypaper would-be intruders and fugitive "souls."

Chichikov eventually effects his escape only with the aid of the eleven-year-old girl Pelageya, whom Korobochka lends him as a guide. Perhaps it is implied that Pelageya, as a child, has yet to undergo the soul-destroying "metamorphosis" suffered by the other females who appear, and thus she retains a knowledge of the road to freedom that they have lost. At least no reference is made to the "hoarseness" of her voice, and perhaps an allusion to this knowledge may be detected in her name, which is derived from the Greek *pelagos* ("sea") and therefore suggests one of the most common romantic symbols of freedom. But although Pelageya still possesses this knowledge, she can no longer use it for her own advantage, and the *Greek* derivation of her name is probably intended to indicate that escape from the "metamorphosis" is no longer possible for her. Lifelong captivity is her unalterable fate, and the main symbol of this fate is the condition of her feet. When she first appears, they are described as "so thickly plastered with fresh mud that from a distance one might have taken them for boots" (58–59); the chapter ends with Selifan muttering to her through his teeth: "Oh, you black-footed creature!" (60). Thus the portrait of Korobochka and her domain appropriately ends, as it begins, with the same expressive symbol of captivity.

Ensnared by the mud, Pelageya is doomed to the fate of every other female in Korobochka's service, and her short journey with Chichikov offers her perhaps her last sight of the freedom she craves. Her conversation with Selifan, when he asks her the way, reflects her inner conflict:

> "To the right, is it?" Selifan asked curtly, addressing the girl sitting beside him, and pointed with his whip towards the road which had turned black in the rain between the freshened, bright green fields.
>
> "No, no, I'll show you," the girl answered.
>
> "Which way, then?" said Selifan when they had driven a little nearer.
>
> "That's the way," replied the girl, pointing with her hand.
>
> "Well, you're a one," said Selifan. "Why, that is to the right. She doesn't know which way is right and which is left!" (59)

The first point worth comment here is raised by Selifan's opening question, for it is noteworthy that in general, whenever the narrator mentions the direction of his turnings, they are to the right. In chapter two he turns right on the advice of the peasant with the wedge-shaped beard who directs him to Manilovka (22), and again he turns instinctively right when he loses the way at the beginning of chapter three (41). He is also urged to turn to the right by the enraged driver of the carriage bearing the governor's daughter in chapter five (90). The impression conveyed by these repeated references to right-hand turns is that in the course of his visits Chichikov is transported clockwise around the circles of a descending spiral, and again the possibility of Dante's influence naturally suggests itself. When Selifan, therefore, in obvious anticipation of an affirmative reply, asks Pelageya whether their path lies to the right, he implies his expectation that the same circular, "infernal" course will be continued. The road to the right, however, is the road of "dead souls"; transformed by the rain into black mud, it is the road of captivity, and Pelageya instinctively rejects it. Yet she has no choice but to take it in the end. For both Pelageya and Chichikov there is no access to the freedom symbolized by the "freshened, bright green fields." The right-hand turning can be postponed but not avoided. Like Dante, the hero must continue along the circular route that confronts him with the splintered facets of his own spiritual malaise, while Pelageya, forcibly restrained by her shackles of mud, must submissively return to her prison.

Having received from the departing Chichikov his assurances that he will not try to carry off Pelageya, Korobochka "began to examine everything in her yard. She fixed her eyes [*vperila glaza*] on the housekeeper, who was carrying a wooden vessel full of honey from the storeroom, and on a peasant who had appeared in the gateway, and little by little she became completely absorbed in the affairs of the estate" (58). The passage provides perhaps the most vivid illustration of Korobochka's eaglelike surveillance of her subjects; it also indirectly "explains" a reference to Chichikov when he first enters her house: "He felt that his eyes were sticking together, as if someone had coated them with honey" (45). The image of glutinous honey is clearly cognate with that of the clinging mud and may be regarded as an extension of the same motif. It reinforces the oblique comparison of Korobochka's realm to an intricate spider's web. And although, as stated, the end of the chapter seems to suggest that Chichikov finally succeeds in shaking himself free, we learn five chapters later that his freedom is simply a mirage. Gogol's vocabulary conveys the truth when he describes Chichikov's reactions to Nozdryov's revelations at the governor's ball:

> He began to feel uncomfortable, ill at ease, just as if he had stepped with a beautifully polished boot into a filthy, stinking puddle—in a word, bad, very bad. He tried not to think about it; he made efforts to distract himself, to amuse himself, and sat down to a game of whist, but everything went wrong like a crooked wheel. (173)

Thus the moment of disaster is signified by Chichikov's metaphorical relapse into the same metaphorical mud that makes him hoglike on the night of his arrival at Korobochka's estate, and three pages later Korobochka herself duly arrives on the scene to finish her victim off. Such is the denouement, the way having been prepared on the novel's first page when the two peasants converse about the durability of the carriage's crooked wheel. Just as Korobochka clings tenaciously to her dead serfs (including "Ivan the Wheel"), so she clings to the wheel of Chichikov's departing carriage, ultimately combining with the remorseless "hunter" to create the "filthy, stinking puddle" in which it finally breaks down. Into the town she brings in pursuit the twin emblems of her prison—mud and noise.

The most obvious emblem, however, of Korobochka's prison is her name, which means "box."[4] Hitherto it has been customary to regard it simply as an allusion to her acquisitive or accumulative instinct—to her habit of thrusting everything that comes her way into boxes, bags, sacks, and sundry containers. Thus in her first appearance, she is characterized as "one of those dear old ladies, small landowners, who . . . accumulate money little by little in multicolored linen bags which they stow away in chests of drawers. In one bag they put nothing but silver roubles, in another fifty-copeck pieces, and in a third twenty-five-copeck pieces" (45). Even the rainwater flowing from her roof falls "into a tub specially positioned for it" (44), and every other substance and object seems likewise to have been ordered, categorized, and assigned an appropriate "box." Since, however, the entire estate with its fences and protective ring of mud is itself a tightly sealed "box," it is quite conceivable that this methodical "boxing" of the inanimate is meant to imply a similar treatment of the estate's inhabitants. The comparison of the roads which lead out of the estate to "captured crayfish emptied from a sack" (60) suggests that Korobochka's containers are primarily, and appropriately, symbols of containment, and it is interesting to observe how the chapter's syntax reflects this implication of the motif.

In chapter four we have noted the correspondence between Nozdryov's disruptive, iconoclastic approach to life and the long, amorphous inventories of heterogeneous objects that punctuate the narrative flow. Chapter three is distinguished by

the recurrence of a sharply contrasting structure in which
everything is rigidly ordered and compartmentalized. The description quoted above of Korobochka's "categorization" of
her money is characteristic of this harmony between syntax
and symbolic theme: "In one bag, . . . in another, . . . and in a
third. . . ." A second example of the same "boxy" syntactic
structure is met earlier in the same paragraph—the description
of the dogs and their barking:

> One brought forth his notes . . .; another was snapping
> away rapidly . . .; between them a restless treble rang
> out . . .; and all this was finally capped by a bass. (44)

And the same type of structure occurs in the description of the
flies that settle on Chichikov's face, rousing him from his
slumbers:

> One sat on his lip, another on his ear, a third was striving
> to work out some way of settling even on his eye, while
> the one which had had the imprudence to sit near his
> nostril he had drawn up while still half asleep into his nose,
> which made him sneeze violently. (49)

Two other examples in the chapter are the narrator's typology
of the various kinds of landowner who each merit a distinct
mode of address (49) and the description of the structure and
contents of Chichikov's box in which, as in a number of other
instances, the transitions from one syntactic "box" to another
are marked by the adverb "then" (*potom*):

> . . . in the very middle was the soap container, and behind
> it there were six or seven narrow little partitions for
> razors; then there were square nooks for a sandbox and an
> inkwell with a little boat which had been hollowed out
> between them for pens, pieces of sealing wax and every-
> thing that was a little long; then came all kinds of com-
> partments, some with lids and others without lids, for
> things that were on the short side, filled with visiting
> cards, funeral cards, theatre tickets, and other cards which
> were kept together as souvenirs. The entire upper drawer

with all its compartments could be taken out, and beneath it was a space filled with piles of papers in folio; then followed a small secret drawer for money, which could be opened imperceptibly from the side of the box. (55–56)

The two levels of the box clearly allude to the two levels of Chichikov's personality—the "cleansed," urbane exterior and its underlying "stench." It is equally clear, however, that the inclusion of this exposé in chapter three is no more fortuitous than the inclusion of Chichikov's meeting with the governor's daughter in chapter five. It is as relevant to Korobochka and her domain as it is to Chichikov. Between the box's numerous partitions and compartments and Korobochka's fences and pens, there is an obvious connection. Like all the other containers in the chapter, the box of Chichikov, which contains in its concealed lower compartment his lists of dead souls, alludes to the large, intricately constructed "box" that is Korobochka's prison.

In the same connection we should also consider the details and events comprising the dramatic introductory section of the chapter, i.e. that which precedes the direct portrayal of Korobochka and her estate and describes the journey of Chichikov and Selifan from Manilovka. Thus we have already noted the symbolic implications of the storm, the thunder, and the mud Chichikov falls into, as well as the relevance to Chichikov's prospective hostess of the "strong words" he uses to scold the besotted Selifan. But the "introduction" is far richer in meaning than these details would suggest. Significant, for example, is Selifan's lengthy response to Chichikov's threats of a beating:

As your worship pleases. . . . If it's to be a whipping, then let it be a whipping. I have nothing at all against it. Why shouldn't you give a fellow a whipping if he's deserved it? That's what a master's power is for. You should administer a whipping, because a peasant takes liberties, and order must be maintained. If he's deserved it, then give him a whipping. Why not whip him? (43)

The unusual garrulity of Selifan at the beginning of chapter three undoubtedly reflects, as stated earlier, his susceptibility to Manilovka's inebriating atmosphere. But there can also be little doubt that his words point toward the new destination to which he is unwittingly conveying his master. His acknowledgment that peasants must be whipped to maintain order can only be regarded as alluding to the discipline that prevails in Korobochka's "box," while the readiness with which he apparently submits foreshadows her regimented subjects' state of mind.

Selifan's passive surrender, however, to the threat of his master's whip is merely a pretense; his actual response is the maneuver that later hurtles Chichikov into the clinging mud. Selifan is threatened with a whip, yet is himself possessor of a whip—the whip he uses to thrash the three horses, displaying in the process a vigor strongly reminiscent of that of Sobakevich's "masculinized" emissaries, Uncle Mityay and Uncle Minyay. The main recipient of his stinging blows is the cunning, dapple-gray side-horse, who excels in concealing his indolence and with whom Selifan is engaged in intermittent conflict throughout the novel; it is noteworthy that the lash is applied to the horse both when Chichikov approaches Korobochka's estate and when he departs at the end of the chapter. The portrait of Korobochka and her domain, then, is framed by the thrashing of the dapple-gray. The allusion, of course, is unmistakable, and we may now understand why, in Selifan's dialogue with Pelageya quoted above, he points to the right—i.e. to the black, muddy road of captivity—with his whip. The whip of Selifan is one of many allusions by which the reader is made aware of Korobochka's invisible whip.

We miss the main implication of the allusion, however, unless we recognize that Selifan's equine victim is, in fact, Chichikov's alter ego. A hint of this relationship is provided in chapter five by the corresponding fascination of Chichikov with the governor's daughter and the dapple-gray with one of the horses harnessed to her carriage. In chapter three, two other hints are offered, the more explicit being the narrator's comment on Selifan's remonstrations with the horse: "If Chichikov had been listening, he would have learnt many details relating to himself personally" (41). The other is in one of the phrases by which Selifan addresses the horse—"you confounded Bonaparte!" (41)⁵—which anticipates the suspicion later entertained by the dignitaries of the town of N. (in the wake of Korobochka's intervention) that Chichikov is Napoleon in disguise. Thus the thrashings of the dapple-gray allude not only to the fate of Korobochka's captive souls, but also to the "thrashing" of Chichikov, which begins with his tumble into Korobochka's mud. This misfortune heralds the downfall of the false Napoleon at the hands of the woman whose sitting room is appropriately adorned with a portrait of Kutuzov (47).

The activity of Korobochka's whip—in particular, its application to Chichikov's broad back—is also conveyed in the introductory section of the chapter by two more allusive details: the rain and the thunder. After the first drops have fallen,

> Finally, a second clap [*udar*] of thunder rang out more loudly and closer, and the rain suddenly poured down [*khlynul*] in bucketsfull. At first it came down in an oblique direction and lashed [*khlestal*] one side of the carriage and then the other. (41)

Besides the ambiguity of *udar*, which means "blow" as well as "clap," the verb *khlestat'* ("to lash") clearly effects the comparison to a whip of this pouring rain, which, of course, produces Korobochka's mud. The verb merely clarifies, however, the implication already apparent in the earlier verb *khlynut'* ("to pour"), for it is noticeable that in describing Selifan's punishment of the dapple-gray, Gogol uses neither *khlestat'* nor its perfective form *khlestnut'*, but a much rarer verb with the same meaning, *khlysnut'*. It is used twice in the first paragraph of the chapter and is again taken up at the end:

> The dapple-gray felt some very unpleasant blows [*udary*] on his broad, plump parts. "Just look how swollen it has become," he thought to himself, slightly twitching his

ears. "He certainly knows where to strike! He won't lash
[*khlysnyot*] you right across the back, but chooses a more
tender spot: stings you on the ears or lashes [*zakhlysnyot*]
you under the belly." (59)

Although *khlynut'* and *khlysnut'* are stressed on different sylla-
bles, their close juxtaposition, the frequency with which *khlysnut'* is preferred to *khlestnut'*, and the reinforcement of their
visual resemblance by the consistent omission of the intermediary consonant *t* (cf. *khlystnut'*), together suggest that
Gogol engages here in a characteristic bout of meaningful word
play, whose suspected implication seems finally confirmed by
the lone intrusion of the verb *khlestat'*. The verbal sequence
khlysnut', khlynut', khlestat' establishes the expressive correlation between Selifan's whip, which varies the direction of its
assault and "chooses a more tender spot," and the whiplike
rain, which comes down first "in an oblique direction" and
then, "changing its mode of attack and coming down quite
straight, drummed right on the top of the carriage; and, finally,
splashes of rain began to fly into [Chichikov's] face" (41). The
whipping of the dapple-gray and the lashing of Chichikov by
the resourceful rain are two symbolic prefigurations of the
sufferings inflicted later in the chapter on the determined seeker
of dead souls, who cries: "Oh, how that confounded old
woman has killed me!" (55) and "felt that he was covered all
over with perspiration, as if he had fallen into a river; everything he had on, from his shirt to his socks, was wet" (55).
However, it is necessary now to probe more deeply into Selifan's role.

The evidence thus far implies that the relationship between
Chichikov and the dapple-gray is paralleled in a similar connection between Selifan and Chichikov's "masculinized" female
persecutor, and it may be noted that, like Korobochka, Selifan
remains a thorn in Chichikov's flesh. Not only does he tip him
into the mud; he also causes the collision in chapter five and, in
chapter eleven, almost prevents Chichikov's escape from the
town. Selifan seems ever at pains to sabotage his master's

carefully laid plans. Yet although Selifan does not join his
master in the mud and plays no part in the scenes enacted
between the arrival and the departure, Gogol plainly shows, as
we have seen, that the visit to Korobochka's realm is hardly
more pleasurable for him than it is for Chichikov. Indeed, the
lash of the rain falls even more heavily on the coachman's back
than on that of his passenger. And in general, of course, as
Chichikov's constant companion, Selifan partakes of all the
misfortunes that befall his master on his eventful travels. This
fact in itself would perhaps suffice to prompt the supposition,
already expressed by Belyy,[6] that like his fellow servant Petrushka, Selifan is a "bearer" or externalization of some aspect
of Chichikov's personality. It is difficult to agree, however,
with Belyy's contention that he personifies the "poetry" in
Chichikov's nature, unless the term *poetry* is used here to
denote an instinctive reluctance to act in conformity with the
dictates of reason. It is precisely this instinctive element, this
element of irrationality in Chichikov's character, that Selifan
appears to personify—the irrationality which constantly frus-
trates the realization of his plans and which is most blatantly
revealed in his attempts to acquire dead serfs from the two
landowners, who plainly regard him as a quarry to be hunted.
The name "Selifan," which is derived from "Silvanus"—the
partly wild, partly civilized, Roman deity of woodland border-
ing on clearings—perhaps alludes to this symbolic role.

   If we accept this connection between Selifan and Chichikov
and agree that the dapple-gray is Chichikov's equine mask,
then it is reasonable to assume that the other two horses of the
troika are the equine masks of Selifan and Petrushka. The nu-
merical coincidence—three horses, three men—is not the only
evidence to support this hypothesis. Another detail that illustrates how deeply embedded in the text are the most revealing
indications of Gogol's meaning is in the seemingly digressive
paragraph which describes Selifan's cries of encouragement to
his steeds. The last sentence reads: "Thus it came to the point
that he finally began to call them secretaries" (42). Critics
normally react to such statements by ammassing superlatives

in tribute to the allegedly glorious surrealism of Gogolian art, and accordingly this particular statement has recently been described as "perhaps the finest of all Gogol's surreal dying falls".[7] However, it is neither "surreal" nor "dying"; it is merely maintained for eight pages in a state of suspended animation from which it is finally roused by Korobochka's announcement to Chichikov that she is a collegiate secretary's widow (50). The equine "secretaries" are thus linked with the deceased collegiate secretary, the pathetic victim of Korobochka's campaign to appropriate the dominant "masculine" role. The significance is that this link, unlike others that have been considered, connects Ivan Petrovich with the dapple-gray (i.e. Chichikov), along with the other two horses (i.e. Petrushka and Selifan), thereby tending to confirm that the three horses are a composite equine symbol of Chichikov's complex personality corresponding to the tripartite "human" form in which it is externalized: the instinctive or irrational Selifan (the light chestnut named "Assessor"), the stinking Petrushka (the bay shaft-horse), and the cunning or "rational" Chichikov himself (the dapple-gray).

As the symbol of Chichikov's irrationality, Selifan stands for no less serious an obstacle than does Korobochka to the fulfillment of his master's ambitions, and the respectively indicated and implied whips of the coachman and landowner are the most obvious signals of this connection between them. We may now understand, therefore, why it is Selifan who propels Chichikov into the trap of Korobochka's mud and why, in his drunken address to the dapple-gray, he describes his master not as a *kollezhskiy sovetnik* ("collegiate councilor") but as a *skoleskoy sovetnik* ("Swheel[8] councilor") (41). By means of this epithet he is linked, as Korobochka is to be later and as he himself is to be once more in chapter eleven, with the image of the crooked wheel that alludes to the failure of Chichikov's "rational," fraudulent scheme. Like the light chestnut, Selifan deeply resents the burden he must take owing to Chichikov's (the dapple-gray's) cunning avoidance of his lawful duty, and he is always looking for chances to right the wrong. He remarks to the dapple-gray:

You think that you are concealing your behavior. No, you must live honorably if you want to be shown respect. Now the servants of the landowner we visited were good people. I will gladly have a chat with a good man. With a good man I'm always on the friendliest of terms, and will willingly have a cup of tea or a bite with him if he's a good man. Everyone will show respect to a good man.

Then follows, in Proffer's phrase, the "ironic twist":[9]

Thus everyone respects our master because, you see, he was in government service; he's a Swheel councilor. (41)

The "twist" highlights the relevance of the admonitions to the "Swheel councilor" with the respectable appearance.

But despite his admonitions, Selifan both administers the whip and, in both his human and his equine forms, receives its blows. Lashing the dapple-gray cannot deflect Chichikov from his chosen course, and Selifan (with Petrushka, who is present only in his equine form) is consequently doomed to endure the same. The question Korobochka asks Chichikov, after she reveals her name and status, alludes to the common fate to which his master condemns him: "You, I suppose, are an assessor?" (50). Having already killed off one "secretary" (her husband), Korobochka is clearly contemplating the destruction of another—the light chestnut "secretary" named Assessor, who is the equine mask of Selifan, one of the three facets of the hero's personality.[10]

While the unfortunate Chichikov is successively portrayed as a horse and a pig, the majority of Korobochka's resident victims undergo two different Ovidian "metamorphoses"— into flies and dead birds. Bearing in mind the parallel series of images in chapter five, one suspects it is not mere coincidence that her "extensive kitchen garden" is well stocked with "cabbages, onions, potatoes, beetroot, and other household vegetables" (48), but in general the imagery of "natural produce" is inconspicuous in this chapter, and the condition of the souls in Korobochka's charge is primarily denoted by the imagery of

birds and flies. The meaning of the ornithological imagery in
the novel has already been determined. Birds—or, more precisely, the smaller species of bird—are symbols of the pure,
"feminine" human soul, and we have seen how Gogol uses
such larger species as geese and tattered or strutting cocks to
signify various forms of the soul's "debasement." Since
"sweetness," therefore, is also closely associated with "femininity" (in both its "authentic" and "superficial" manifestations), it is appropriate that the "sweet" produce of Korobochka's fruit trees should be a constant lure to the sparrows and
magpies and that Korobochka, oppressor of free souls, should
confront them with a screen of nets and a scarecrow wearing
one of her own bonnets (48). As suggested, however, by
Chichikov's telling her that she might wish to retain her dead
souls to "frighten the sparrows at night in your kitchen garden" (54), the spiderlike Korobochka is less interested in
frightening birds than in killing them, in sucking the life from
them just as the citizens of N. suck the tea from their teacups
which, lying on the waiter's tray, are compared in chapter one
to "birds on the seashore" (9). The evidence of her success is
her question to Chichikov shortly before his departure:
"Perhaps you will be needing some birds' feathers?" (57), and
ten pages earlier is the more graphic evidence of Chichikov's
bed, which "almost reached the ceiling." When he climbs onto
it, the narrator records, "it sank beneath him almost down to
the floor, and the feathers, forced out of their case, flew into all
corners of the room" (47). The thickness of the mattress attests
to the high mortality rate of birds in Korobochka's prison. Only
the flying feathers remain to signify their erstwhile freedom.

    Among the chapter's other references to birds, in addition to
the turkey hens supervised by the magisterial cock and the
chick consumed by the porcine Chichikov, are the pair of birds
(eagle and partridge) that Ivan Petrovich is transformed into
during his shift from departmental chief to grain of sand, and
Chichikov's short-tempered rejoinder to the cock (49), which
suggests that even he undergoes a brief ornithological existence
on his way to becoming a sow. Thereby, of course, his affinity
with Korobochka's husband is strengthened still further. It is

also notable that among the first objects to catch his eye in
Korobochka's sitting room are the pictures of birds on the
walls, significantly framed by the background of striped
wallpaper. On waking the next morning, he takes another look
at them: "Glancing around the room, he now observed that the
pictures were not all of birds; among them hung a portrait of
Kutuzov" (47). The juxtaposition calls to mind that of
Sobakevich's thrush and his portrait of Bagration, and it
throws some light on the additional implications of the name
"Bonaparte" with which Selifan abuses the dapple-gray. The
name alludes to the defeat of Chichikov-Napoleon by
Korobochka-Kutuzov, and also to the suppression of freedom,
to the imprisonment (or "masculinization") of the free soul. As
in Pushkin's poem *To the Sea (K moryu)* (1824) and Lermon-
tov's *The Last House-warming (Posledneye novosel'ye)* (1841), the
image of the sea (Pelageya) is linked with the greatest romantic
symbol of freedom—Napoleon.

Thus while the porcine Chichikov's "femininity" connotes
his subordination to the emphatically "masculine" cock, the
Napoleonic Chichikov has an affinity with the birds over
whom Kutuzov stands guard. Ironically, the sow who gobbles
chicks is associated with the notions of freedom and purity of
soul. A sure indication of the intentional irony here is seen in
the flies that settle on the sleeping Chichikov's face. The passage has already been quoted in part:

> . . . the flies, which the day before had been sleeping peace-
> fully on the walls and the ceiling, all turned to him [*ob-
> ratilis' k nemu*]. One sat on his lip, another on his ear, a third
> was striving to work out some way of settling even on his
> eye, while the one which had had the imprudence to sit near
> his nostril he had drawn up while still half asleep into his
> nose, which made him sneeze violently, and it was this
> circumstance which caused him to wake up. (47)

The scene clearly reminds us of the Homeric simile in chapter
one in which the dancers are likened to flies settling on a loaf of
sugar, and since the simile, together with the contrast between

"fat men" and "thin men" that follows it, offers at least some idea of the meaning we should attach to the image of the fly, it obviously needs to be reconsidered in relation to this episode.

Having noted the connection between the "sugar" and the symbolic theme of "femininity," we may infer that the fly image is associated with the purity of soul which the theme symbolizes. The flies are attracted to the sugar just as the thin men are attracted to their female partners. Too, the image of the fly plainly conveys another feature of the thin men that has already been mentioned regarding the portrait of Feoduliya Ivanovna—their "lightness," "airiness," and "complete insecurity," i.e. their position of intrinsic weakness or subservience in relation to their "antifeminine" brethren, who regard their dancing with scorn. This connotation of subservience may explain why the image is used not only to characterize the serfs of Sobakevich and Plyushkin as well as those of the "masculine" Korobochka, but also to mark the final stage in the sequence of metamorphoses undergone by Ivan Petrovich before he is finally reduced to a grain of sand. The image expresses, therefore, two main ideas: an association with or craving for "femininity" and a state of oppressive subservience.

The comparison of Ivan Petrovich to a fly in the penultimate phase of his descent is yet another allusion, of course, to his connection with Chichikov, for the Chichikov who has no intention of visiting Korobochka and yet finds himself stuck in her glutinous mud himself bears an obvious resemblance to a fly that has carelessly flown into a spider's web. But what possible meaning resides in the settling of Korobochka's flies on Chichikov's face and thus in the implicit comparison of his face to the sugar lump in the Homeric simile? The clue is the analogy between the sow who inadvertently consumes the chick and the sleeping Chichikov whose nose inadvertently "consumes" the fly. The import seems to be that the flies see Chichikov just as the chick does, not simply as a visitor from the world outside the prison but, more significantly, in the "feminine" guise denoting purity and freedom. Unlike the vicious insects of Nozdryov, they are consequently drawn not to attack, but for the same purpose that attracts their predecessors in chapter one to the "femininity" of the sugar and the sparrows and magpies to the "sweetness" of Korobochka's fruit. As the verb *obratit'sya* (which can mean "to appeal") suggests, they turn to him for salvation, and their comrade's disappearance up his nose evidences their grievous error. "The matter isn't worth an eaten egg," declares Chichikov as he struggles desperately to persuade his tormentress to release her souls (55)—such is this unlikely savior's attitude to captive souls. Chichikov does not save them; whether souls appear as eggs, chicks, or flies, he eats them. Although for Korobochka he is merely a substitute for Ivan Petrovich, his box, which houses their names, marks his more significant affinity with the spider whose web ensnares their bodies. Korobochka is no less a facet of Chichikov's personality than Sobakevich, Nozdryov, and Manilov.

For reasons, however, which have emerged clearly, the resemblance we are most conscious of when reading the chapter is between Korobochka and Sobakevich. Their portraits, as we have seen, are linked by numerous common details and allusions—above all, by the evidence of their common "canine" instincts. Indeed, these instincts, unfortunately for Chichikov, seems to be even stronger in Korobochka than in the landowner with the "canine" name. Moreover, although the "ursine" (i.e. Russian) element is not revealed explicitly in Korobochka's portrait, its presence is unmistakably conveyed by the same oblique procedure that Gogol employs in chapter five—by repeated generalizations about alleged Russian customs and "virtues." Are we not reminded, for example, of the "digression" on the "aptly uttered Russian word" by the "digression" on Russian modes of address which begins: "It must be said that if in Russia we have not yet caught up with foreigners in some things, we have far outstripped them in our ability to address people" (49)? Similarly, the spectacle of Selifan propelling the horses with his whip in the pitch darkness prompts the narrator to remark: "Instead of eyes the Russian driver has a good sense of smell. As a result he sometimes races along at full speed screwing up his eyes and always finishes up somewhere" (43). And the song Selifan sings to the strokes of the whip is likewise invested with a broad national relevance: "Everything went into it: all the encouraging and stimulating cries with which horses are regaled from one end of Russia to the other" (42). In this typically indirect manner the image of the whip is fused as expressively with the image of Russia as it is with the image of Korobochka; thus Korobochka is herself linked with Russia in exactly the same way as Sobakevich. Her "masculinized" realm is exposed as another symbolic micro-cosm of despiritualized Russia, and it is to this association, it seems, that Gogol is alluding in the sentence which describes Selifan's search for the gates:

> He [Chichikov] sent Selifan to look for the gate, which undoubtedly would have taken a long time if it were not for the fact that in Russia the job of porters is done by spirited dogs, which announced his arrival so resonantly that he raised his fingers to his ears. (43)

Given Korobochka's general antipathy to intruders, it is hardly surprising that she partakes in full measure of Sobakevich's xenophobic attitudes. Herein lies yet another implication of the portrait of Kutuzov and its kinship with Sobakevich's portrait of Bagration. Although she does not echo Sobakevich's abuse of the French, we may perhaps deduce from one of her remarks that she shares his contempt for Gallicized Russia, i.e. St. Petersburg. Thus her instinct is, on noticing the excellent workmanship of Chichikov's box, to inquire whether he bought it not in St. Petersburg but in the ancient capital of "indigenous" Russia, Moscow; and his affirmative reply evokes her recollection of the impressive quality of some children's boots made in Moscow that her sister once brought her (56)—boots that were swiftly commit-ted, if we may judge from the "mud boots" of Pelageya, to the safety of one of her boxes.

A final common feature evident in the portraits of Korobochka and Sobakevich is a suggestion of the author's favorable attitude to their competence as administrators. It is a virtue, of course, which distinguishes them sharply from the other three landowners and one to which Gogol clearly attached some importance. Perhaps it is not coincidental, therefore, that these two portraits alone contain hints of the possibility of rebirth—the coloring of Sobakevich's thrush, and Korobochka's Christian name Nastas'ya, which is derived from the Greek word for "resurrection." But again it must be emphasized that the praise is more apparent than real, for in both contexts efficient administration is merely a prerequisite for efficient "masculinization." It implies the discipline and dictatorial control whereby "feminine" souls are winnowed from masculine or "masculinized" bodies and transformed into captive birds, flies, or vegetables.

Caution should likewise be exercised when considering the comparison with her sister from which Korobochka seems to emerge in an almost favorable light.

> You might even begin to think: enough! Does Korobochka really stand so low on the endless ladder of human perfectibility? Is the gap really so great that separates her from her sister, inaccessibly enclosed by the walls of her aristocratic house, with its fragrant, cast-iron staircases, its shining brass, its mahogany and carpets, who yawns over some unfinished book as she waits to pay a visit to fashionable, witty society? There she will have the scope to shine with her intelligence and express well-rehearsed views which, according to the laws of fashion, engage the town's interest for a whole week, views which have nothing to do with what is happening in her house and on her estates, ruined and entangled in debts due to her ignorance of how to manage them, but rather concern the impending political revolution in France or the direction taken by fashionable Catholicism. (58)

The difference between the two sisters may well appear to be as great as the difference between Korobochka and Manilova, but the question at the beginning of the second sentence makes it

explicit that the differences are distinctly less important than is
the similarity they tend to obscure. The passage is not an
exculpatory appendage to Korobochka's portrait, but a preliminary allusion to her fundamental affinities with her "sisters" in the town of N., the nature of which is to be clarified
later—in the portrait of the ladies of the town in chapter eight.
The sister behind the walls of her aristocratic house is essentially, despite all the superficial differences, a replica of the
Korobochka who holds sway behind the fences of her rural
realm, and it is perhaps to this metamorphosis of the chapter's
heroine that Gogol is alluding in the remarks that conclude the
comparison:

> But away, away! Why is it that in the midst of unthinking,
> gay, carefree moments a quite different, strange feeling
> suddenly comes over one? The laughter has hardly had
> time to vanish from one's face when one is suddenly
> transformed into someone else among the same people,
> and one's face is illuminated by a different light. (58)

Although, however, Korobochka differs less significantly
from her sister than appearances suggest, she does differ in one
important respect from Sobakevich, and the difference may be
attributed to her sexual ambivalence. While Sobakevich is
"masculinity" personified and inconceivable in any position
other than one of "masculine" primacy, the primacy of
Korobochka, as we have observed, is the result of conquest.
She is a usurper, ever conscious that her "masculine" position
may be challenged at any moment. Perhaps the most revealing
insight into her state of mind is provided by her highly imaginative description of Chichikov's arrival at her estate as told
later to the wife of Father Kiril; it is reported by the "agreeable
lady" in chapter nine:

> Suddenly, in the dead of night, when everyone in the
> house was already asleep, there was the most terrible
> knocking at the gates that you could possibly imagine.
> "Open up," they shouted. "Open up, or else we shall

break down the gates!" . . . Just imagine, he arrives armed
from head to foot like Rinaldo Rinaldini and demands:
"Sell me all your souls who have died". (183)

The armor in which she mentally clothes the mud-bespattered
Chichikov reflects her view of his intrusion as a challenge to her
position, and we have noted how she responds to it. But it is
clear from this account that her initial response is fear—an
emotion to which Sobakevich is seemingly immune.

Korobochka is prey to a nagging fear of everything that
eludes her grasp or lies beyond her fences and nets, and Gogol
tries to make this reaction more plausible by conveying the
impression that Korobochka's hostility to the intruders whom
she cannot control is matched by a hostility of equal inten-
sity. Thus the flight of the sparrows, for example, which attack
her fruit trees is described in terms that evoke the description of
the rain which batters Chichikov: ". . . the sparrows . . . flew
from one place to another in huge oblique clouds" (48), i.e.
seeking to find in her defenses the most "tender" spot. As a
force she cannot control, they are ipso facto a threat and therefore a source of fear. They are akin in this respect to the forces
of nature that ruin her harvests and to the physical afflictions
about which she complains to Chichikov. But the source of her
greatest fears is clearly the element of fire, from which she
seems to be under perpetual assault. The first oblique allusion
to these assaults is in Gogol's "digression" about the contents
of Korobochka's chest of drawers:

> . . . in appearance it seems as if there is nothing in the chest
> of drawers except linen, nightdresses, reels of cotton, and
> an unpicked woman's coat which was destined to be trans-
> formed later into a dress, if the old one should somehow
> have a hole burnt through it while she was baking cakes
> and all kinds of meat pies for some festive occasion or
> should simply wear out by itself. (45)

The most vivid illustration, however, of fire's capacity to pick
out her "tender spots" is her account of the death of her
blacksmith:

... he caught fire himself. Somehow a fire started inside
him. He had drunk too much. A blue flame came from
him, and he smoldered, smoldered and turned as black as
coal. And he was such a skillful blacksmith. And now I've
nothing to drive out in. There's no one to shoe the horses.
(51)

Initially, of course, we assume that Korobochka fears fire as a
destroyer of the material possessions she values so highly, but
the distinctly "fantastic" character of the blacksmith's death
suggests an additional explanation and prompts us to recon-
sider what significance Ivan Petrovich's point of departure may
have in his sequence of metamorphoses. Before beginning his
descent from the status of man, Ivan Petrovich is compared to
Prometheus. He is identified with the Titan who was the friend
and benefactor of man and gave him fire, thereby bringing
upon himself the wrath of Zeus, who wished to destroy the
human race and replace it with a new species. Thus Prometheus, the giver of fire, and therefore fire itself are implicitly
associated with man. Fire becomes a metaphor of the human
spirit, which Korobochka-Zeus is bent on destroying. Like the
transformation of Ivan Petrovich from Prometheus into a grain
of sand, the emergence of the "blue flame" from the
blacksmith's body signifies the destruction of the free human
spirit. What remains is the blackened body, the color of which
is in harmony with the dominant color of Korobochka's
realm—with the blackness of the night on which Chichikov
arrives, with the gloom of the house in which the mirrors are
small and set in "dark frames" (45), and with the darkness of
Korobochka's dress (49), which contrasts so markedly with
the dress of Manilova. The extinction of fire is thus paralleled by
the extinction of light, in which we may likewise perceive an
allusion to the "masculinization" of the "feminine" human soul.
Hence the servitude of the maid Fetin'ya, whose name, a popular form of Fotin'ya, is derived from the Greek word for "light."

The motifs of fire and light, therefore, directly relate to the
motif of birds. All three motifs allude to the free human spirit,

which Korobochka engages in unrelenting conflict—a conflict in which she enjoys a grim success, but which presents her with tormenting reminders that however formidable her defenses may be, they are not impregnable. The assaults of the birds and the flames instill the painful consciousness of her vulnerability, which explains the inclusion in her portrait of such seemingly discordant features as her insomnia and addiction to fortune-telling, evidence of her craving for assurance that she will ultimately prevail.[11] And it is precisely the "ambiguous" element of fire, with its connotations of hell as well as of the spirit, that assumes in her dreams the form of the devil, ironically compelling her to burn a candle before her icon and to solicit the support of God with the aid of the Church which, in the person of Father Kiril, is subservient to her will. Such is the most striking pair of metamorphoses in the most "Ovidian" of the novel's chapters: the free human spirit is equated with the devil, while the representative of God is the ally of its ruthless oppressor.

5

Plyushkin

After examining the portraits of the first four landowners, we can reject conclusively the view that they "are completely unconnected with one another."[1] Are we similarly entitled, however, to reject the argument that they "occur without logical order"?[2] Although this question has not been raised thus far, it is already clear that the argument is a fallacy. It is surely inconceivable that the artist who devoted so much "consideration" to the composition of these portraits was not equally concerned with their arrangement. A closer look at the text enables us to base our supposition on more substantial grounds.

Perhaps the first impression gained by the reader is that the portraits are arranged according to the principle of contrast, and our interpretations of the first four would seem to support this view. Thus the portraits of the "canine," earth-bound Korobochka and Sobakevich are preceded and separated by portraits that reflect sharply contrasting attitudes to earthly possessions—attitudes of total disregard (Manilov) and total disrespect (Nozdryov). But although this contrast is repeated, it cannot be regarded as the main determinant of the order in which the portraits appear, for the sequence of alternations is broken by the portrait of Plyushkin, who plainly has much more in common with Korobochka and Sobakevich than with Manilov or Nozdryov.

In the third of his four letters on the novel, Gogol referred to a quite different reason for the arrangement, indicating a sequence based on increasing degrees of spiritual mortification (*poshlost'*).[3] Critics have tended to accept the statement only up

to a point—presumably because it seems to accord only partially with the facts. Thus we can accept that the first and last
landowners (Manilov and Plyushkin) are respectively the least
and most squalid of the five, but is there really much to choose
between Korobochka, Nozdryov, and Sobakevich? The answer, quite simply, is that there is, but to recognize it we must
note two progressions—the progression of symbolic themes
and the progression of the motifs Gogol uses to represent dead
souls. Manilov and Korobochka are distinguished from one
another, as we have observed, not only by their contrasting
attitudes to earthly possessions, but also more basically by the
contrasting "sexual identities" with which these attitudes are
associated. The "superficially feminized" male is contrasted
with the "masculinized" female, and it is clear that in the
descending symbolic hierarchy which denotes degrees of
spiritual corruption the former "identity" stands higher than
the latter. Although, however, Korobochka is contrasted with
Manilov, she also shares with him the crucial feature of a sexual
"metamorphosis." Though "masculinized", she remains a
woman both physically and even, in one respect, emotionally,
for she displays a susceptibility to fear that is decidedly untypical of the authentic "masculinity" personified by Nozdryov
and Sobakevich.

The second two landowners, therefore, differ from the first
two in that they are free from sexual ambivalence. They also
are contrasted with one another, but the contrast embraces
merely different manifestations of essentially the same spiritual
condition—the psychologies of the "canine hunter" and the
"canine bear," which represent the two poles of the "masculine" psychological spectrum. At the same time a new development in chapter five illustrates that "masculinity" does
not mark the lowest point in Gogol's hierarchy. This development is the notably extended role of the "natural produce"
motif, which seems to explain why Sobakevich follows Nozdryov and to foreshadow the transition to the portrait of
Plyushkin. The beginnings of this motif, as stated, may be
traced to the vegetables in Korobochka's "extensive kitchen

garden" and perhaps even to the "nuts" (*orekhi*) mentioned in chapter one that are sold from stalls in the main street of the town of N. (11), but in general the motif plays no significant part in chapters one through four. Its further development is postponed till chapter five, in which for the first time it is more commonly employed to denote the state of the soul than the imagery of birds and flies, and even Sobakevich himself is presented as a creation of nature.

Although, therefore, the special skill of Sobakevich is his ability to "masculinize" his dependents, the motif of "natural produce" reveals his capacity for subjecting them to a still more rigorous process. In our study of chapter five we tended to view this process simply as an extension of "masculinization", but now, in this introduction to our study of chapter six, we must regard it as a distinct process denoting the maximum degree of mortification to be inflicted on the human soul in Gogol's "inferno"—the process of "naturalization". By repeated references to "natural produce" in similes and popular sayings, Gogol indirectly effects in the portrait of Sobakevich the transition to the symbolic theme that completes his symbolic typology of dead souls. The descending hierarchy of "superficially feminized" and "masculinized" souls ends logically in chapter six with the portrait of a "naturalized" soul in which even the few remaining human attributes implied by the term "masculinity" are replaced by the attributes of a plant.

At the mention of chapter six one thinks of its most celebrated passage—the description of Plyushkin's garden, from which Gogol himself, it seems, after subjecting it to more changes than any other part of the work, derived a special satisfaction.[4] It merits quotation in full, however, not simply because of its intrinsic excellence, but, more pertinently, because it is the cornerstone of the entire chapter and of the portrait of its central figure:

> An old, extensive garden, which stretched behind the house and reached beyond the village and then, overgrown and neglected, disappeared into the fields, alone

seemed to refresh this large village, and it alone was truly picturesque in its splendid wildness. The tangled tops of the trees, which had spread out freely, lay in green clouds and asymmetrical cupolas of quivering leaves against the horizon. The huge white trunk of a birch tree without its top, which had been broken off by a gale or a thunderstorm, rose up from this dense green mass and stood in the air like a round, symmetrical, shining marble column, and the slanting, pointed fracture, in which it came to an end at the top instead of a capital, showed up darkly against its snowy whiteness like a cap or a black bird. The hops, which were stifling the bushes of elder, mountain ash, and hazel below and then ran along the top of the entire fence, finally climbed upward and twined halfway up the broken birch tree. On reaching the middle of the tree, they hung down and were already beginning to clutch the tops of other trees or simply hung in the air, twisting into coils their delicate, clinging, hooklike tendrils which swung gently in the air. In places the green thickets, lit up by the sun, parted and revealed an unlit chasm between them, yawning like the dark open mouth of some wild beast; it was plunged in darkness, and in its black depths could be seen with difficulty the track of a narrow path, broken-down railings, a tumbledown summerhouse, the hollow, decaying trunk of a willow tree, a gray caragana which thrust out from behind the willow, like dense bristles, its tangled, crisscrossed leaves and branches which had withered in the terrible, stifling atmosphere, and, finally, the young branch of a maple, stretching sideways its green, clawlike leaves, one of which was suddenly transformed by the sunlight, which, God knows how, had penetrated beneath it, into a transparent, fiery leaf, gleaming marvelously in that dense darkness. On one side, at the very edge of the garden, a number of tall aspens, rising above the level of the other trees, bore huge rooks' nests on their quivering tops. Branches had been pulled from some of them, but they were not completely severed and they hung down with their withered leaves. In a word, it was all beautiful. (112–113)

Almost every detail in this passage is echoed in other parts of the chapter, and it is necessary to refer back to it often. But before tracing the threads that bind together the various sections of the chapter, we must consider the most curious feature of the description—namely, the contradiction between its details and the epithets the narrator applies to the garden in its entirety: "picturesque" (*zhivopisen*) and "splendid" (*kartinnom*)[5] in the first sentence and "beautiful" (*khorosho*) in the last. Although these epithets are not exactly inapt, they do convey, like the verb "to refresh" in the opening sentence, a misleading impression of the garden's essential character. Even if we concede that the scene does have a certain picturesqueness, perhaps even beauty, it is not at all the kind of beauty that the epithets seem to imply, but rather an "inhuman" beauty, the beauty of savagery, destruction, and death. The birch tree is decapitated; the bushes are stifled; the gap between the thickets resembles the maw of a wild beast; the willow and caragana are withered and decaying; the leaves of the maple are compared to claws; and some of the aspens have been almost dismembered. These are not the kind of details we would normally term beautiful or picturesque, and it seems scarcely credible that attempts have been made to interpret the garden as a scene of beauty designed to highlight by contrast the squalor of Plyushkin's domain.[6] Its role is really quite different. Not only is the garden an integral part of the domain; it also enshrines the spirit of its master. It is the key to the mystery of Plyushkin's mind, an oblique psychological exposé of the chapter's protagonist.

Gogol's object in creating this scene was apparently to embody the spirit of nature, which is implicitly contrasted with the spirit of man. The description, in short, is primarily symbolic, and its dominant symbol is the image of the hops (*khmel'*). In the realm of nature, the description implies, there is no peace; there is only the spectacle of a ceaseless battle between predators and victims, and in the "dark open mouth" of the thickets and the "claws" of the maple we perceive allusions to the savagery of this battle. Supreme among the predators, however, are the hops, which demonstrate how nature conquers and kills—by gradual encroachment and slow asphyxiation. With the aid of the verb "twined" (*obvival*) and the noun "coils" (*kol'tsami*), Gogol again evokes the image of the snake to convey the insidious movement and power of the "clinging, hooklike tendrils [*tsepkiye kryuch'ya*]" that wind themselves around everything in their path, condemning to death, like the spreading thickets, both their victims in nature and the creations of man: the narrow path, the broken-down railings, the tumbledown summerhouse.

The image of the spreading, voracious hops has a direct parallel in the description of Plyushkin wandering through the streets of his village and peering into every nook and cranny, "and everything that he came across," we read, "an old sole, a woman's rag, an iron nail, a piece of broken earthenware,[7] he bore off to his house and deposited on the pile which Chichikov had noticed in the corner of the room" (117). Here Plyushkin is portrayed as the grasping spirit of nature incarnate, relentlessly extending its dominion, like the hops, over the material relics of a once prosperous human community. It has been customary to regard him simply as a miser, but here the acquisitive instinct is merely a manifestation of the rapacious spirit of nature that has supplanted his human soul. Avarice is not the cause of his inhumanity, but rather its dominant symptom, just as Nozdryov's passion for hounds is a symptom of his ebullient "masculinity."

The name provides a revealing clue. Derived from the noun *plyushch* ("ivy"), it alludes to the "naturalization" of its bearer's soul, to his metamorphosis from man into plant. Like the terrible phrase that Gogol applies to him—"a gaping hole [*prorekha*] in humankind" (119)—it denotes the collapse of his human identity. As the Greek root, signifying "fertility," of the two village priests' names, Karp and Polikarp, alludes to nature's victory in this domain over the human spirit, so the name *Plyushkin* expresses the resemblance between the

wizened old man who when a boy used to "climb fences" with
the president of the court (126) and the hops that run "along the
top of the entire fence." And in the narrator's references to the
meandering route Chichikov must take through the village,[8]
we perceive another allusion to the same affinity. As a projec-
tion of Plyushkin's personality, the village mirrors his ivylike
soul.

The connection between Plyushkin and the garden is reinforced by several details in his physical portrait and in the
description of his attire. Thus, the growth on his chin, which
"resembled the kind of currycomb made of iron wire with
which horses are groomed in a stable" (116), calls to mind the
"dense bristles" of the grey caragana, and his hand, in the act of
writing, seems to be driven, like the tendrils of the hops, by
nature's hatred of a vacuum: ". . . he began to write . . ., continually restraining the movement of his hand which was galloping all over the paper, sparingly forming one line after
another, and thinking not without regret that there would still
remain a lot of blank space" (127). Moreover, his nose displays
the capacity of the hops for generating new shoots:

> "Oh, my dear fellow! Oh, my benefactor!" cried
> Plyushkin, not noticing in his joy that a piece of snuff was
> peeping most unpicturesquely [*nekartinno*] from his nose
> like coffee grounds, and that the skirts of his dressing
> gown had flown open, revealing clothing which was not
> entirely proper for inspection. (123)

Particularly striking here is the reappearance of the epithet
kartinnyy ("picturesque"), which Gogol now employs in negated form. The possibility of coincidence, of course, cannot be
discounted, but it is interesting that the synonym *zhivopisnyy* is
similarly taken up again and negated in the description of the
"little balconies" of the peasant cottages on the estate which,
we read, "had turned black," like the jagged top of the birch
tree in the garden, "in a manner that was not even picturesque
[*dazhe ne zhivopisno*]" (112). Since Gogol is not normally given
to repeating words in this way without significant cause, we

may interpret the echoes as signals of the central distinction that he is intent on drawing here—that between the human and the "natural," which both in Plyushkin's domain and in Plyushkin himself is no longer clearly discernible. What Gogol seems to be saying is that the "picturesque" in nature is by no means "picturesque" in man.

We may also suspect with some justification that the reference to the "shoot" of snuff (*tabak*) is not by chance coupled with a reference to Plyushkin's dressing gown, for the skirt or tails of this remarkable garment are a transparent allusion to the tendrils and foliage of the ivy like hops. "At the back," we read earlier in the chapter, "four tails were dangling instead of two, and cotton wool [*khlopchataya bumaga*] was sticking out of them in tufts" (116).[9] And if the noun *bumaga* ("cotton") alludes here to "leaves," we may perhaps impute a similar role to it when it appears with its more common meaning "paper," e.g. in the reference to the "papers [*bumazhek*] covered with small writing" on Plyushkin's bureau (115). Although Gogol does not actually use the noun *list* here, he seems to be indulging in the kind of play with its two meanings ("leaf" and "sheet of paper") repeated in chapter seven in the simile that conveys the noise of scratching pens in the government offices: "A loud rustling came from the pens which resembled the passage of several carts full of brushwood through a forest six inches deep in dead leaves" (142). And an extension of this meaningful word play may be seen in the references to Plyushkin's habit of covering objects with pieces of paper, e.g. the "scrap of paper [*loskutok*]" with which he covers the wine glass (126) and the ironically allusive "triangle of blue sugar paper" stuck over one of the house's windows (112).[10] Do we not perceive here further allusions to the leaves of the spreading hops, and a parallel between the encroachment of the hops on man's creations in the garden and the encroachment of the metaphorical leaves of the "naturalized" man on the house and its contents?

Nature, in Gogol's depiction, does not rend and tear. Hence Plyushkin's lack of teeth (121). Like Sobakevich, he consumes with relish his cabbage soup and buckwheat porridge, but there is no saddle of mutton to complete the meal. The method of nature is simply to envelop and suffocate, and in the domain of Plyushkin the suffocation of the human element is everywhere in evidence. Here the sturdy fences of Sobakevich and Korobochka are conspicuous by their absence. The fences of Plyushkin have collapsed before nature's advance (112). The boundary that once existed between nature and the house has disintegrated, like the boundary that separated the once cultivated garden from the fields into which, "overgrown and neglected," it has now "disappeared." And with the disintegration of this boundary everything human has died. The suffocated house, which is "so long, so inordinately long" (i.e. thin),[11] has become a "decrepit invalid" (112), a "gaping hole in humankind," like its owner, which nature has remorselessly filled. Just as the "tendrils" of Plyushkin's dressing gown occasionally part to expose his emaciated frame, so the walls of the house "showed in places the bare laths under the plaster" (112). Its windows (i.e. eyes) are described as "half-blind," and in the entrance hall Chichikov is struck by a "cold breeze," which is compared to the chill of a cellar (*pogreh*) (114). The allusion, as Proffer has noted, is to the "grave" (*grob*); the human element has been "buried" (*pogrebyon*).[12] Commenting on the drawing room, the narrator observes: "It would have been quite impossible to say that a living creature was dwelling in this room, had not his existence been announced by an old, threadbare skullcap which lay on the table" (115).

Although the clock of Korobochka, like the hops, bears indirect likeness to a snake and is an instrument of ruthless oppression, it nevertheless functions with supreme efficiency. Though transformed into a source of pain, the concept of time remains as a signal of human control. In the realm of Plyushkin, however, it has ceased to have meaning. While the watch that he briefly considers giving to Chichikov as a reward for his "generosity" is "slightly damaged" (130), the pendulum of the clock in the house has long been still. From a tool of man it has been transformed into a tool of nature, into the home of the spider, which has covered it with its web

(115). Similarly the decanter is "covered in dust as if it were wearing a jersey" (125), while the linen cover over the chandelier "had come to resemble because of the dust the cocoon of a silkworm" (115).[13] Light, like time, has been extinguished. It has been "suffocated" by the linen cover, its coating of dust and the boards, shutters, and "sugar paper" over the windows. The house has fallen prey to the darkness and "terrible, stifling atmosphere" of the garden, to the gloom of the "unlit chasm" between the thickets, which resembles "the dark open mouth of some wild beast". Hence the name of the housekeeper Mavra, derived from the Greek root meaning "dark," and the darkness of the entrance hall that leads into a room "which was also dark and only barely lit by the light from a wide crack at the bottom of the door" (114).

If light is the element of man, then youth is the time of light in human life, and old age is the time of its fading. The contrast between youth and old age is inferred on the opening page of the novel in the statement that just as Chichikov "was neither too fat nor too thin," so "he could not be said to be old, but he was not too young either" (7). In the context of chapter six, this is the most important of all the contrasts that are linked with the fundamental one between the human and the "natural," and the narrator's recollections of his youth in the long opening paragraph should be regarded less as his momentary surrender to elegiac reminiscence than as a preparation for this sustained symbolic theme. The transition from youth to old age is a metaphor of dehumanization, of the "naturalization" of Plyushkin's soul, which indirectly explains why the description of the garden begins with the adjective "old" (*staryy*). As he watches Plyushkin's hand jumping over the sheet of paper, the narrator reflects:

As you emerge from the tender years of youth and pass into bleak, embittering manhood, take with you on your journey all the human emotions! Do not leave them on the road, for you will not pick them up later! Old age, which lies ahead of us, is terrible and menacing, for it

gives nothing back, it returns nothing! The grave is more
merciful than old age. On the grave will be written:
"Here a man is buried," but you will read nothing on the
cold, insensitive features of inhuman old age. (127)

In an earlier draft of the passage old age is endowed with
"claws that cannot be prized open [*nerastsepimymi kogtyami*]"
(769)—an allusion to the "clinging, hooklike tendrils [*tsepkiye
kryuch'ya*]" of the hops and the "clawlike leaves" of the
maple, which merely confirms that here "inhuman old age" is
simply a mask of "inhuman nature."

Once more Gogol employs in this famous passage the device
of couching a revealing statement about a character in a
generalization. A comment on Plyushkin is masked as a comment on Everyman.[14] When the narrator calls on us to avoid
leaving our emotions "on the road," the appeal makes an
impact not because it expresses some general truth about old
age, but because it reminds us of Plyushkin's booty-hunting
expeditions in his village, after which, we read, "there was no
need to sweep the street" (117). It reminds us of Plyushkin's
remark to Chichikov: "You can't put a condolence in your
pocket, you know" (122). It refers, in other words, to the lost
capacity to feel or to recognize feeling that is symptomatic not
of the aging process per se, but simply of the symbolic aging
process that has taken place in Plyushkin. As part of nature,
man's body is subject to the organic process of aging, but he
retains to the end the capacity to think and feel by which he is
distinguished from nature. In Plyushkin this distinction has
been lost. The aging of his body coincides with the aging of his
emotions, implying that, like the hops, the caragana, and the
maple, he consists of organic matter alone.

The prominence of the theme of aging in Plyushkin's portrait is explained precisely by this view of the process as an
exclusively physical process, as a process primarily affecting
the organic, i.e. "natural," element as distinct from the emotional, i.e. human, element. And it is this same view of the
process that seemingly explains Gogol's decision to give him a

fairly detailed biography. The inclusion in the portrait of this record of his body's transition from youth to old age implies that his life, like that of a plant, is interesting solely as an illustration of this transition. The biography is an allusion to the exclusively physical, organic, or "natural" character of his existence. True, it reveals a certain evolution even in the emotional sphere, but its importance has been grossly exaggerated. As the young father of three children, Plyushkin had the good fortune to be married to a woman of exceptional qualities, and Gogol shows plainly that the real source of life[15] and light[16] on the estate was this friendly, hospitable female. The features of Plyushkin, by contrast, even then "did not reflect any strong emotions" (118), and the estate, though efficiently managed, was already in the grip of a spider: "The sharp eye of the master was everywhere, penetrating into everything, and like a hard-working spider he would rush about restlessly but efficiently from one end of his industrial web to the other" (118). Moreover, since even the parts of the fence around the house that still stand are described as "low" (112), we may infer that even the young Plyushkin, who presumably had them built, was not unduly concerned to detach the house from its "natural" surroundings.

The biography, in reality, records not the death of Plyushkin's emotions (for they had never really been alive), but merely the progressive realization of the potentiality disclosed by his name. It confirms that the administrative efficiency of the young Plyushkin is related to the destructive greed of the aged miser not as the opposite pole of a contrast, but simply as a preliminary stage in the development of a single, continuous process. It should not be thought that the old widower is less industrious than the young family man or less insistent on increasing production. The difference is simply that production has now become a means not of accumulating wealth but rather of gratifying the spider's "natural" urge to grasp, possess, and suffocate, which after the death of his wife[17] and with age has acquired an even more sovereign hold over his being, becoming his sole raison d'être. Commenting on the changes that followed his wife's death, the narrator remarks: "The master's miserliness began to reveal itself more noticeably, and the flecks of gray in his rough hair promoted its further development, for gray hair is the faithful companion of greed" (118). The gray, "rough hair" is doubtless another allusion to the gray (or "gray-haired" [*sedoy*]) caragana's "dense bristles." But the essential point is that the changes which followed the death of Plyushkin's wife should not be construed as fundamental changes in Plyushkin himself. Her death merely removed his last remaining link with humanity, the last restraint on his complete submission to "natural" instinct. It marked the final surrender of the house to the rapacious, egocentric spirit spirit of "inhuman nature." Hence the death soon afterwards of his younger daughter and the departure of his son, his elder daughter, the French tutor, and the French governess. As nature took over, so man withdrew, leaving Plyushkin "the sole keeper, guardian, and master of his riches" (119), happily acquiescing in the rotting (i.e. "stifled") state of the crops in his barns, declining the most generous offers of dealers, and acting solely in obedience to the possessive instinct of the ivylike hops.

As he enters the village, Chichikov catches sight of two churches behind the rotting stacks of wheat—"a wooden church which was deserted and a brick one with yellow walls which was stained and cracked" (112). Why, we may ask, are there two churches? Surely one would have sufficed. The answer, of course, is that the churches form a contrast—a contrast, moreover, of considerable importance in the chapter which, like the contrast between old age and youth, directly relates to the fundamental contrast between the human and the "natural." Wood is contrasted with other materials used for structural or manufacturing purposes (particularly brick, stone, marble, and iron); wood is associated with nature (old age) and the other materials with man (youth).[18] While the wooden church is the church of "inhuman nature" and is therefore deserted by man, the stained, cracked walls of the brick church, like the tumbledown state of the summerhouse in the garden, present additional evidence of nature's triumph over the human.

The opening paragraph of the chapter conveys the narrator's recollections of his youth, and also gives a certain prominence to man-made structures of brick and stone. Gogol begins, in other words, by combining, and thereby linking, the "human" poles of the chapter's two principal symbolic contrasts. He writes:

> Every building, everything that simply bore the mark of some noticeable peculiarity—everything caused me to stop in amazement. Whether it was a brick public building of the well-known architectural design with half its windows blind, standing all alone among a mass of the local citizenry's rough-hewn, timbered, one-story dwellings, or a round symmetrical cupola covered all over with white sheets of iron, rising above a whitewashed new church as white as snow . . . nothing eluded my fresh, keen attention. (110)

Here the brick public building and the iron-clad cupola of the church rise high above the timbered cottages, for this is the realm of man, a fitting sight for the eyes of youth. In the realm of Plyushkin, however, not only is brick replaced by wood, but the "symmetrical" (*pravil'nyy*) cupola's sheets of galvanized iron (literally "leafy iron" (*listovym zhelezom*)) give way to the "green clouds" and "asymmetrical cupolas of quivering leaves [*nepravil'nymi trepetolistnymi kupolami*]," which plunge the garden into darkness.[19] The three emblems of man—symmetry, the static "leaves" of iron, and the chromatic symbol of the human soul, white, which links the church and its cupola with the symbolic figure of the governor's daughter—are supplanted by contrasting emblems of nature: asymmetry;[20] the tangled leaves of the trees, "which had spread out freely"; and green. White is reserved for only one object in the garden—the "huge white trunk" of the birch tree, which seems to have been inserted as a direct parallel to the church in the opening paragraph. The whiteness of both is compared to the whiteness of snow; both "rise up" above their surroundings; and both are endowed with the "human" qualities of "roundness" and "symmetry." And it is significant that the only reference to the "human" art of architecture in the description of the garden is when the narrator speaks of the birch. But instead of a "symmetrical capital" the birch now displays a "slanting, pointed fracture," which "showed up darkly against its snowy whiteness like a cap or a black bird," i.e. like a "darkened soul,"[21] and the hops, we read, "climbed upwards and twined halfway up the broken birch tree." Like the remaining material vestiges of human habitation on the estate—the railings, the summerhouse, and the iron nails, rags, and pieces of broken earthenware, etc. assiduously garnered by Plyushkin— this shining, churchlike symbol of the human spirit, which seems to be made of marble rather than wood, is doomed to "suffocation."

Just as every other important motif in the novel enters inconspicuously before acquiring prominence in one particular chapter-context, so the motif of "wood" wends its way unnoticed through the early chapters before finally becoming a major expressive element in chapter six. It first appears, of course, in chapter one, when Chichikov's eye is drawn to the "interminable wooden fences" in the town and to the dark gray of its wooden houses (11), but it begins to catch the reader's eye in the portraits of the two landowners whose acquisitive urge intensifies to a level that directly presages the Plyushkinian extreme—Korobochka and Sobakevich. Thus while the house of Manilov is made of brick (22) and the materials of Nozdryov's house are passed over in silence, Chichikov's arrival at the house of Korobochka is immediately marked, as we have seen, by the collision of his carriage with her wooden fence, and one of the first references to the house is to the loud pattering of the rain on its "wooden roof" (44). In chapter five, wherein the transition to the symbolic theme of "naturalization" is already partly effected, the motif appropriately gathers considerable momentum. The house of Sobakevich is made of wood and

flanked by woods (93), and in the courtyard with its "strong
and inordinately thick wooden fence" the stables, barns, kitch-
ens, and well are constructed of "stout, heavy beams that
would stand for centuries" and of "the strong oak which is
usually used only for mills and ships" (94). These details comprise, as it were, the overture to the motif's greatly intensified
development in chapter six.

The allusions to wood in Plyushkin's physical portrait have
already been indicated. We have noted the oblique comparison
of his hand, while he is writing, to the spreading wood of the
hops and the allusive analogy of the house's exposed wooden
laths and his ribs exposed by the gaps in his dressing gown.
Equally significant are the "literal" implications of the
metaphor "wooden" in the following reference to his face:
". . . not a minute passed before the joy which had appeared so
instantaneously on his wooden face vanished just as instantaneously, as if it had never existed, and his face once more
assumed a thoughtful expression" (123). And no less
"wooden," it seems, than the master of the estate are the
"souls" in whom the state of his own soul is clearly
refracted—the serfs who, when serving as watchmen, are obliged to beat "with wooden spades on empty barrels instead of
a sheet of iron" (130). While the boy Proshka is "as stupid as a
block of wood [*kak derevo*]" (124),[22] Mavra is not only "dark",
but also *zanozistaya* (127)—a term meant by Plyushkin in the
figurative sense of "nagging," but which retains on the allegorical level its literal meaning of "splintery."

The climax of the motif, however, is encountered in the
description of Plyushkin's work yard:

> If anyone had peeped into his work yard, where he had
> stockpiled all kinds of woods and utensils which were
> never used, he might have thought that he had somehow
> found his way to the timber market in Moscow, whither
> efficient mothers-in-law repair every day, followed by
> their cooks, to lay in their household supplies and where

every kind of wood—dovetailed, turned, joined, and wattled—rises in white heaps: barrels, half-barrels, tubs, buckets, jugs with and without spouts, round wooden vessels, bast baskets, pails in which women keep their mops and other rubbish, boxes of thin, bent aspen, cylindrical boxes of woven birch bark, and many other things that go to meet the needs of rich Russia and poor. For what purpose, one might ask, did Plyushkin need such a mass of these wares? He could not have used them all in his lifetime even on two such estates as his, but even this was not enough for him. (117)

Here the motif of "wood" alone suffices for Gogol to restate once more the fundamental contrast of the chapter, and he does so by pretending to compare Plyushkin's yard and the Moscow timber market while, in fact, contrasting them. In both the yard and the market the wooden articles are symbols of nature, but they are clearly distinguished from one another. In Moscow they are unequivocally the tools of man. Housed in a market,[23] they are sold to man (or, more precisely, to man in his feminine, more emphatically "human," form) and are bought by man to be used for the purposes for which man designed them. Accordingly they are characterized by the color symbol of the human soul, white. The wooden articles of Plyushkin, however, have ceased to be tools. The functional role for which they were made has become irrelevant. They have been restored to the "natural" element from which they came, and there, like everything else in nature's realm, they exist simply as matter, as a potential prey of the grasping, spreading ivy.

As in the description of the birch tree, Gogol clothes the most revealing clue to his meaning here in a color symbol, and these two examples of the device indicate the greatly extended role of color symbolism in this highly complex chapter. As a symbol of the "human" (as distinct from the "natural"), "white"[24] is combined several times with "red," chiefly associated with "man-made" structures of brick. Thus recalling the kind of scene that used to gladden his eyes in his youth, the narrator states in the opening paragraph:

> From a distance I would catch fleeting, inviting glimpses of the red roof and white chimneys of a manor house through the green foliage of the trees, and I would wait impatiently for the orchards surrounding it to part [*razoydutsya*] and for the whole exterior of the house to be revealed, which in those regrettably departed days was far from vulgar [*poshloyu*]. (111)

Not only are the red and white of the house contrasted here with the green of the foliage, but, like the white in the description of the Moscow timber market, they convey the impression that in this distant, "human" time of youth man was in full control. When the orchards "parted," they duly revealed the "far from vulgar" spirit of man. When, by contrast, in the present "natural" time of old age the green thickets "part" (*raskhodilis'*) in Plyushkin's garden, they reveal "an unlit chasm . . . yawning like the dark open mouth of some wild beast." The contrast certainly seems intended,[25] and it is particularly interesting for the light it casts on the vice of *poshlost'* ("vulgarity") to which Gogol scholars have devoted so much attention. Its effect is to equate the vice with the triumph of nature over the soul of man.

In choosing red to accompany white, Gogol was evidently influenced by its association with blood. The red blood of man was to be contrasted with the green "blood" of nature. The basis for this assumption is an earlier description of the path in Plyushkin's garden:

> Where the green, cloudy masses parted, two-hundred-year-old limes displayed their bent, hollow trunks which were the width of three men, and between them a path was visible unlit by the sun and overgrown with green, and here and there reddish, almost bloodlike spots stood out, testifying that it had once been covered all over with small bricks or strewn with sand." (759)

Again, red is connected with the material of brick, which is linked far more explicitly here with the "human" pole of the contrast than in any part of the chapter's final version. Here the bricks and the sand are the last surviving drops of blood of the "suffocated" man-made path. Perhaps Gogol judged that in this case the allegory had obtruded too far.

Analogous to the association between red and structures of brick is a similar association between green and structures of wood. "A green mold," we read, "had already covered the rotting wood of the fence and gates" (113), signaling yet again nature's invasion of man's domain. And just as white is complemented by red, so green is complemented by yellow, the color symbol of "human" decay and "aging," which denotes the transition from white to green. This intermediate stage in the process of "naturalization" is illustrated by the "yellow walls" of the "stained and cracked" brick church on the estate, by the "yellowed engraving" on the sitting-room wall (115), by the "small yellow grooves filled with glue" exposed by the dislodged pieces of mosaic on Plyushkin's bureau (115), and by "the toothpick which had turned quite yellow and with which the master had perhaps picked his teeth in the days before the French invasion of Moscow" (115)—a detail which suggests that Plyushkin finally lost his teeth in 1811 or 1812.[26] In an earlier draft the "stone paperweight" on the bureau was also described as "yellowed" (761), but Gogol evidently decided that complete "naturalization" was a more appropriate fate for an object in close and constant contact with heaps of paper "leaves." In the final version it becomes "a marble[27] paperweight which had turned green" (115).

Throughout the chapter the contrasting pairs of color symbols continually intertwine with the other pairs of contrapuntal motifs already noted: youth and old age, brick and wood, symmetry and asymmetry, light and dark, time and timelessness, warmth and cold. Perhaps the most graphic illustration of this interlocking is the "digression" in which the narrator turns briefly from the "naturalized" domain of the miser Plyushkin to the "human" domain of an allegedly typical aristocratic spendthrift:

A passer-by, who had never seen anything like it before, would stop in amazement at the sight of his abode, wondering what mighty prince had suddenly settled among those small, benighted landowners. His white stone buildings with their countless chimneys, belvederes, and weather vanes look like palaces, and are surrounded by numerous wings and all kinds of lodgings for his guests. What does he not have there? Theatrical performances, balls, and all night the garden is brilliantly lit by lights and lampions and is filled with the thunder of music. Gay and dressed up, half the province strolls under the trees, and in this unnatural illumination no one thinks it weird and threatening when a branch, lit up by the artificial light and stripped of its bright green color, leaps out theatrically from the thicket of trees, and the night sky above appears darker, bleaker, and twenty times more menacing [*grozneye*],[28] and the austere treetops, rustling their leaves in the distant heights and withdrawing deeper and deeper into the impenetrable darkness, express their indignation at the tawdry brightness which illuminates their roots from below. (120).

In no other part of the chapter is the hostility of nature to man conveyed so dramatically. Again "white stone buildings" are juxtaposed with nature's greenery, the former bathed in brilliant light and the latter "withdrawing deeper and deeper" into "impenetrable darkness," and twice Gogol emphasises the "man-made" character of this light, its "unnaturalness" and "artificiality," perhaps implicitly contrasting it with the shaft of "natural" sunlight that in the garden of Plyushkin momentarily transforms one of the maple's "claws" into a "transparent, fiery leaf."[29] But just as significant as the implications of the epithets "unnatural" and "artificial" is the tone they inject into the passage—the impression they convey of the narrator's somewhat disparaging attitude to this "human" light and the "theatrical" scene it illuminates. It is a tone which recalls that of the chapter's opening-paragraph reference to the "well-known architectural design" of the "brick public building," and it is

strongly reinforced at the end of the passage by the phrase
"tawdry brightness."

How can we reconcile this apparent disapproval of the "human" scene, and implicit condonement of nature's hostility to
it, with the accumulated evidence that man and nature are
respectively the positive and negative poles of the chapter's
fundamental contrast? The answer, of course, is that we cannot, for the simple reason that this discord between tone and
content is Gogol's principal means of disguising the allegory. It
is precisely for this reason that the most numerous examples
are met in the passage on which the allegory hinges—the
description of Plyushkin's garden. Here the discordant effect of
the verb "to refresh"[30] and the adjectives "picturesque" and
"beautiful" has already been noted, but far more striking is that
of the famous concluding sentence, which critics have always
insisted on taking literally:

> In a word, it was all beautiful as neither nature nor art can
> contrive, but as happens only when they come together,
> when nature passes its final cutting edge over the often
> senselessly heaped up labor of man, lightens the heavy
> masses, destroys the crudely palpable symmetry and the
> clumsily conceived gaps [*prorekhi*] through which the un-
> concealed, naked plan may be glimpsed, and imparts a
> wonderful warmth to everything that has been created in
> the cool of a measured purity and neatness. (113)

Not only are "human" symmetry and the coldness of human
reason referred to here in the same disparaging manner as
"human" light in the later description of the spendthrift's
contrasting garden, but also the "human" (art) and the
"natural" are associated throughout with qualities totally at
variance with those implicitly ascribed to them in the preceding detailed description. Thus just as the phrases "heaped up
labor" and "heavy masses" are far more applicable to the
creations of nature in the garden—e.g. the "green clouds" and
"asymmetrical cupolas" of "quivering leaves," the "green
thickets," and the caragana with its "dense bristles"—than to

the pitiful remains of man's creations, so the image of the cutting edge or chisel (*rezets*) evokes more readily the incisiveness and "neatness" of human reason than it does the slow, "stifling" encroachment of nature. Moreover, in the rest of the chapter it is nature that is identified with "coldness"; it is the "asymmetry" of nature rather than the "symmetry" of man that is "crudely palpable"; and it is nature's gaps—above all, the "gap" formed by the "naturalized" Plyushkin, the "gaping hole in humankind"—that are "clumsily conceived," resembling "the dark open mouth of some wild beast." In the light of these inconsistencies we can only conclude that when Gogol wrote the sentence, his tongue was once more lodged firmly in his cheek.

The addition of art to the various other interrelated symbols of the "human" is another noteworthy common feature of the two passages. In the sentence appended to the description of Plyushkin's garden art presumably refers to the disappearing traces of the original "human" design, but by the time we reach the "digression" on the garden of the spendthrift its meaning has been expanded to encompass theatrical performances, dancing, and music; other direct and oblique references to these art forms are met repeatedly, clearly denoting on each occasion a principle profoundly alien to Plyushkin and nature. Thus one of the reproaches Plyushkin heaps on a neighboring captain is that he allowed "some actress" to filch his money (122); Chichikov too is suspected of having "gadded about with actresses" when he "recklessly" offers to pay the costs of the deed of purchase (123). In both cases the motif of art is associated, as in the "digression" on the spendthrift, with the "unnatural" phenomenon of profligacy. It implies a sense of freedom and release, and, perhaps as a signal of the craving for release, it reappears in the following reference to Plyushkin's bootless serfs:

> If anyone had glanced out of the window in the autumn, especially in the mornings when the light hoarfrosts were beginning, he would have seen all the house-serfs execut-

ing such leaps as the most lively dancer could scarcely
manage at the theatre. (124)

Of particular interest is the connection between the art and
military motifs that is forged by Plyushkin's reproach to the
neighboring captain. The connection is reinforced on the following page by his suspicion that Chichikov had not only
"gadded about with actresses," but "had probably been an
army officer" (123), and it illuminates the significant change in
the "military motif" in this chapter—a change comprehensible
only in the light of the distinction that Gogol is intent on
drawing between Plyushkin and his four predecessors. Perti-
nent here is his emphasis on the rarity of the "Plyushkin type"
in the "digression" on the aristocratic spendthrift:

> It must be said that such people are rarely encountered in
> Russia, where everyone would sooner show what he can
> do than draw in his horns, and it is all the more surprising
> because right there in the vicinity you might meet a land-
> owner making merry with all the recklessness of a Russian
> aristocrat and burning the candle, as the saying goes, at
> both ends. (120)

Plyushkin is distinctive, we have seen, as the only one of the five
landowners whose deviation from the ideal of "pure femininity" involves complete dehumanization, a metamorphosis into
a different species. As a result, the contrast that is the basis of
his portrait is quite different from the contrasts which underlie
the portraits of Manilov, Korobochka, Nozdryov, and Sobakevich. The implied contrast is no longer between "feminine"
and "masculine" conditions of the human soul, but rather
between the human soul ("masculine" and "feminine") and the
"nonhuman" or "inhuman" soul (i.e. "naturalized"). The attributes, therefore, of "masculinity" are now associated with
the positive pole of the contrast, and the motifs expressing this
symbolic theme—above all, the "military motif"—are accordingly endowed with unfamiliar "positive" implications. In
fact, only once in chapter six is the "military motif" used in the

customary manner. The example occurs in the reference to the
French tutor of Plyushkin's children, "who shaved mag-
nificently", we read,[31] "and loved shooting. He always
brought back black grouse or ducks[32] for dinner, but sometimes only sparrows' eggs, from which he would have an
omelet made for himself, for no one else in the house would eat
them" (118). The allusions to the destruction of souls (female
birds and eggs) are self-evident, and it may seem rather curious
that only the tutor is engaged in this activity. The explanation,
however, is equally self-evident, for the period concerned is the
time in Plyushkin's life when the "feminine" virtues personified by his wife were still the dominant influence on the
estate. Against this background "Nozdryovian" violence inevitably appears in its usual "negative" light.

In every other case, however, the "military motif" alludes
less to "Nozdryovian" violence than to "Nozdryovian" ebullience and high spirits, to the qualities of recklessness and
profligacy that are anathema to the grasping spirit of nature as
personified by the "aged" miser. The main connotations of the
motif, in other words, are directly comparable to those of the
youth motif, and this explains perhaps why the yellowing of
Plyushkin's toothpick, i.e. the termination of his "masculine"
youth, is linked with the French invasion of Moscow. It might
also explain why the narrator inserts into the recollections of
his youth in the opening paragraph the memory of "an infantry
officer, walking by himself, who had been transferred to this
dull provincial outpost from God only knows what province"
(110).[33] In the context of chapter six, as the rosy complexion of
Plyushkin's military neighbor (122) suggests, the "military
motif" is a protracted metaphor of human vitality, and we may
assume it is exactly the "suffocation" of this vitality in
Plyushkin's domain that impels his elder daughter to elope
with "a captain of God only knows what cavalry regiment"
(118) and his son to disobey him and risk his paternal curse by
joining the army rather than the civil service (119).

Plyushkin's instinctive antipathy to soldiers, therefore, expresses the same idea as does the indignation of the "rustling

treetops" at the "tawdry brightness" of the scene in the aristocratic spendthrift's garden. Appropriately enough, the "military motif" and the motifs of light and youth are repeatedly
interwoven. Functioning, however, as a kind of common de-
nominator of all three motifs is another, which in this chapter
serves even more prominently as a symbol of the spirit of man
than in chapter three—the motif of fire, which also has an
obvious connection with the color symbol "red." Not supris-
ingly, this motif also makes its first appearance in the context of
the narrator's youthful reminiscences, where it is introduced
by the reference to the sulphur visible "through the door of
some greengrocer's shop" (110). Its association with youth is
later indicated more explicitly in the "digression" on the "fiery
[*plamennyy*] youth of today," who would "recoil in horror if he
were to be shown his own portrait in old age" (127). Similarly
the penchant of the aristocratic spendthrift for "burning the
candle at both ends"[34] indicates its association with the "vitality" of the brightly lit scene in his garden, while in the reproaches Mavra receives from her "wooden" master, for
whom fire is naturally a source of profound terror, Gogol
remarkably succeeds in linking it with the motif of iron:

> You just wait! On the Day of Judgment the devils will
> roast you for this on gridirons. You'll see how they'll roast
> you! . . . The devils will roast you all right. They'll say:
> "Take that, you scoundrel, for deceiving your master!"
> and they'll roast you on hot irons. (127)

Moreover, in one instance the motif is even connected with the
motif of brick—in the comparison of the stacks of wheat
behind the cottages in the village to "old, badly baked bricks"
on top of which "all kinds of weeds were growing, and even
bushes had clung to their sides" (112). The suggestion seems to
be that if the "bricks" had been "young" and properly baked,
the onset of nature would have been successfully resisted.

The motif is used perhaps most expressively, however, in
two passages in which its presence is simply inferred from
closely related motifs that Gogol uses as substitutes. Thus we

are told that Plyushkin's "yellowed engraving" depicts the scene of "some battle with enormous drums, yelling soldiers in three-corned hats, and drowning horses" (115), and we naturally relate the scene at once to the "military motif," but at the same time the drowning of the horses suggests the image of an extinguished flame. Similarly, in the following description of Plyushkin's face the role of the fire motif is played by the motifs of light and warmth, the "drowning" of which inspires one of Gogol's most celebrated similes:

> . . . suddenly a ray of warm light glided over that wooden face; there was not so much an expression of feeling as a pale reflection of a feeling, a phenomenon like the unexpected appearance of a drowning man on the surface of the waters, evoking a shout of joy in the crowd thronging the bank. But in vain do his rejoicing brothers and sisters cast a rope from the bank and wait to see whether his back will appear again or his arms wearied by the struggle—that appearance was the last. Everything is still, and now the becalmed surface of the mute element becomes even more terrible and desolate. So Plyushkin's face, after the feeling that had glided over it for an instant, became even more insensitive and vulgar [poshleye]. (126)

The simile, of course, like the intrusion of water into the "military motif" on the engraving, represents the "suffocation" of Plyushkin's humanity by the "mute element" of nature.

Finally, we might note the implications of the motif of fire in Plyushkin's lament to Chichikov: "In the last three years a confounded fever has exterminated large numbers of my peasants" (121). Here the motif appears in yet another disguise— that of the noun goryachka ("fever"), which is related to the verb goret' ("to burn"). The implication is that Plyushkin's peasants have succumbed to a fever not of the body, but of the mind—to a "feverish" craving for freedom, light, and vitality. We may therefore infer that although Plyushkin chooses to regard these peasants as having been "exterminated," they are not dead, but are, in fact, the "fugitive souls" (*beglyye dushi*) whose names Chichikov acquires later, together with those of their dead brethren. Indeed, Gogol seems to confirm this point with the phrase that he uses for "large numbers"—*zdorovennyy kish*—which means literally "a robust lot." In this case he apparently concluded that the reader needed a little extra assistance, for the adjective *zdorovennyy* was a later substitution for *bol'shoy* ("big") (766).

Among the other allusions to the fate of the "souls" in Plyushkin's charge, familiar images of "natural produce" predictably reappear. Examples are the "stacks of wheat" overgrown with weeds and resembling "old, badly baked bricks," and the "dried up lemon no larger than a hazel nut [*lesnogo orekha*]" on Plyushkin's bureau (115)—an image that evokes once more the significant color yellow, and also reminds us of the "stifling" of the hazel (*lesnogo oreshnika*) by the hops in Plyushkin's garden. Inseparably related to these details, of course, are the scattered references in the chapter to birds and flies. Thus alongside the lemon on the bureau Chichikov observes "two quills" (*dva pera*)[35], which are described as both "dried up as though from consumption," and "ink-stained" (*zapachkannyye chernilami*) (115), and may therefore relate to the "black bird" (*chornaya ptitsa*), i.e. the "darkened soul," to which the jagged top of the white birch tree is compared. He also notices on top of the paperweight a small artificial egg, which has turned green, and "a wineglass containing some liquid and three flies," which is "covered with a letter" (115), a sheet of paper in which we may recognize yet another "stifling" Plyushkinian leaf. Twelve pages later the allusions are repeated when Plyushkin sits down to compose his letter for Chichikov: ". . . he dipped the quill into an inkwell containing some moldy liquid and a multitude of flies at the bottom" (127). Such are the disfigured remains of the "souls" whose names cover his lists "as thick as flies" (125)—names that express the human qualities he has destroyed, e.g. Paramonov ("loyal, true"); Panteleymonov ("kind, compassionate"); and Pimenov ("the shepherd"). Concluding the list is Grigoriy

"Never-Get-There" (Grigoriy Doyezzhay-ne-doyedesh') who was seemingly "stifled" while poised for flight.

Despite the "giant lock" (*zamók-ispolin*) (114) that secures the gates of Plyushkin's "manor" (*zámok*),[36] escape from his prison clearly poses fewer problems than escape from Korobochka's because of the lowness and broken state of his fences. But Plyushkin has another deterrent, which he seems to operate more rigorously than Korobochka—the removal of his serfs' boots, and allusions to it comprise yet another motif in the chapter that merits attention. They include, for example, the reference to the "old soles" that Plyushkin gleans, together with the "iron nails" and "pieces of broken earthenware," during his "street-cleaning" forays (117); the comparison of the greasy, shiny sleeves and skirts of his dressing gown to "the soft leather of which boots are made" (116); and the juxtaposition of the green mildewed egg on the paperweight with "an ancient book in a leather binding with a red edge" (115). Leather, like the color red, is another symbol of the "human"; it is another "human" material that the "ivy" has appropriated. In the form of boots it denotes contact with the world of man, which Plyushkin is bent on severing.

Like the "dead souls" of Sobakevich, however, the still-surviving "souls" of Plyushkin are chiefly portrayed as mirror images of their master. Thus the peasant cottages, which consist of little else but "a ridge pole on the top and riblike poles at the sides" (111), reflect the same concern with breaking down the barriers between man and nature as the walls of Plyushkin's manor, which show their "bare laths" (i.e. ribs) through the veneer of cracked plaster. Likewise Proshka, as noted above, is accredited by his "wooden-faced" master with the stupidity of "a block of wood," while the "husky-voiced housekeeper" Mavra is physically a counterpart of Plyushkin in almost every detail, even to the revealing nicety of "a large tear [*prorekhoyu*] in her skirt" (114). When Chichikov first meets her, we read: "For a long time he could not make out the figure's sex, whether it was a man or a woman" (114), and since he later mistakes Plyushkin for Mavra, we may take it that the state-

ment applies equally to him, confirming that the dominant
symbolic theme here is neither the "emasculation" of man nor
the "masculinization" of woman, but the reduction of both to
the asexual, indeterminate condition of "inhuman nature."

Nor should we assume that the final section of the chapter—
the description of Chichikov's return to the town—is an independent section which bears no relation to this symbolic
theme. It opens significantly with the statement: "The dusk
was already thick when they approached the town," and the
scene that greets Chichikov's eyes is described as follows:

Light and darkness were completely intermingled, and it
seemed as if the objects themselves had also become intermingled. The parti-coloured turnpike had assumed an
indeterminate color. The moustache of the soldier standing on sentry duty seemed to be on his forehead and much
higher than his eyes, while his nose seemed to have vanished completely. . . . The street lights had not yet been lit,
and here and there lights were only just beginning to
appear in the windows of the houses, while in the lanes and
back streets the kinds of scene and conversation were
taking place which are inseparable from this time in all
towns where there are many soldiers, cabmen, workmen,
and peculiar kinds of creatures in the form of ladies in red
shawls and shoes without stockings who dart over crossroads like bats. . . . From time to time the sound of apparently women's voices reached Chichikov's ears exclaiming: "You're lying, you drunkard! I never allowed him to
take such liberties!" or "Don't you knock me about, you
boor! Be off with you to the police station. There I'll prove
it to you! . . ." In short, the kind of words that are like a
deluge of boiling water to a twenty-year-old youth lost in
his dreams as he returns from the theatre with his head full
of a street in Spain, the night, and the marvelous image of a
woman with curls and a guitar. What thoughts and
dreams are not passing through his head? He is in heaven
and has paid a visit to Schiller, when suddenly the fatal

words ring out above him like thunder, and he sees that he
is back on earth, and even in the haymarket and near a
tavern, and once more life in its humdrum manner goes
flaunting itself before him. (130–131)

On being transposed, therefore, from the darkness of
Plyushkin's realm to the dusk of the town, Chichikov is confronted again with the spectacle of indeterminate physical
forms. Black and white are no longer distinguishable from one
another on the turnpike, and the face of the sentry is grotesquely distorted, suggesting a similar distortion of the "human" attributes that the "military motif" in this chapter, as we
have seen, symbolizes. Similarly the women darting over the
crossroads take the form of "peculiar kinds of creatures" which
bear more resemblance to bats, and the speakers whose voices
rend the air cannot even be definitely identified as female.

The town, therefore, to which Chichikov returns significantly resembles the domain he has left, and to signal this
likeness Gogol appropriately reintroduces the motif of youth
in the familiar form of the twenty-year-old, who passes from
the "human" world of art, light, and "pure femininity" into
the disfiguring dusk in which these symbols of the "human"
are "drowned" in boiling water. At the same time the affinities
with Plyushkin's realm coexist with obvious differences. Although dusk has fallen, the darkness is still "intermingled"
with light, and "here and there" lights are "beginning to appear
in the windows of the houses." Moreover, the women have
shoes if not stockings; their shawls are red; and their voices,
even if only *apparently* those of women, are not so completely
indeterminate as the voice of Mavra. If, in conjunction with
these details, we take into account the fact that Plyushkin not
only represents, on Gogol's admission, an exceptionally rare
breed, but is also the only one of the five landowners who does
not visit the town in the course of the novel, we may conclude
that Gogol is as intent on contrasting the town and the estate as
on establishing a parallel between them, and the implication
would seem to be that although the town has contracted some

of the symptoms of "naturalization," it has still not succumbed entirely. As yet the state of its inhabitants' souls is mirrored in the souls of the four landowners who mix in their society. The affinities with Plyushkin's realm, like the motif of "natural produce" in the portrait of Sobakevich, merely point to the future, to the final stage on the downward course to which they are blindly committed.

Since the town, therefore, is compared and contrasted with Plyushkin's realm, it acquires in this chapter, like the "military motif," certain "positive" associations that are apparent in no other part of the novel. Hence the ambivalence in the description of Chichikov's arrival at the inn, in which Gogol again indicates resemblances to Plyushkin's realm while placing greater emphasis on contrasting features. Thus the statement that "the carriage, after executing a considerable leap [*poryadochnyy skachok*], passed through the gates of the inn as if it were dropping into a hole" (131) seems to echo, in part, the reference to Chichikov's entry into Plyushkin's village: "He was soon made to take notice of this . . . by a very considerable jolt [*preporyadochnyy tolchok*] caused by a roadway made of logs . . ." (111), to which the narrator adds "compared to which the stone cobbles of the town were as nothing," thereby specifying from the beginning, both explicitly and symbolically (i.e. by means of the implied contrast between the "stone" cobbles and the "wooden" logs), that the more signficant relationship between the town and the village is one of contrast. At the end he reemphasises this contrast with the aid of three separate details: the passing mention of Petrushka's attempts to hold up the skirts of his coat "for he disliked seeing them fly apart" (i.e. unlike Plyushkin) (131); the reference to the candle with which the waiter lights the way for Chichikov;[37] and the waiter's announcement that room sixteen has been allocated to a newly arrived army lieutenant, which reflects a patently "un-Plyushkinian" attitude to soldiers. The three details confirm that Chichikov has reentered a world which, at least compared with Plyushkin's realm, is one of people—a world in which he can fall safely into "that marvel-

ous sleep which is enjoyed only by lucky people who know
nothing of hemorrhoids, fleas, or excessively strong intellectual capabilities" (132).

6

The Masters and the Slaves

Gogol uses the portraits of the five landowners to establish connections in our minds between specific patterns of details and specific types of spiritual degradation; in each of the five portraits, as we have seen, a plurality of such patterns intersect and are transformed into signals of the type of degradation that the landowner embodies. Having firmly established these connections, Gogol can then detach the patterns of details from the figures in whose portraits they acquire their signalling capacity and use this capacity in new contexts. This, in effect, is what he does in the remaining chapters of the novel, which differ from the "portrait chapters" in that the characters encountered by the hero are portrayed less as individuals than as representatives of social and sexual groups. Certainly new patterns of details or motifs continue to emerge in each of these chapters, but they no longer have the primary function of signalling conditions of the soul. Henceforward this role is mainly performed simply by new combinations of the motifs with which we are now familiar.

Perhaps the most obvious result of the switch from individual portraits to group portraits is the even greater use that Gogol makes in the next three chapters of contrast, for in addition to the customary implicit contrast between the ideal and the deviations from it there are the contrasts between the groups. There are three such groups, which may be called the "slaves," the "masters," and the "ladies," and the structure of these three chapters is based on a contrast between two of

them. In chapter seven the first and second groups are contrasted; in chapters eight and nine it is the second and third. At
the same time the change from individuals to groups, combined with the return to the urban setting, produces no sense of
discontinuity. This pitfall is avoided not only by using familiar
motifs, but also by including in the groups that are contrasted
in chapter seven characters who are already well known to us.
Thus the group of "masters" includes, along with the dignitaries and senior civil servants of the town, Manilov and
Sobakevich, while the category of "slaves" embraces not only
the junior civil servants, but also the dead and fugitive serfs
whose names are recorded on Chichikov's lists.

Most familiar of all, however, in the second half of the novel
is Gogol's creative method, which continues to display the
same dominant features as in the "portrait chapters." Again
each chapter confronts the reader with a highly digressive
narrative in which the real relations between words are skillfully disguised, and again the discovery of these relations reveals an unexpected unity of theme and conception. The
replacement of individual figures with contrasting groups may
make these chapters seem even more loosely constructed than
chapters two through six, but again appearances are calculated
to deceive. On turning to chapter seven we find once more that
passages which seem to have a completely independent existence (e.g. the "digressive" introductory section) are sprinkled
with details binding them inseparably to their contexts, and
that in the light of these connections the meanings normally
ascribed to them will require radical reassessment.

The superstructure of chapter seven is divisible into seven
main parts; the short opening paragraph, in which the narrator
dwells on the happiness of the traveler who has returned from
an arduous journey to the bosom of his family; the contrast in
the following long paragraph between two types of writer; the
next brief paragraph, which introduces the contrast between
"laughter" and "tears" and seems to point forward to the
ensuing development of the "epic"; the description of
Chichikov's daydreams inspired by the names on his lists; the

account of his visit with Manilov to the government offices to legalize his purchases; the depiction of the festivities arranged in his honor by the president of the court and the chief of police; and, finally, the description of his return to the inn. It can be seen, therefore, that four of the seven parts are already completed before the narrative resumes its forward movement, and that the first three bear little apparent relation to what follows. But like the narrator's reminiscences of his youth at the beginning of chapter six, these three opening parts are genuinely introductory. They comprise, in fact, a single tripartite introduction to the two central themes of the chapter, the first of which, as stated, is the contrast between the "masters" and the "slaves." We may begin our examination of the chapter, therefore, by considering each of the three introductory parts in turn and its connections with the four parts that follow.

The opening paragraph reads:

> Happy is the traveler who, after a long and tedious journey [*dorogi*] with its cold, slush, and mud, its half-asleep post-masters, jingling bells, repairs, squabbles, coachmen, blacksmiths and all kinds of villains of the road [*dorozhnymi podletsami*], sees at last the familiar roof and the lights rushing toward him and encounters the familiar rooms, the joyful cries of the people dashing out to meet him, the noise and scurrying of his children, and the calming, gentle words interrupted by passionate kisses which have the power to eradicate all melancholy thoughts from his memory. Happy is the family man who has such a home, but woe to the bachelor! (133)

The traveler, of course, is Chichikov, and we naturally assume that the passage refers to his return to the town at the end of chapter six. We also assume that the term *bachelor* similarly refers to Chichikov and that the happiness of the "family man" is evoked to offset the bachelor's misery. These assumptions, however, immediately pose the question: how can we reconcile this misery with the obvious pleasure that Chichikov derives from his return? Certainly the narrator informs us at the end of chapter six that "it is not known whether Petrushka rejoiced at his master's arrival" (131), but the ease with which Chichikov consumes the sucking pig and sinks into a "marvelous sleep" leaves little doubt that he himself is delighted to be back. His state of mind, in other words, seems to have much more in common with that of the "family man" than that of the " bachelor," suggesting that we should associate him with the former. Yet how could the term *family man* possibly be applied to a man whose bachelor status is emphasized in the very first sentence of the novel? The later sections of the chapter provide the answer, confirming that this opening paragraph is related less to the conclusion of chapter six than to the ensuing events of chapter seven.

Although "joyful cries," "calming, gentle words," and "passionate kisses" are conspicuously absent from the greeting Chichikov receives on his return to the inn, they are part of the greeting he receives on entering the office of the president of the court. The impact of his arrival (in the company of Manilov) is described as follows:

> The arrival of the visitors gave rise to an exclamation, and the presidential armchair was moved back noisily. Sobakevich also half-rose from his chair and became visible from all sides with his long sleeves. The president embraced Chichikov and the office resounded with kisses. They enquired about each other's health. (144)

Moreover, these are not the only kisses bestowed on the hero. A similar scene follows his meeting shortly before with Manilov on the street:

> They immediately embraced one another and remained on the street in this position for about five minutes. The kisses they bestowed on each other were so powerful that the front teeth of both of them ached for almost the whole day. (140)

The two scenes clearly echo the greeting received by the "family man." But granted that the echoes are not coincidental, what possible connection can be established between Chichikov and "the noise and scurrying of his children"? The answer is supplied by a single word in the description of the president's exuberant conduct at the festivities in the penultimate section of the chapter:

> The president, who was a most delightful man when merry, embraced Chichikov several times, exclaiming in a heartfelt effusion: "My dear fellow [*dusha ty moya*]! My poppet!" and even set off dancing around him, snapping his fingers, and singing the well-known song "Oh, you are such a Kamarinsky peasant!" (151)

The word proving that the "noise" and "scurrying" of the children who greet the traveler are, in fact, allusions to the president's singing and dancing is the Russian word for "poppet"—*mamen'ka*—which presents yet another example of Gogolian word play with the literal and figurative meanings. The context obviously demands the figurative meaning "poppet," but far from being submerged, the literal meaning "mother," which momentarily converts the president into Chichikov's child, is used by Gogol to forge this comic connection between the two widely separated parts of the chapter.

Although it will therefore be necessary to return to this point later, it no longer seems implausible to suggest that the traveler with whom Chichikov should be identified in the opening paragraph is the "family man" rather than the "bachelor." The term *family* in this context is an ironic allusion to the powerful and privileged group of "masters"—Manilov, Sobakevich, the president, the chief of police, and the various other dignitaries and landowners—of which Chichikov, by virtue of his recent acquisitions, can now consider himself a member. It denotes the company of the successfully corrupt who instantly recognize in the newcomer a kindred spirit. But if Chichikov is the "family man," who is the "bachelor"?

The most important clue in the opening paragraph to the "bachelor's" identity is the noun *doroga,* which is used here in the sense of "journey," but which basically means "road."

Again, of course, we are initially inclined to identify it with the road Chichikov has traversed on his way from landowner to landowner and back again to the town, but repetitions of the noun in a later section of the chapter suggest that once more the allusion points forward rather than backward. The section concerned is that in which Chichikov surveys his lists of dead and fugitive serfs and, choosing names at random, tries to imagine the conditions of their lives and the circumstances in which they met their deaths. Thus contemplating the name of Korobochka's serf, Pyotr Savel'yev "Disrespectful-of-Troughs," he asks: ". . . and how did you meet your death? Was it in a tavern, or were you run over by a clumsy cart while asleep in the middle of the road [*seredi dorogi*]?" (136). And a similar question is prompted by the name of Plyushkin's Grigoriy "Never-Get-There": "Was it on the road [*na doroge*] that you gave up your soul to God . . . ?" (137). The interesting point is that although both these serfs died in their respective "prisons," Chichikov is still disposed to associate them with the image of the "road," to imagine them, like the fugitive serfs, as travelers, and it is similarly as travelers and vagabonds that he visualizes the other dead serfs, e.g. Stepan Probka, who is imagined striding "through all the provinces with an axe in his belt and his boots slung over his shoulders" (136), and Maksim Telyatnikov, who ends his days "loafing about the streets" (137).

But the fate of these travelers, as Chichikov pictures it, is plainly very different from that of the "family man." Not for them the joy and kisses of a welcoming family; on the contrary, both dead and fugitive serfs are imagined moving in the opposite direction—away from their homes and their wives toward the solitude of the road and death. The surname of Nikita Volokita and his son Anton, which signifies a "homeless vagabond,"[1] defines their common situation. Even the Volga boatmen, who are joined by the most fortunate of them, Abakum Fyrov, are obliged as they set sail to "bid farewell to their mistresses and wives" (139). The result is the ironic paradox that while the bachelor Chichikov is suddenly en-

dowed with a "family" (which, significantly, is exclusively
masculine), the married serfs, detached from all feminine society, are involuntarily transformed into "bachelors."

The contrast, therefore, between the "family man" and the
"bachelor" is an allusion to the contrast between Chichikov
and his serfs which, in its turn, is related to the central contrast
of the chapter between the "masters" and the "slaves." We
must now consider the possible relevance to this contrast of the
second part of the chapter's "introduction"—the contrast between the two kinds of writer. The first writer is described as
follows:

> Happy is the writer who avoids tedious and disagreeable
> characters, who make an impression with their dismal
> reality, and turns to characters who manifest the lofty
> dignity of man, the writer who from the great maelstrom
> of daily revolving images has chosen only the few excep-
> tions, who has never once betrayed the sublime pitch of
> his lyre, who has never stepped down from his pinnacle to
> his poor, insignificant brethren and, without touching the
> earth, has immersed himself completely in his exalted
> images, which are so far removed from it. His fortunate
> lot is doubly enviable: among them he seems to be among
> his own family [*on sredi ikh kak v rodnoy sem'ye*], and
> meanwhile his fame spreads far and wide. He has clouded
> men's eyes with an intoxicating vapor; he has flattered
> them wonderfully, concealing the sadness of life and
> showing them the goodness of man. Applauding,
> everyone tears after him and races after his triumphal
> chariot. They call him a great, universal poet, soaring high
> above all the other geniuses of the world as an eagle soars
> above the other high-flying birds. At the mere mention of
> his name young, fervent hearts are filled with trepidation;
> tears gleam in response in every eye. . . . He has no equal
> in power—he is a god. (133–134)

The conventional view is that Gogol is describing in this
passage the kind of writer from whom he dissociates himself,

and that his personal position and attitudes are reflected in the following passage on the second kind of writer. Once more, however, the later development of the chapter prompts us to revise our initial impressions and even to question whether these passages tell us anything about Gogol himself, for it confirms conclusively that he is contrasting here not so much two types of writer as the two types of character to whom the chapter is chiefly devoted.

A careful examination of the later sections of the chapter leaves little doubt that the passage on the first kind of writer alludes ironically to the "masters" as represented by their two most prominent members in this chapter—the president of the court and the chief of police. The image of the "pinnacle," for example, from which the writer "has never stepped down . . . to his poor, insignificant brethren" points forward to the "pinnacle" in the government offices on which the president is perched high above the heads of his "tedious and disagreeable" subordinates, sitting there "in solitude like the sun" (144) and meriting comparison with Homer's Zeus (139). Such is the eaglelike[2] "god" who fills "fervent hearts" with "trepidation." The official who escorts Chichikov and Manilov to the office is likened to Virgil who "had once served Dante," and just at the pre-Christian bard was obliged to leave his charge at the summit of Purgatory, so "the new Virgil felt such reverence" on opening the door that "he did not venture to set foot there" (144). Admission to paradise is restricted to the "exalted images" of the "family" of "masters."[3]

The notion of the "family," however, is most conspicuously reinvoked in reference to the chief of police, Aleksey Ivanovich, of whom we read:

> The chief of police was in a certain sense the father and benefactor of the town. Among the citizens he seemed just as if he were among his own family [*on byl sredi grazhdan sovershenno kak v rodnoy sem'ye*], and he visited the shops and the bazaar as if they were his own larder. . . . His chief admirers were the merchants, who liked him just because

he was not proud; and indeed he stood godfather to their children and was on friendly terms with them, and although he occasionally fleeced them terribly, he somehow did it very cleverly: he would pat them on the back, burst out laughing, give them a cup of tea, promise to come for a game of checkers, and inquire about everything, how business was going and how they were getting on. (149–50)

Here Gogol reveals the true nature of the "intoxicating vapor" with which the eyes of men are "clouded"—a pat on the back, a cup of tea, a few beguiling words, and a game of checkers, the "Nozdryovian" implications of which are already known to us. The checkers of the "good man" conceal the "swords" of the villain—the "sadness of life." The passage continues:

He would set off in his droshky to maintain law and order, and at the same time he would drop a word to this or that passer-by. . . . Meanwhile, even the shop assistants, doffing their caps, would usually look at one another with pleasure as if wishing to say: "Aleksey Ivanovich is an excellent chap!" In short, he succeeded in gaining universal popularity, and it was the opinion of the merchants that although Aleksey Ivanovich "will fleece you, he will never let you down." (150)

Thus the "great, universal poet" with the "triumphal chariot" and the throng of fervent admirers is exposed as the eloquent, "universally popular" policeman with the droshky and the "family" of admiring merchants.

The "hearts" of the "poet's" admirers, however, are not only "fervent"; they are also "young," and in the "trepidation" of these "young hearts" we may perceive yet another allusion to the later portrayal of the "masters" and their new recruit— an allusion to their contempt for youth, voiced on several occasions. Thus in reference to the two "still youthful" clerks who insist on knowing the details of Chichikov's purchases before agreeing to direct him to the appropriate office we read:

"Chichikov saw at once that, like all young civil servants, the clerks were simply curious and wished to add more weight and importance to themselves and their work" (142). And when the president congratulates him on his purchases, Chichikov is moved to observe: "... a man cannot determine his aim in life unless he has finally stood with a firm foot on a sound foundation and not on some free-thinking chimera of youth." The narrator adds: "And here he very aptly chided all young people for their liberalism, and it serves them right" (146). The motif of youth, of course, has the same connotations here as it does in chapter six and in the portrait of the governor's daughter, but here youth is contrasted not with old age (which denotes, as stated, a degree of decay peculiar to Plyushkin), but with middle age, and the two poles of the contrast are respectively associated with the "slaves" and the "masters." Hence the announcement of Sobakevich: "I'm over forty and not once have I been ill" (145) and the narrator's comment on the senior official Ivan Antonovich: "It was immediately apparent that he was a man of sensible age and no young chatterbox and gadabout. Ivan Antonovich seemed to be well over forty" (143).

Having been informed on the first page of the novel that Chichikov "could not be said to be old, but he was not too young either" (7), we can see that he is as admirably qualified by his age for admission to the "family" of "masters" as by his new acquisitions. At the same time the narrator makes plain to us in chapter seven that Chichikov does not always conduct himself in a manner befitting his age. We are told, for example, that on rising from his bed, he "forgot his dignity and the proprieties of middle age and took two leaps across the room" (135). Nor is Chichikov the only middle-aged "master" susceptible to such lapses, for his "leaps," as we have seen, are later imitated in the dance of the president. And since these two "masters" are capable of forgetting the "proprieties of middle age," might we not suspect that Ivan Antonovich is equally liable to do so, that he is capable of being not only a "chatterbox," but also a "gadabout," the Russian term for which, vertoplyas, significantly combines the notions of "gyrating" and "dancing"? Furthermore, it is noteworthy that as soon as the festivities begin, Chichikov's strictures about the "liberalism" and "free-thinking chimeras of youth" are swiftly forgotten. The narrator records: "They forgot completely about whist; they argued, shouted and talked about everything—about politics and even military matters—and expounded free-thinking ideas for which at any other time they would have thrashed their own children" (151). Thus the reprehensible habits that the middle-aged "masters" attribute to youth are subsequently practiced by the "masters" themselves, providing a further indication not only of the irony that pervades their entire portrait, but also of the means by which the ironic effects are principally achieved, for these are merely a few examples of Gogol's recurrent procedure of associating the "masters" either with practices they condemn in the "slaves" or with deviations from the lofty standards previously ascribed to them.

Another example of the same procedure is indicated by the last of the statements that we need consider in the passage on the first type of writer—the claim that he "has never once betrayed the sublime pitch of his lyre." Is this not an ironic allusion to the president's drunken rendering of "Oh, you are such a Kamarinsky peasant!" and the various other high-pitched noises the "masters" are associated with—noises that seem implicitly contrasted with the "song as endless as Russia herself" (139) sung by Abakum Fyrov and the Volga boatmen? Thus while Chichikov directs his invective against the liberalism of youth, Manilov, "enchanted by his phrases, merely nodded his head approvingly with pleasure, while settling into the kind of position which a lover of music assumes when a female singer outdoes the violin itself and shrills a note which is so thin that even a bird's throat could not manage it" (146–147). And in the final section of the chapter the "snore of unprecedented richness" emitted by Petrushka and Selifan is discordantly accompanied by the "creaking"[4] of Chichikov's bed and his "thin, nasal whistle" (153). Such, it seems, is the "sublime pitch" of the "masters'" lyre.

The general conclusion, therefore, to which all this evidence leads is that the passage on the first type of writer is composed almost entirely of forward-pointing allusions that provide a basis for the ironic portrayal of the "masters." An examination of the somewhat longer passage on the second kind of writer shows that it provides a similar basis for the portrayal of the "slaves":

> . . . quite different is the fate of the writer who has dared to summon forth into the light of day everything that is continually before our eyes and that indifferent eyes fail to see—all the dreadful, shocking morass of trivialities in which our life is entangled, the whole profusion of cold, split-up, everyday characters with whom our sometimes bitter and tedious earthly path [*doroga*] teems, and who has dared with the mighty power of his implacable chisel to exhibit them graphically and vividly before the eyes of the whole nation. He is not fated to receive the people's applause or to behold the grateful tears and the unanimous delight of the souls that he has stirred; no sixteen-year-old girl will fly to meet him with her head turned and full of heroic enthusiasm; he will not find oblivion in the sweet fascination of the sounds he has extracted; nor, finally, will he escape the judgment of his contemporaries [*sovremen-nogo suda*], the hypocritical and callous judgment of his contemporaries, which will call his cherished creations insignificant and despicable, assign him a contemptible place in the ranks of writers who insult humanity, ascribe to him the qualities of the characters he has portrayed and rob him of heart, soul, and the divine spark of genius. For the judgment of his contemporaries does not recognize that the glasses which behold suns and those which reflect the movements of unnoticed insects are equally marvelous; for the judgment of his contemporaries does not recognize that great spiritual depth is needed to illuminate a picture taken from contemptible life and raise it into a pearl of creation; for the judgment of his contemporaries

does not recognize that sublime, ecstatic laughter is
worthy to stand beside sublime lyrical emotion and that
there is a whole world of difference between it and the
antics of a *skomorokh*[5] at a fair. The judgment of his contemporaries does not recognize this, and it will turn everything into a reproach and abuse of the unrecognized
writer; without reciprocated feeling, without response,
without sympathy, he will remain alone in the middle of
the road [*posredi dorogi*] like a traveler without a family.
Hard is his calling, and bitterly will he feel his solitude.
(134).

The reference to the "cold, split-up, everyday characters
with whom our sometimes bitter and tedious earthly path
teems" and similarly the predicament of the writer himself
standing "alone in the middle of the road like a traveler without
a family" are immediately recognizable allusions to the plight
of Chichikov's "bachelor slaves," as his imagination subsequently recreates it. The writer and his "cherished creations"
share a common "fate," which is likewise the "fate" of the
characters spawned by Chichikov's fantasy. Separated from
the feminine society of their families, the "slaves," unlike the
"happy family man" Chichikov, are not fated to be greeted by
any sixteen-year-old governor's daughter[6] or by the "grateful
tears" and "unanimous delight" inspired by the chief of police.
Their "fate" is to be deprived of the "divine spark" of freedom
and life[7] and to be confronted with the "indifferent eyes" of the
"masters", by whose "judgment" they are condemned to be
"entangled" in the "dreadful, shocking morass of trivialities."
Significant here is not only the term "morass" (*tina*), which
reminds us of Korobochka's clinging mud, but also the term
sud that Gogol uses for "judgment" and which also means
"trial" and "court." There is a reason, we may assume, for the
term to be used six times. The repetitions are Gogol's means of
conveying to us that the source of this "judgment" is the
president of the court (*predsedatel' suda*). Accordingly, the
"morass of trivialities" may perhaps be interpreted as the web

of legal snares that the fugitive "slaves," e.g. Plyushkin's house-serf Popov, seek vainly to evade. While the chief of police is rewarded for fleecing his "family" with "universal popularity," Popov's rewards for two alleged thefts are the stocks and a cell, and the involvement of the president of the court in imposing these penalties is conveyed in the same indirect manner. Addressing Popov in his thoughts, Chichikov observes:

> And now you live in prison until your case is heard in court [*v sude*]. And the court [*sud*] decrees that you be taken from Tsarevokokshaysk to a prison in such-and-such a town, and the court [*sud*] there decrees that you be sent to some town called Ves'yegonsk. (138)

Repetitions of the noun *sud,* however, are not the only way that Gogol links the fate of the "slaves" with the figure of the president. For while the "movements of unnoticed insects," which evoke once more the image of the fly,[8] are patently an allusion to the "travels" of the "slaves," the "glasses which behold suns" can only refer to what Chichikov sees on entering the president's office—the president seated "like the sun" at his desk "behind two thick books and a *zertsalo*" (144).[9] And a further allusion to the president may be discerned in the implied association of the "masters" with "sublime lyrical emotion," which contrasts with the similar association of the "slaves" with "sublime, ecstatic laughter" and "the antics of a *skomorokh* at a fair." Here again the irony resides in associating each of the contrasting groups with actions and sentiments that are later shown to be more typical of the other, for genuine "lyrical emotion" is encountered solely in the references to the sufferings of the "slaves" and is merely parodied, as we have seen, in the effusive greetings that Chichikov receives from the president and Manilov. Likewise the "laughter" and "antics" (*krivlyan'ye*) are plainly untypical of the "cold, split-up, every-day characters" to whom they are attributed and can only be related to the merriment of the "masters" at the later festivities and to the president's sprightly dance.

The phrase "the antics of a *skomorokh* at a fair" points forward to a whole complex of details in the portrait of the "masters" that present yet another vivid illustration of the labyrinthine manner in which Gogol expands his motifs. It is this phrase, for example, which foreshadows the bizarre actions of Chichikov on rising from his bed:

> He lay for two minutes or so on his back and then snapped his fingers and remembered with beaming face that he now had almost four hundred serfs. . . . He did not look now either at his chin or at his face, but proceeded at once, just as he was, to put on his morocco boots with cutout patterns in all sorts of colors, in which the town of Torzhok does a lively trade thanks to the idle inclinations of the Russian nature, and in the Scottish manner, wearing nothing but his short nightshirt and forgetting his dignity and the proprieties of middle age, took two leaps across the room, slapping himself very cleverly with his heel. (135)

Thus, having acquired his own "slaves" and thereby achieved the status of "master," he launches at once into the "antics" that mark this status, demonstrating by his leaps and snapping of fingers his elevation to kinship with the dancing, finger-snapping president.

Even more arresting, however, are the "antics" of the lieutenant from Ryazan', whose arrival at the inn is announced at the end of chapter six. His second and last appearance, which, according to Erlich, is included in the narrative "with a supreme lack of concern for relevance or coherence,"[10] is delayed until the end of chapter seven, signifying by its position the considerable importance in the chapter of the motif to which his actions are related. The scene is described as follows:

> Soon afterwards everything settled down, and the whole inn was enveloped in a deep sleep. Only in one little window could a light still be seen, where some lieutenant, the one who had arrived from Ryazan', was living. He was

evidently a great lover[11] of boots, for he had already ordered four pairs and was continually trying on a fifth. Several times he walked up to his bed to throw them off and lie down, but he could not bring himself to do so; the boots were indeed well made, and he continued for a long time to lift his foot and inspect the deftly and wonderfully turned heel. (153)

Although the lieutenant is neither dignitary nor landowner, the close association between the "masters" and the military throughout the novel creates the necessary basis for applying to him one of the motifs that chiefly characterize the "masters." If any doubt remains that his pacing and raising of his foot are meant to manifest the same emblematic activity as the "dances" of Chichikov and the president, then it is surely removed by the repetition of the boot motif, from which the implications of the "antics" motif may be plausibly deduced.

The inception of the boot motif can be traced back to the "boot trees" (*sapozhnyye kolodki*) that are unpacked from Chichikov's case in chapter one (8)[12] and to the pictures of boots that he observes on shop signs during his first walk round the town (11). We have also noted the detail of the "mud boots" of Pelageya in chapter three and Plyushkin's tactic of removing the boots of his serfs in chapter six, which suggest that the motif is closely connected with the idea of freedom. The most elaborate development of the motif, however, is postponed until chapter seven, where the references to the boots of Chichikov and the lieutenant comprise one of the two frames in which the narrative section of the chapter is expressively set. The basis for this development, of course, is established in the preceding introductory paragraphs by the motifs of travel and the "road," and since these two motifs are chiefly associated with the "slaves," it is not surprising that boots figure as prominently in the portrait of the latter as in that of the "masters."

References to boots are particularly numerous, for example, in Chichikov's meditations on Sobakevich's serf Maksim

Telyatnikov, who, a cobbler by trade, allegedly tried to make a quick fortune in Moscow by selling at low prices boots he had made from cheap leather. Unfortunately, the predictable tendency of the boots to burst prematurely brought his spectacular initial success to a speedy end and his business soon collapsed—a result that he promptly ascribed, in the spirit of his xenophobic master, to the unfair competition of his treacherous German rivals. Lexical and phraseological echoes make it quite clear that the failure of Maksim's attempt to "fleece" his public is intended to contrast with the successful "fleecing" of the citizenry by the chief of police. Thus the description of the cobbler as a "marvel" (*chudo*) (137) by his first employer echoes the two references to the chief of police as a "miracle-worker" (*chudotvorets*) because of his ability to organize Gargantuan feasts at the drop of a hat (148–149). And the ability of the "father and benefactor of the town" to arrange matters "so cleverly that he received an income which was double that of all his predecessors" (149) is briefly matched by Maksim's success in making "twice as much on each boot" (137) with the aid of his cheap leather. But whereas Aleksey Ivanovich's "fleecing" wins him "the affection of the whole town" (149), Maksim draws "the vilest abuse" (137).[13]

Although, however, boots play such a notable part in the brief story of Maksim, the implications of the *motif* of boots are not disclosed by the episode. More revealing in this respect is Chichikov's supposition that Stepan Probka "must have traveled through all the provinces with an axe in his belt and his boots slung over his shoulder" (136), which suggests that his boots were so inferior they could not withstand a long, arduous journey and so had to be carried. A similar idea seems to be expressed in the order issued after Popov's interrogation: "Hammer the stocks on his feet and take him off to prison" (138). Since the Russian word for "stocks" is the same as the word for "boot trees"—*kolodki*—the suggested meaning is that Popov has no boot trees (and, implicitly, no boots) and that the stocks are a kind of substitute. In other words, the "slaves" who are obliged to brave the hardships of the "road" in their quest for freedom are characterized by having either no boots at all or boots of such inferior quality that they cannot be used. And it may be noted that their "colleagues" in the government offices are threatened with similar deprivation, for Chichikov and Manilov arrive just in time to hear "a more majestic voice, doubtless belonging to one of the superiors, announce imperiously: 'Here, write that out again or else your boots will be removed and I'll keep you sitting here for six days without food' " (142).

The position of Chichikov and the lieutenant is plainly very different. While Chichikov is the proud possessor of "morocco boots with cutout patterns in all sorts of colors", the lieutenant has five pairs of surpassing magnificence. The mark of good quality is similarly detectable in the "lacquered jackboots" of the "smart" policeman who is summoned by the chief of police to prepare the food for the guests (149). Yet the only significant purpose to which this resplendent footwear is put is the intermittent cavorting that Gogol calls "antics." Apart from these occasional paroxysms of bizarre activity, the "masters" seem to be almost completely immobile embodiments of the "idle inclinations of the Russian nature" to which Gogol ironically attributes the lively trade in boots in the town of Torzhok. Hence the bedroom settings with which the narrative section of the chapter both begins and ends, and the sprinkling of details that might be generically referred to as the motif of the "sedentary life." The most obvious example is encountered in the initial exchanges between Chichikov and the president: "They inquired about each other's health, and it turned out that they both had a pain in the small of the back which was immediately ascribed to a sedentary life" (144). Other examples are the term *sidel'tsy* (literally "sitters"), which Gogol uses for the "shop assistants" who form part of Aleksey Ivanovich's "family" and also the statement relating to Aleksey Ivanovich himself, which might be rendered as: "In general, he was the right man, as they say, in the right place," but which reads literally: "In general, he sat [*sidel*], as they say, in his place" (149). And, finally, we might note the comments of

Sobakevich on the various officials whom he suggests as possible witnesses to the signing of the purchase deeds:

> Send word right now to the public prosecutor. He's a lazy man and is [literally "is sitting" (*sidit*)] probably at home. . . . The inspector of the public health authority is also a lazy man and is also probably at home, if he has not gone somewhere to play cards, and there are many more who live nearer. (146)

While it is appropriate that these remarks should be voiced by Sobakevich, the apostle of physical prowess, it is also significant that shortly afterwards the "bear" is himself reduced to complete immobility by the weight of the phenomenal sturgeon that he consumes.[14] In response to Chichikov's recitation of Werther's letter in verse to Charlotte, Sobakevich "merely looked blank as he sat [*sidya*] in his armchair, for after the sturgeon he felt a profound urge to sleep" (152).

These widely scattered details comprise the fourth and last of the various motifs Gogol relates in the chapter to the pivotal motif of boots, and its connections with the other motifs are sufficiently self-evident to require little further comment. It is clear that the motifs of "antics" and the "sedentary life" in the portrait of the "masters" correspond to the motifs of travel and the "road" in the portrait of the "slaves," and the recurrent source of irony is the adaptation of each of the two groups' footwear to the needs of the other—that of the "slaves" to the insignificant demands of "antics" and the "sedentary life," and that of the "masters" to the exacting demands of travel and the "road." The only journey, in fact, of any consequence that any "master" must make is Chichikov's journey on foot to the government offices, and even then, thanks to Manilov, his morocco boots turn out to be almost superfluous. "At every small elevation," the narrator notes, "whether it was a small mound or a step, Manilov supported Chichikov and almost lifted him with his arm, adding with a pleasant smile that on no account would he allow Pavel Ivanovich to bruise his little feet" (140).

Reverting, therefore, to our point of departure, we can see that "the antics of a *skomorokh* at a fair" is yet another phrase which confirms the genuinely introductory function of its context—the passages on the two types of writer. It now remains only to consider the final part of the introductory section which includes some of the most frequently quoted words in the novel:

> And for a long time yet I am ordained by a wondrous power to walk hand in hand with my strange heroes, to view the whole immensity of life as it rushes past me, to view it through a laughter which is visible to the world and through invisible tears which are unknown to it. And as yet far off is the time when an awesome storm of inspiration will arise like some gushing spring from a head swathed in sacred terror and brilliance and men will hear, in confusion and trepidation, the majestic thunder of different words. (134–135)

The usual consensus is that while the first sentence of the passage provides insight into Gogol's general approach to and treatment of his subject, the second alludes to the later volumes of the "epic" in which the "dead souls" were seemingly to be purified and resurrected. It is an entirely plausible view and there seems little cause to challenge it, but like so many traditional views of the novel, it takes account of only one of two coexisting levels of meaning. In the light, for example, of our observations on the preceding paragraphs of the introductory section, is it not equally plausible that the famous pronouncement on "laughter" and "tears," which echoes the contrast in the passage on the second kind of writer between "sublime, ecstatic laughter" and "sublime lyrical emotion," relates more to the content of chapter seven (i.e. the two contrasting group portraits) than to that of the novel as a whole? Lexical echoes again provide some justification for this contention. Thus the Russian for the verb "to view" in the passage is significantly *ozirat'*, the highly literary, and therefore rather conspicuous, verb that Gogol has already associated obliquely with the "masters" by means of the quoted allusion to the president in his office: ". . . the glasses which behold suns [*styokla, ozirayushchiye solntsy*]." Moreover, the image of this Zeuslike or sunlike figure is again evoked by the reference to the "head swathed in sacred terror and brilliance." Similarly, the author's reference to walking "hand in hand" with his "strange heroes" seems to prefigure the journey of Chichikov and Manilov to the government offices, the description of which includes the statements: "For about a quarter of an hour he [Manilov] held the hand of Chichikov in both his hands and made it terribly hot. . . . The friends took each other by the arm and set off together" (140). And finally, while the "majestic [*velichavyy*] thunder of different words" reminds us of the "more majestic [*velichavyy*] voice, doubtless belonging to one of the superiors" which threatens the clerks in the government office with the removal of their boots, the "trepidation" (*trepet*) that it will allegedly inspire directs our attention once more to the "trepidation" (*trepet*) which fills "young, fervent hearts" at the mere mention of the "great, universal poet" behind whose mask we have detected the chief of police.

Although, therefore, the traditional views of this passage cannot be discounted, its lexical composition suggests that we should regard it primarily as the concluding part of Gogol's introduction to his ironic portrait of the "strange heroes" in whom we may recognize the distinctive features of the "masters." It is possible, of course, to view such a phrase as "the whole immensity of life as it rushes past me" as little more than a solemn rhetorical flourish, but it seems much more consonant with the general character and tone of the chapter's "introduction" to regard it as an ironic allusion to the conspicuously immobile or sedentary mode of existence that is repeatedly associated with these "strange heroes." And as if to confirm this as indeed his intended meaning, Gogol a few lines later effects the same ironic juxtaposition by evoking once more the image of the "road" before passing directly to the description of Chichikov in bed:

On with the journey [*dorogu*]! On with the journey! Away
with the wrinkle that has assailed the brow and the severity that has darkened the face! Let us all at once plunge into
life with all its muffled crackle and ringing bells, and let us
see what Chichikov is doing. (135)

The image of "ringing bells" (*bubenchikami*) merely reinforces
our argument that the "introduction" remains to the very end
an amalgam of ironic, forward-pointing allusions, for bells
were essential equipment of the *skomorokh*.

In this examination of the opening paragraphs of the chapter
as a characteristically oblique Gogolian introduction, we have
observed that the author contrasts the "masters" and the
"slaves" principally by filling the portrait of each of the two
groups with details that are echoed in the portraits of the other.
As the chapter advances, these echoes become more numerous,
and the details concerned are often separated by considerable
intervals. Thus fourteen pages after Chichikov has informed us
that Stepan Probka made his way through the provinces eating
"a farthing's worth of bread and two farthing's worth of dried
fish [*sushonoy ryby*]" (136), we read that Sobakevich, having
surreptitiously consumed the sturgeon, "kept quiet, as if he
were not to blame, and going up to a plate which lay some
distance from the others, he prodded a small dried fish
[*sushonuyu malen'kuyu rybku*] with his fork" (150–151). The
implication, it seems, is that the food which constitutes almost
the total rations of the "slave" is an object of fastidious contempt for the sated "master."[15]

We have also observed, however, that these echoes are most
frequently contrived by identifying the "masters" with attitudes or vices that have previously been ascribed to the
"slaves"—indirectly in the "introduction," directly in the account of Chichikov's daydreams. Particularly striking are the
repeated allusions in this account to the weakness of the
"slaves" for drink. Addressing himself, for example, to Pyotr
Savel'yev "Disrespectful-of-Troughs," Chichikov asks, as

noted above, whether he met his death in a tavern, and shortly afterwards we are told that Grigoriy "Never-Get-There" "called at a tavern, and then went straight to a hole in the ice" (137). It is also alleged that Maksim Telyatnikov, after the collapse of his business, "took to drink" and, appropriately, became "as drunk as a cobbler" (137). Quite apart from the fact that drunkenness would not have been tolerated by Sobakevich in any of his serfs, it is obvious that Chichikov can have no evidence for his suppositions, and the reason for their inclusion becomes apparent only toward the end of the chapter when the "masters" confirm by their libations at the feast that their own weakness for drink, by contrast, is completely genuine. "The chief of police," we read, "apparently did not like to spare the wine, and there were innumerable toasts. . . . After the champagne they uncorked the Hungarian wine, which put them in even higher spirits and made the party even merrier" (151). And as a parodic appendage to this scene, Gogol describes the expedition to the tavern of Chichikov's "doubles," Petrushka and Selifan, filled with details that also allude to their master's other experiences on this day of triumph—his journey to the government offices with Manilov,[16] their ascent up the stairs of the building,[17] his return to his bed,[18] and, as already indicated his "thin, nasal whistle."

Even without reference to the nature of the vices concerned, having Chichikov initially attribute to the "slaves" vices which are really the prerogative of the "masters" is itself significant, for it alludes to the most salient of the "masters' " character traits—their blatant hypocrisy, the perpetual discord between external appearance and inner substance. Many details in the chapter are designed to highlight this fundamental characteristic. Among them are the references to the "sincere love" that Chichikov feels for his face (135) and to his sprinkling himself with eau de Cologne (139), which frame the record of his daydreams, and it is as an ironic comment on these idiosyncrasies that we should consider again the reintroduction of his "inner substance" at the end in the customary, less appealing form of the malodorous Petrushka. Another example of the same discord is the contrast between the contents of Manilov's rolled-up list on the one hand and, on the other, the "neatness and beauty of the writing" and the pink ribbon with which it is tied (140). Just as the personalities of the rural "masters" infuse their houses, so the hypocrisy of their urban brethren is mirrored in the discordant character of the government offices. Appropriately guarded by "a soldier with a gun" and surrounded by "long fences" (141), they present to Chichikov and Manilov from the outside the spectacle of a "large, three-story brick building, the whole of which was as white as chalk, probably to signify the purity of soul of those who performed their duties there. . . . From the windows of the second and third stories the incorruptible [*nepodkupnyye*] heads of the priests of Themis occasionally showed themselves and immediately hid themselves again" (141). The inside produces a rather different impression:

> Neither in the corridors nor in the rooms were their eyes struck by the spectacle of cleanliness. People still did not bother about cleanliness in those days, and what was dirty remained dirty, without any effort being made to improve its appearance. Themis received her visitors simply, just as she was, in negligee and dressing gown. (141)

Quite apart from the more obvious irony conveyed by the name of the ancient Greek goddess of law and order, it is perhaps appropriate to mention once more the connotations of "soullessness" that "pagan", mythological images often seem to possess in the novel.

Equally striking is the manner in which the epithet "incorruptible" is used by Gogol to indicate that this symbol of hypocrisy relates to Chichikov, for as he prepares to examine his lists after executing his "two leaps," he rubs his hands in front of his box "with the same kind of pleasure with which an incorruptible district magistrate [*nepodkupnyy zemskiy sud*] embarking on an investigation rubs them as he approaches a snack lunch" (135). Moreover, we may recognize in the "incorruptible district magistrate" the figure of the president partaking of the savories assembled by the chief of police. More generally, however, it is clear that the epithet "incorruptible" alludes ironically to the eminently corruptible nature of the entire "family" of "masters" as they are portrayed in this chapter—to the "corruptibility" and capacity for swindling not only of Chichikov, the president, and the chief of police, but also, for example, of the "sensible" Ivan Antonovich, who "instantly covered with a book" the note Chichikov lays before him (143–144), of the attorney Zolotukha ("Scrofula"), who is described by Sobakevich as "the worst scrounger in the world" (146), and also of Sobakevich himself, the arch foe of "scoundrels," whose cunning insertion of the name "Yelizavet Vorobey" in his list prompts Chichikov to exclaim: "Here too Sobakevich, the villain, has swindled me!" (137).

The contradiction, therefore, between the adjective "incorruptible" and the actions of those to whom it refers provides another illustration of the consistently oblique methods of characterization Gogol uses to offset ironically the "masters' " hypocrisy. In this respect the adjective serves the same purpose, as our analysis has indicated, as almost every other detail in the chapter. Yet far from nearing completion, the analysis is still seriously deficient, for nothing has yet been said about an aspect of the chapter that is more elusive and perhaps even more important than the contrast which has been examined. This second aspect is concerned wholly with the position of Chichikov, and it illustrates perhaps more vividly than any other part of the novel Gogol's remarkable ability to convey at least two quite distinct meanings simultaneously. The critics' failure to recognize this second level of meaning explains the major criticism to which this chapter has been subjected—the charge so often leveled that Chichikov's day dreams are implausible.[19]

Throughout the novel, of course, Chichikov remains a uniquely ambivalent figure, but in no other chapter is this ambivalence so dramatically and extensively conveyed as it is in chapter seven. The positioning of this emphasis is not coincidental. By the end of chapter six he has completed his visits, acquired his "slaves," and thereby gained admission to the "family" of "masters." The admission is gained, however, on false pretenses. His status as "master" rests on a nonexistent foundation. Hence the irony of his statement that "a man cannot determine his aim in life unless he has finally stood with a firm foot on a sound foundation and not on some free-thinking chimera of youth"—a statement to which the narrator adds: "But it was noticeable that there was a certain lack of firmness in his words, as though he were saying to himself at the same time: 'Good heavens, my dear fellow, you're talking nonsense—what's more, the most arrant nonsense!' " (146).

Chichikov's position, therefore, presents yet another example of discord between appearance and reality, and it is curious that critics have not borne this obvious fact in mind when assessing the functions of the various parts of the chapter. For in the light of this fact it may now be seen, for example, that the contrast between the "family man" and the "bachelor" in the opening paragraph not only prefigures the contrast between "masters" and "slaves," but also alludes directly to the hero's ambivalence. The former term alludes to the appearance, the latter—to the reality. And since the term "bachelor" also alludes to the "slaves," it implies that Chichikov is likewise a "slave"—a "master" in appearance, a "slave" in reality—thus explaining why the president later addresses him, in the song that he sings at the feast, as a "Kamarinsky peasant." Unless this distinction is fully recognized, it is impossible to understand either the motivation and true significance of Chichikov's daydreams or the additional implications of the motif that frames the narrative section—the motif of sleep. It has been observed that the narrative section both begins and ends with scenes of Chichikov asleep in his bed, and we have noted the obvious relevance of this frame to the motif of the "sedentary life" in the portrait of the "masters." Equally important, however, is its particular relevance to Chichikov himself, for sleep implies dreams, and it is precisely the unreality of a dream that characterizes his position as "master." This is essentially the point that Gogol seeks to emphasize in the

description of his merry conduct after his return from the
festivities to the inn:

> ... for a long time he kept muttering all sorts of nonsense
> about a fair-haired bride with a rosy complexion and a
> dimple in her right cheek, his Kherson estates and his large
> sums of capital. Selifan was even given some instructions
> about the running of the estates, such as assembling all the
> newly resettled peasants in order to take a roll-call of
> them. . . . But at last his boots were removed, the master
> was properly undressed, and, after tossing and turning for
> a while on the bed which creaked unmercifully, he fell
> asleep like a genuine Kherson landowner. (152)

The passage implies that his position as a "master" becomes a
reality only in the dreams induced by potent beverages.

In chapter seven, therefore, the propensity to dreaming is a
feature of central importance in Chichikov's portrait. But this
in itself would clearly not suffice to make his dreams about his
serfs entirely convincing. Their plausibility remains questionable until it is recognized that in addition to evoking the unfortunate lot of the "slaves" and imparting to them hypocritically
the vices of the "masters," they are also a revelation of
Chichikov's subconscious fears—the fears of the "family man"
and "master" who in reality, like the subjects of his dreams, is
himself a "bachelor" and "slave," a creature of the "road."
They are a dramatic record of his fears that his deception might
be discovered, and since these fears are ultimately realized, they
accordingly acquire importance as predictions of his eventual
fall. In other words, the fictitious situations in which be places
his "slaves" are essentially metaphors of the actual situations in
which he ends up himself. In his dreams he projects his own
fate onto the fate of the "slaves," whose position reflects the
reality of his own.

Let us consider, for example, in this connection the curious
hypothesis of Chichikov about the fate of Stepan Probka,
whom he addresses as follows:

Did you clamber beneath the church cupola for a bigger
profit, or perhaps you even dragged yourself to the cross
and, slipping from it, from the crosspiece, tumbled to the
ground, and only some Uncle Mikhey, who was standing
beside you, scratched the back of his head and said: "Oh,
Vanya, what on earth made you do it?" and tying a rope
round his waist, climbed up to take your place? (136)

Uncle Mikhey's use of the name "Vanya," a diminutive of
"Ivan," reveals at once that Chichikov's thoughts here are cen-
tered not on Stepan only, and since the name cannot possibly
refer to either of the two characters in the novel who bear
it—Korobochka's husband, Ivan Petrovich, and her serf, Ivan
Koleso—we may reasonably conjecture that it is the dream-
mask of the dreamer himself, Pavel *Ivan*ovich Chichikov. But
this is by no means the only justification for regarding
Chichikov's hypothesis as a symbolic dream-picture of his
own subsequent fate in the novel. In Stepan's aspiration to a
"bigger profit," for example, we may perceive an allusion to
Chichikov's aspiration to the proceeds from the mortgage of
his nonexistent serfs or perhaps, more generally, to the status of
"master" that these proceeds would give him. But how can we
reconcile the steps that Chichikov must take to realize this
aspiration with the action of "clambering" beneath a church
cupola? The answer is suggested by the first of these steps—
namely, his visit to the top floor of the government offices to
complete the formalities. Since this building is inhabited by
"the priests of Themis" and is thus implicitly likened to a pagan
temple, the description of its top floor—or perhaps, more
precisely, the office of the Zeus-like president—as a "cupola"
would not seem inappropriate. And since the cross in the
dream appears to be located at the highest point of the church,
we may recognize in Stepan's attempts to reach it an allusion to
Chichikov's struggles to reach the summit of the temple, i.e. to
secure his position in the "family" of the elect. But like the
corklike Stepan, the bubblelike Chichikov is doomed to
plummet to earth just when the pinnacle seems to have been

reached, to fall swiftly and ironically from the cross of his dreams to the real cross formed by the symbols of his real personality—by the bodies of the drunken Petrushka and Selifan as they collapse on the former's bed after their return from the tavern. The scene is described in the final paragraph as follows:

> Petrushka stopped for a moment before his low bed, wondering how he might lie more decorously, and he finally lay right across it so that his feet rested against the floor. Selifan lay down too on the same bed, placing his head on Petrushka's stomach. (153)

The cross of Petrushka and Selifan parodies the cross to which their master aspires, just as their "snore of unprecedented richness" parodies the "sublime pitch" of his "masterly" nasal whistle.

Like the comic episode in which Petrushka "almost pulled his master to the floor" while struggling to remove his boots (152), thereby reducing him to the "bootless" status of a "slave," these parodic details expose the futility of Chichikov's exalted dreams, confirming that however convincing the "masterly" appearance may be, reality will inevitably reassert itself. The dreams are fated to turn to dust, like the dust with which Petrushka fills the corridor when beating his master's trousers and "gleaming cranberry-colored dress coat" with the riding crop (152). And we may conclude that it is Chichikov's subconscious realization of this fact which prompts him to cast himself, in the guise of Stepan, as a "slave" of the most suspicious and least gullible of all the *real* "masters"—Mikhail Semyonovich Sobakevich, whose presence in the dream the name "Uncle Mikhey" immediately discloses. It is to this aspect of the dream that Gogol is alluding later when, after Chichikov's boasts in the president's office about the river and pond on his lands, he follows with the adjunct:

> Having said this, Chichikov glanced inadvertently at Sobakevich, and though Sobakevich remained motionless

as before, it seemed to him that he could read in his face the words: "Oh, you're lying! I doubt whether there is a river and a pond there or any land at all!" (148)

And as if to reemphasize this link between Chichikov's fears and Sobakevich, Gogol almost repeats this scene four pages later in the description of the "masters' " feast:

> Chichikov had never felt in such a merry mood. He imagined that he was already a real Kherson landowner, spoke of various improvements—of the three-field system of agriculture and of the happiness and bliss of two souls—and began to read to Sobakevich Werther's letter in verse to Charlotte, in response to which Sobakevich merely looked blank as he sat in his armchair, for after the sturgeon he felt a profound urge to sleep. (152)

We can now see, therefore, that Gogol was not simply intent here on adding another detail to the satirical motif of the "sedentary life." The effect of Chichikov's inebriation is momentarily to invest his hopes and ambitions with the quality of reality. At the same time, however, like his earlier surrender to the power of dreaming, it also momentarily relaxes rational control over his subconscious fears, and from the depths of his personality rise the words of Werther in which those fears are unequivocally expressed. As Smirnova-Chikina has persuasively argued, Gogol probably had in mind here not the Werther of Goethe, but the hero of the short poem by V. I. Tumansky, *Werther to Charlotte (an Hour before His Death)* *(Verter k Sharlotte [za chas pered smert'yu])*, which had appeared in 1819 in the journal *Blagonamerennyy (The Well-Meaner)*. It reads:

> The lamp of my melancholy days is fading, Charlotte! I feel that my silent hour has come. For the last time your faithful friend gazes on the places where he tasted happiness.[20]

Unfortunately, having identified the source, Smirnova-Chikina proceeds to interpret Chichikov's recitation of the poem as an implausible indication of sentimentality.[21] Actually, like his daydreams, it reflects his direst presentiments.

Another reasonable assumption, therefore, is that the reappearance of the name Grigoriy "Never-Get-There" among the serfs' names that catch Chichikov's eye is not coincidental, for it expresses succinctly the idea or theme of failure which is undoubtedly the central theme of the daydreams. Insofar as it is associated with the "slaves," of course, the theme offsets the contrasting one of success in the portrait of the "masters," but more significantly it also expresses the dreamer's own fears that failure is equally his predestined lot, that the "laughter" of the "family man" will ultimately give way to the "tears" of the "bachelor," and that his *kolodki* will ultimately be transformed from "boot trees" into "stocks." For the fate of the house-serf Popov, who cannot prove his identity, is yet another symbolic preannouncement of the ambivalent Chichikov's own fated fall. His interrogation by the captain of police, who persistently hurls at him the monosyllable *vryosh'*, is not only inserted as an ironic contrast to Chichikov's later interrogation by the president; as his name confirms, it also reflects Chichikov's dread of being again subjected to the kind of interrogation that followed his most ambitious swindle of the past—the customs swindle in chapter eleven, which failed over an argument with his accomplice provoked by the term *popovich* ("son of a priest") with which they abused one another (237). The symbol of past failure foreshadows the imminent failure, and in the figures of the two "old soldiers" who don the stocks we may discern a vivid premonition of the two Nozdryov-like ladies in chapter nine whose passion for rumor and gossip ensures the debacle.

The second level of meaning we have observed in the record of Chichikov's daydreams is also found in the chapter's other major allusions to the position of the "slaves"—above all, in the introductory passage on the second type of writer. Indeed, the relevance of the "introduction" specifically to the position of Chichikov may possibly explain, in part, why Gogol chose to begin the chapter with the distinction between the two types of writer, for it is as a writer that Chichikov is first presented to us. "He decided," we read in the first paragraph that follows the introductory section, "to draw up the deeds of purchase himself, to write them out and make a copy, so that he would not have to pay the clerks" (135). However that may be, there are numerous indications that the contrast between the two types of writer, like the contrast in the opening paragraph, alludes not only to the contrast between "masters" and "slaves" but also to Chichikov's failure to translate his dreams into reality. Thus when Gogol writes in reference to the second kind of writer that "no sixteen-year-old girl will fly to meet him with her head turned and full of heroic enthusiasm," we may suspect that he alludes as much to Chichikov's conspicuous failure to turn the head of the governor's daughter in chapter eight as to the good fortune he enjoys as a "master" in having the opportunity to meet her. Moreover, given the "masterly" connotations that high-pitched sounds are endowed with in the chapter, we may possibly interpret the statement that the second type of writer "will not find oblivion in the sweet fascination of the sounds he has extracted" as another prediction that Chichikov's "masterly" status is doomed to be shortlived. And each statement that follows in the passage progressively reinforces the impression that the idea of Chichikov's impending failure dictated the choice of phraseology. A few examples will suffice:

. . . nor, finally, will he [Chichikov] escape the judgment of his contemporaries, the hypocritical and callous judgment of his contemporaries [i.e. the judgment of the genuine, hypocritical "masters"], which will call his cherished creations [i.e. the dead "slaves" resurrected by Chichikov's imagination] insignificant and despicable, assign him a contemptible place in the ranks of writers who insult humanity [i.e. who attempt to deceive the "masters"], ascribe to him the qualities of the characters he has portrayed [i.e. will utlimately discover that Chichikov himself, like his "cherished creations", is, in reality, a "slave"]. . . .

The conclusion, therefore, in brief, is that each of the three contrasts with which the chapter begins performs a dual role. Foreshadowing the contrast between "masters" and "slaves," they have the additional function of foreshadowing the ambivalence of Chichikov's position. The related images of the "family man," the first type of writer, and "laughter" allude to the "masters" and Chichikov's *apparent* position; the images of the "bachelor," the second type of writer, and "tears" allude to the "slaves" and Chichikov's *actual* position. In other words, the two contrasting series of images refer simultaneously to the two contrasting social groups and to the two contrasting aspects of the hero, providing the basis for yet another remarkable synthesis of superficial digressiveness and fundamental coherence.

7

The Masters
and the Ladies

In chapter seven of the novel the "masters" are contrasted with their subordinates, and the emphasis in their portrait is placed on two main features: their hypocrisy and their apparent omnipotence. Hence the conspicuous roles in the chapter of the two landowners in whose individual portraits these features are represented as dominant characteristics—the "hypocritical" Manilov, whose external refinement conceals an inner void, and the "omnipotent" Sobakevich. In chapter eight, however, the "masters" are contrasted with the ladies of the town, and their omnipotence is abruptly exposed as an illusion. Their position in this new context is one of unequivocal subservience to the females, whose portrayal the chapter is chiefly devoted to. In the portrait of the ladies the dominant attributes of the absent Manilov and Sobakevich are significantly complemented by those of Nozdryov and Korobochka, who now appropriately reappear to herald the presence of a more formidable "masculinity" with which the "masters" are powerless to compete. And to offset this renewed emphasis on the "masculinization" of females, Gogol reminds us once more of the ideal that has been perverted by reintroducing the governor's daughter.

Although Korobochka's intervention is delayed till the end of the chapter, her "presence" is sensed almost from the beginning, for the earlier sections of the chapter are sprinkled with motifs which call her instantly to mind. An obvious example is the noun "bags" (*meshki*) to which Gogol effectively draws our

attention by using it in unusual contexts. Thus the narrator refers
to the postmaster's predilection for lacing his speech with short
auxiliary phrases "by the sackful [*meshkami*]" (157), and he
notes in reference to the word *millionaire*: ". . . in the sound
alone of this word, quite apart from the money bags [*mimo
vsyakogo denezhnogo meshka*], there is something which has an
effect on people" (159). Similarly Korobochka's habit of com-
plaining about her poor harvests is recalled in Chichikov's
critical comment on the townspeople: "The harvests in the
province are bad, everything is dear, and here they are clamor-
ing for balls!" (174).

Korobochka's arrival also seems foreshadowed in the chapter's repeated allusions to her main adversaries in life besides
men—birds. Commenting, for example, on the occasional deviations in the ladies' attire from Parisian standards of fashion,
the narrator observes: "Only here and there some bonnet
which had never been seen on earth before or some feather
which was almost as large as a peacock's would thrust itself
forward in opposition to all fashion and in accordance with
individual taste" (163–164). A few lines later Chichikov is
passed by "a lady with a pale blue feather" and "a lady with a
white feather" (164), and shortly afterwards the narrator
directs our attention to the feather on the "oriental turban" of
the governor's wife (168). And perhaps we might add to these
anticipatory details the narrator's criticism of his readers for
"pronouncing English in a birdlike fashion"; he adds:
". . . they will even try to look like a bird and even laugh at
anyone who is unable to look like a bird" (165). Finally, we
might note the reappearance of the cock image in the long,
complex sentence culminating in the announcement of Korobochka's entry into the town:

> But while Chichikov was sitting in his hard armchair,
> disturbed by his thoughts and insomnia . . . , while the
> blind, dark night stared at him through the windows . . . ,
> and while in the distance the cocks were crowing to one
> another, and in the town, which was fast asleep, some
> victim of misfortune, of unknown class and rank, was

trudging along somewhere in a frieze overcoat, knowing
only the road which has been worn, alas, into too many
holes by the reckless folk of Russia—at this moment an
event was taking place at the other end of the town which
was about to increase the unpleasantness of our hero's
position. (176)

The crowing of the cocks, the insomnia, the "blind, dark
night"—all three details are extensions of motifs that are an
integral part of Korobochka's portrait in chapter three.[1] Here
the damage inflicted at the ball by the "hunter's" disclosures is
about to be compounded by the persecutor of males, and the
image of the "victim of misfortune" in the frieze overcoat
foreshows its effects. The mask of the false "master" is finally
about to be stripped off, revealing the face of a wretched
"slave" doomed to rejoin his brethren on the "road."

When Korobochka finally appears, the anticipatory details
are appropriately repeated and amplified. Her carriage, we
note, is "crammed with bags [*meshkami*] of loaves," and
"chicken pies . . . even peeped out at the top" (176). And while
the "fat-cheeked, bulging watermelon" to which the carriage is
compared reminds us of the symbolic overtones of the vegetables in her kitchen garden and of her affinities with the "bear"
with the pumpkinlike face, her entry is heralded by yet another
emblem of her ominous presence—ear-shattering noise:

> The noise and creaking of the iron clamps and rusty
> screws woke up a policeman at the other end of the town
> who, though only half-awake, picked up his halberd and
> cried out with all his might: "Who goes there?" but seeing
> that there was no one and hearing nothing but a clanking
> in the distance, he caught some kind of beast on his collar
> and, going up to a light, executed [*kaznit*] it at once on his
> nail. (176–177)

Once more an apparent digression conveys details that are
singularly apt. While the brief appearance of the policeman
reintroduces the idea of guards or sentries and thus evokes the
image of the canine sentinels in chapter three, his execution of
the insect not only reminds us of the fate of flies in Koroboch-

ka's domain, but also directs our thoughts to the "Korobochkan" severity of the town ladies who, according to the
narrator, "punished [*kaznili*] all weaknesses without mercy"
(158). Needless to say, the "weaknesses" are those of their
menfolk.

Significantly, the house that is Korobochka's destination in
the town belongs to Father Kiril's wife.[2] The detail is yet
another allusion both to the dominant position of females in
this urban society and to the incompatibility of Korobochka
and males. And in general it may be noted that just as
Korobochka appears in the novel almost exclusively in the
company of females (except, of course, for her confrontations
with Chichikov), so Father Kiril's sole appearance is in the one
chapter where females play no active part—chapter seven
(148). Since the relation of his wife to Korobochka compares
with that of Uncle Minyay to Sobakevich, we may infer that he
is perfectly content to let her dwell in the solitude of her
personal abode. "Be off with you, you old priest's wife!" the
postmaster cries, according to chapter one, whenever he plays a
queen at whist (16). These sentiments are doubtless Father
Kiril's too.

As soon as the carriage halts, the daunting "masculinity" of
the "Korobochkan" female is demonstrated. "A maidservant," we read, "with a kerchief on her head and wearing a
padded jacket climbed out of the carriage and struck the gates
so powerfully with both fists that one might have thought it
was a man . . ." (177). The fate of the male at the hands of such
women is epitomized in the treatment meted out to the footman: ". . . the fellow in the brightly colored cotton jacket was
then dragged out by the legs, for he was fast asleep" (177). The
dormant state of this unfortunate creature, "with an unshaved
beard lightly touched with gray," denotes the same degree
of exhaustion that drove Ivan Petrovich to a premature grave
and caused Korobochka's blacksmith to emit a blue flame.
Hence the rendering of "*fast* asleep" by the adverb *mertvetski*,
which means literally "like a corpse."

Just as the archpriest's wife is an extension of Korobochka's
personality, so her residence is a miniature replica of Korobochka's distinctive prison. Every detail in its brief description

provides eloquent testimony to the fact—the image of the
sturdy gates on which the maidservant's "Sobakevichan" fists
(*kulaki*) beat their violent music, the barking of the dogs, the
"chicken coops" in the "narrow yard," and the "little sheds"
(*kletukhi*) which in Russian differ only in their suffix from
"cages" (*kletki*). The house is the culminating symbol of Korobochka's urban "presence," of the "Korobochkan" element in
the psychology of the town's most powerful females, which
both explains the submissiveness of the "masters" in their
presence and foreshadows the ladies' decisive contribution to
Chichikov's downfall. Describing the ladies' attire at the ball,
the narrator observes that "each of them bared her possessions
to an extent which made her feel convinced that they were
capable of ruining a man" and that their " 'modesties' concealed in front and behind what could not possibly inflict ruin
on a man and yet made one suspect that it was precisely there
that disaster lay" (163). Passing from their dress to their eyes,
he remarks that they alone "are such a boundless realm that if a
man were to enter it, he would simply vanish into thin air. You
wouldn't drag him out of there by hook or by crook" (164).
Their glitter, he adds, "will clutch at the heart and play upon
the soul as if with a violin bow" (164). And commenting on the
ladies' indignant reaction to Chichikov's imprudent interest in
the governor's daughter, he confides: "There are cases in which
a woman, however weak and feeble in character she may be
compared with a man, suddenly becomes harder not only than
a man, but than anything in the whole world" (170–171). Each
of these scattered statements signals the common affinity of the
ladies with the sexually ambivalent destroyer of males. And we
may now appreciate the meaning of the catalogue of individuals who allegedly have already had the pleasure of hearing the
"highly agreeable" remarks that Chichikov addresses to the
governor's daughter:

> . . . he told her about many highly agreeable things
> which he had already had occasion to remark on in similar
> circumstances in a variety of places: namely, in the prov-
> ince of Simbirsk at Sofron Ivanovich Bespechnyy's,

where there were at the time his daughter, Adelaida Sof-
ronovna, and her three sisters-in-law, Mar'ya Gavrilovna,
Aleksandra Gavrilovna, and Adel'geyda Gavrilovna; at
Fyodor Fyodorovich Perekroyev's in the province of
Ryazan'; at Frol Vasil'yevich Pobedonosnyy's in the province of Penza, and at the house of his brother, Pyotr
Vasil'yevich, where there were his sister-in-law Katerina
Mikhaylovna and her second cousins, Roza Fyodorovna
and Emiliya Fyodorovna; in the province of Vyatka at the
house of Pyotr Varsonof'yevich, where there were the
sister of his sister-in-law, Pelageya Yegorovna, and her
niece, Sof'ya Rostislavna, and her two half-sisters, Sof'ya
Aleksandrovna and Maklatura Aleksandrovna. (170)

Only Perekroyev and Frol Vasil'yevich Pobedonosnyy, it
seems, whose names suggest "reshaping" and "victory," have
escaped the female invasions that various marriages have un-
leashed on the others, doubtless condemning them to be eventually transformed into grains of sand. The catalogue merely
confirms that N. is a microcosm of all Russia, that in Simbirsk,
Ryazan', Penza, and Vyatka the "feminine" soul has likewise
been "masculinized."

As stated, however, the attributes of Korobochka form only
the first of the four distinct strands that in the portrait of the
ladies are tied into a single knot. The second is the "Nozdryovian" strand. Particularly important in this connection is the
timing of Nozdryov's intervention at the ball, for like the
intervention of Uncle Mityay and Uncle Minyay in chapter
five, it has the effect of rudely awakening Chichikov from his
absorption in the spectacle of the governor's daughter. On the
symbolic level, therefore, it is another illustration of the instinctive antagonism of the corrupt, "masculinized" soul to the
principle of pure "femininity." The timing of the assault, however, is also significant for another reason, for Nozdryov materializes precisely when the ladies' hostility toward the governor's daughter, provoked by Chichikov's over-zealous attentions to her, has begun to express itself in "Nozdryovian"

violence. Thus one of them, we read, "even grazed the fair-haired girl rather carelessly with the thick *rouleau* of her dress and arranged her scarf, which was fluttering about her shoulders, in such a way that the end of it flapped right into the girl's face" (170). And in the sentence directly preceding the announcement of Nozdryov's entrance, the narrator informs us: "The indignation increased, and in various corners of the room the ladies began to talk about him [Chichikov] in the most unfavorable manner, while the poor schoolgirl was completely annihilated and her sentence had already been signed" (171). The impression is conveyed, therefore, that Nozdryov is conjured into being, as it were, by some inner demand of the ladies, that he presents himself as an emanation or embodiment of their burning resentment against the girl and the middle-aged cavalier who shortly before had been the object of their unstinting adulation.

In his opening remarks to Chichikov, Nozdryov displays his unique capacity for harboring two violently conflicting sentiments at once. "Listen, Chichikov," he cries, "you know, you're—I'm speaking to you as a friend, for we're all your friends here, including his Excellency here—I would hang you, I swear I'd hang you!" (172). Although, however, this combination of the incompatible is entirely typical of Nozdryov, we should not miss its relevance to the ladies—to the volte-face that has taken place in their attitudes toward the hero. And a further indicator of his connection with the ladies is his request that Chichikov permit him to plant a kiss (*beze*) on his "snow-white cheek" (172). The implications of this request can be determined only by reference to the narrator's disclosure nine pages earlier that some of the ladies at the ball wore "a scarf that was lighter than the puff pastry which is known by the name of 'a kiss [*potseluy*]'" (163) and to the indicated ability of one of their number to "arrange" her scarf in such a way that "the end of it flapped right into the girl's face." In the kiss, therefore, that Nozdryov is anxious to plant on Chichikov's cheek, we may recognize a counterpart of the blow that the lady's kiss inflicts on the face of the governor's daughter. Once more Nozdryov seems to be acting as the instrument of the ladies' innermost desires.

True, the relationship between Nozdryov and the ladies is represented as one of mutual contempt. We are told, for example, that in the middle of the cotillion "he sat down on the floor and began to grab at the dancers' skirts which, in the words of the ladies, was quite unheard of" (174). Here Nozdryov (the inveterate enemy of females) and the ladies (the inveterate enemies of males) face one another as natural foes. Yet underlying this opposition, as we have seen, there is a bond that indirectly explains the suddenness and savagery with which the ladies direct their hostility not only against the male Chichikov, but also against the "purely feminine" governor's daughter, and Nozdryov's intervention as the instrument of their hostility is not the only indication of this bond.

Having ascertained, for example, the distinctly "Nozdryovian" associations of the terminology of gambling and cards, we can readily appreciate the force of the author's remark that for the ladies "a visiting card, even if written on a two of clubs or an ace of diamonds, was a very sacred thing" (158), and the following sentence appropriately cites an example of the kind of violent, "Nozdryovian" quarrel to which such cards could sometimes give rise. Equally in evidence is the ladies' "Nozdryovian" competitive spirit, which reveals itself in their frantic attempts to outdo one another in the splendor of their attire (160) and in the refinement of their dancing (168). In such a context, therefore, echoes of the "military motif" are no surprise: to learn that each of the ladies "had inwardly resolved to use all the various weapons [*orudiya*] which hold such danger for our hearts" (167) and that initially they detect in Chichikov's face "even something martial and military," which, "as is well known," comments the narrator, "is very pleasing to women" (165). And once more the "Nozdryovian" signal is followed in the next sentence by a "Nozdryovian" action:

They were even beginning to quarrel a little over him: observing that he usually stood near the door, some of

them, vying with one another, hastened to occupy a seat
by the door, and when one of them had the good fortune
to get there first, there was nearly a most unpleasant scene,
and to many who wished to do the same such impudence
seemed rather disgusting. (165–166)

Seen against the background of these details, the illusion of an
almost telepathic relationship between the ladies and Nozdryov when the latter appears seems entirely plausible.

Turning now to the "Sobakevichan" element in the portrait
of the ladies, we notice that it differs significantly from the
similar element in the portrait of the "masters" in chapter
seven, for Gogol is now far more attentive to the physical
aspect of "Sobakevichism." In chapter seven allusions to the
physique of the "masters" are conspicuously rare, and although we are reminded in chapter eight that they are "fat
men" by the reference to their wives' habit of addressing them
as "Dumpy," "Fatty," and "Paunchy" (157), the diminutive
forms in which these names appear (*kubyshka, tolstunchik,
puzantik*) are probably intended less to suggest endearment
than inferiority; physically the "masters" are completely over-
shadowed by their female partners.

Describing the ladies' attire at the ball, the narrator remarks:

The waists were closefitting and had the most firm and
pleasant shapes for the eyes to feast on (it should be noted
that, in general, all the ladies of the town of N. were rather
plump, but they laced themselves up so skillfully and had
such an agreeable manner that it was quite impossible to
notice how fat they were). . . . The long gloves were not
pulled up as far as the sleeves, but deliberately left bare
those titillating parts of the arm above the elbow, which in
many cases were of an enviable plumpness; the kid gloves
of some ladies had even split in the attempt to force them
up higher. (163)

In the figures of the ladies, therefore, Gogol reproduces the
ample contours of Sobakevich's Bobelina, and allusions to this

likeness may be perceived in the reference to the "beautiful Greek nose" of one of them (168) and in their general "Sobakevichan" contempt for "thin men," whom they scornfully dismiss as "toothpicks" (159–160).

Particularly striking is the irony in Gogol's descriptions of the ladies, effected by using both meanings of the adjective *tonkiy,* which means "thin" and "refined." While continuing to remind us of their plumpness, he refers repeatedly to the "refinement" (*tonkost'*) of their tastes and principles, crediting them, for example, with "a multitude of the most refined [*tonkikh*] proprieties" (158) and prompting Chichikov to detect in them "something elusively refined [*tonkoye*]—oh, how refined!" (164). But as usual, of course, the contours of the body convey the truth. Contrasting with the "refinement" of the ladies is the genuine refinement of the governor's daughter with her "delicate [*tonen'kimi*] features" (166) and her "slender, slender [*tonkiy, tonkiy*] figure" (169). The narrator observes, "She alone stood out white and radiantly translucent from the dull, opaque throng" (126), thus repeating the fundamental contrast of chapter five. Now the hard-shell soul of Sobakevich is replaced by the "dull, opaque throng" of females, which is similarly offset by the "whiteness" and "translucence" of the girl with the "charmingly rounded oval face, such as a painter would take as a model for a Madonna and such as is rarely found in Russia, where everything that exists likes to assume large dimensions: mountains, forests, steppes, faces, lips and feet" (166). Again Sobakevich's attributes, as reproduced now in the portrait of the ladies, are emphatically identified with Russia.

The vain attempts, however, of the ladies to disguise their plumpness and to produce an impression of "refinement" indicate a preoccupation with externals which evokes the image not of Sobakevich but of Manilov, and specific allusions to Manilov are liberally sprinkled throughout the portrait. Examples are the adjectives the narrator uses to describe their "glitter"—"moist, velvety, sugary" (164)—and the passage in which he abruptly terminates his discussion of the ladies'

spiritual qualities before he has scarcely begun, on the pretext
of suffering from shyness—the same shyness, we may assume,
that intervened in chapter two to cut short his discussion of the
character of Manilova (26). The ladies' varied scents, their
"kisses," their "small crimped pieces of fine [*tonkogo*] cambric"
known as "modesties" (163), the chiffons in "pale, fashionable
colors" (163) evocative of Manilova's "pale dress," the "light
headdresses," which "seemed to be saying: 'Look out, I'm going
to fly away and I'm only sorry that I can't take the beautiful
creature with me!' " (163)—each of these details forms part of
an elaborate "superficially feminine" façade erected to conceal
the physical evidence of "Sobakevichan masculinity." The
contrasting attributes of Manilov and Sobakevich, like those of
Korobochka and Nozdryov, are now fused into an expressive
synthesis.

The "Manilovan" element in the portrait of the ladies is
particularly apparent in their distaste for crude speech. The
narrator offers the following illustration:

> In no circumstance could one say: "This glass or that plate
> stinks." It was even forbidden to say anything that gave a
> hint of this; one said instead: "This glass conducts itself
> badly," or something of the kind. (159)

Wholly in tune with this "Manilovan" language is the florid
phraseology of the unsigned love-letter, which rewards
Chichikov with such insights as: "What is our life?—A vale of
sorrows" (160). The style, of course, suffices to identify the
writer as a member of the "dull, opaque throng," and apparently to confirm the fact, Gogol repeats the noun "vale"
(*dolina*) a few pages later in one of the questions the ladies ask
Chichikov at the ball as he struggles to catch a second glimpse
of the governor's daughter: "May we know the name of the
one who has plunged you into this sweet vale [*dolinu*] of
reverie?" (167). But although the language of the letter betrays
an incapacity for genuine feeling, it is far from meaningless.
Indeed, it ironically discloses the reason for this incapacity.
Concluding his summary of its content, the narrator informs

us: "Then the writer mentioned that she was moistening the
lines with tears for a tender mother who had left the world
twenty-five years before" (160). Here the death of a mother
corresponds to the death of a wife in the portraits of Nozdryov
and Plyushkin as a symbol of the death of the writer's
"feminine" soul, and it is as an extension of this symbol that we
should read the metrically defective quatrain that ends her
letter:

> Two turtledoves will show
> Thee my cold ashes,
> Cooingly languidly, they will tell thee
> That she died weeping. (160)[3]

Like the "glitter," therefore, of the ladies' attire, the
"refinement" of their language is a mask of spiritual vacuity
and physical crudity. Shunning the physical, it ironically betrays an existence that is exclusively physical. But this restraint
is observed only in their discourse in Russian. In French, the
narrator remarks, "they permitted themselves words far
coarser than those that have been mentioned" (159). The implication seems to be that whereas discourse in Russian can be
"refined" only by purging its content, the intrinsic splendor of
the Gallic veneer is immune to the grossest crudities. And in
this preference of the ladies for French we perceive another
allusion not only to their "Manilovan superficial femininity,"
but also to their affinities with the iconoclastic Nozdryov,
whose own partiality for French is again reflected in his replac-
ing *potseluy* with *beze* (i.e. *baiser*).

Viewed as a whole, therefore, the portrait of the ladies is an
intricate mosaic of details drawn from four different sources,
and although the generally satirical character of the portrait is
entirely self-evident, it is clear that an awareness of these
sources is imperative if we are to appreciate fully the implications of the details and the continuity of the symbolic themes
and motifs that comprise the allegory. We must now consider,
however, the relationship between this portrait and that of the
"masters" with which the chapter begins. Again we must
determine whether an apparently self-sufficient opening sec-

tion is as independent of the remainder of the chapter as it seems to be or whether, in reality, it is a veiled introduction to the more extensive portrait that follows.

The long opening paragraph of the chapter consists mainly of extracts from a conversation among the "masters" about Chichikov's purchases and his proposed resettlement of his serfs in the Ukraine. Two basic views are distinguishable in which we may again detect indications of the contrasting "Manilovan" and "Sobakevichan" aspects of the "masters' " personalities. Some suggestions, the narrator notes, "savored too much of military harshness and perhaps excessive severity, but there were also opinions imbued with gentleness" (155–156). The distinctive features of the latter opinion are "Manilovan" high-sounding sentiments and an appropriately elevated style. Thus, commenting on the possible outcome of the resettlement, one of the speakers opines:

> . . . it must be taken into account that there are certain moral considerations here, that there is a moral aspect to this question. At present they are rogues, but when they have been settled on new land, they may suddenly become excellent subjects. There have been many such instances, both in the modern world and in history. (154–155)

This theme is duly taken up by the most "erudite" of the "masters," the postmaster Ivan Andreich, to whom is attributed an intimate knowledge of Edward Young's *Night Thoughts* and Eckartshausen's *Key to the Mysteries of Nature*,[4] and whose fervent xenomania is further indicated by the alleged tendency of the other "masters" to append the rhyming phrase "Sprechen Sie deich?" to his name. He now recognizes an admirable opportunity to display his familiarity with another "nonindigenous" source of wisdom:

> The postmaster remarked that a sacred duty lay before Chichikov, that he could become, as he put it, a kind of father to his peasants, and he spoke most favorably on this occasion of the Lancaster school of reciprocal education.[5] (156)

The opposite, "Sobakevichan," view is voiced by the superintendent of factories, who advocates ruling the peasants with a rod of iron, expresses "Sobakevichan" misgivings about the foreign (i.e. Ukrainian) influence to which they are about to be exposed, and issues the following advice to the absent Chichikov: "It is essential . . . that he should rely on no one else and that where it is necessary he should himself give them a sock on the jaw or a clip on the back of the head" (155). Significantly, however, the superintendent is the sole proponent of this view. Every statement that he makes evokes an immediate "Manilovan" riposte, and the final word is left to the postmaster. This would suggest, therefore, that the main purpose of the conversation is to establish at the very beginning of the chapter the point Gogol is clearly intent on conveying throughout—that the daunting physcial aspect of "Sobakevichan masculinity" is less characteristic of the "masters" than of the ladies. Supporting evidence for this conclusion is forthcoming from a number of individual details.

The remark of the superintendent about the need for physical intimidation is followed by yet another of those typically Gogolian sequences which, though not illogical, seem entirely pointless in their immediate context and become intelligible only in the light of details that often appear many pages later. It begins with the "Manilovan" rejoinder to the superintendent's words: "But why should Chichikov take the trouble to do this himself? He might find an estate manager" (155).[6] The superintendent promptly replies that "it would be impossible to find a good estate manager for less than five thousand roubles" (155), to which the president of the court, again for no apparent reason, responds with the comment that "one could find one for as little as three thousand" (155). It is almost twenty pages before Gogol discloses the meaning of these statements—in the disgruntled Chichikov's diatribe against balls toward the end of the chapter and, in particular, against the expenditure they involve. He muses:

It's nothing for a woman to spend a thousand roubles on adorning herself! And all at the expense, you know, of the peasants' quitrent or, what's even worse, at the expense of the consciences of the likes of us. It is well known why men take bribes and act against their consciences: it's to get enough money for their wives to spend on a shawl or on all kinds of crinolines, the devil take them, whatever they're called. And why? So that some depraved Sidorovna will not say that the postmaster's wife is wearing a better dress, and because of her, bang goes a thousand roubles. (174)

Since it is implied here that the economic health of the "masters'" estates is determined to a significant degree by the passion of their wives for balls and dresses, we may conclude that their wives are, in fact, the true managers of the estates and, consequently, that "estate manager" in the earlier exchanges is a metaphor of "wife." The statement, therefore, that Chichikov "might find an estate manager" may be linked with the "masters'" avowed intention of finding him a wife, while the dispute between the superintendent and the president as to whether five or three thousand roubles would suffice to attract an estate manager reflects, in reality, their uncertainty as to whether a good wife may be baited with five dresses or three. If this interpretation is correct, then the implied suggestion that "clips on the back of the head" are best administered by estate managers is a means of associating the ladies once more with a capacity for inflicting violence that to most of the "masters" is evidently distasteful.

An additional indication that "estate manager" here means "wife" is provided by the superintendent's reply to the president's assessment of the required sum. Rejecting the claim that three thousand roubles would suffice, he asks: "Where will you find him? Surely not in your nose?" (155). The key to this curious remark is a reference to Chichikov's nose nine pages later as he stands among the throng of ladies at the ball: "Standing before them, Chichikov thought: 'Which one is the writer of the letter?' and he prepared to thrust out his nose" (164). Thus trusting in his own "Nozdryovian" hunting instincts, Chichikov looks to his nose for the decisive clue to the letter-writer's identity, thereby implying that ladies, i.e. estate managers, can be found "in one's nose." Translated, therefore, into more readily intelligible language, the superintendent's brief question may perhaps be rephrased: "Surely you don't expect that for three thousand roubles you will find *a lady* who is prepared to be your estate manager?"

The conversation of the "masters," therefore, would seem to have the introductory function of highlighting their predominantly "Manilovan" inclinations, while foreshadowing the later emphasis on the contrasting element of crude, physical "masculinity" in the portrait of the ladies. It prepares the way for the ironic reversal of conventional masculine and feminine attributes to which Eckartshausen's subtitle *Key to the Mysteries of Nature* conceivably alludes. Apart from the estate manager recommended by the president of the court—Pyotr Petrovich Samoylov—whose surname (literally "the hunting of herself") suggests a "Nozdryovian" attitude to females, only the superintendent, it seems, has successfully avoided reduction to the status of "garrison soldier" or "mousey little stallion" (165). Every other "master" is comprehensively tarred with the same brush of "superficial femininity" in all its various manifestations. Thus the governor, whose skill at embroidery has already been brought to our attention, is now depicted twice: first, "standing beside the ladies and holding in one hand a candy wrapper and in the other a lap dog" (162); second, stopping Chichikov to ask him "to arbitrate in an argument that he was having with two ladies as to whether a woman's love is lasting or not" (171). We are also reminded again of the "masters'" tendency, already demonstrated by the president in chapter seven, to address one another as "mommy" (*mamen'ka* or *mamochka*)" (156), and it is observed that although they occasionally felt constrained to intervene on their wives' behalf in the "violent scenes" provoked by their efforts to outdo one another, they preferred dirty tricks to duels as a means of expressing their indignation (158).

Certainly, however, the most obvious indicator of the "Manilovism" of the "masters" is the veneration of "refined" form, which they share with the ladies. It reveals itself most comically in the president's moving recitations from Zhukovsky's narrative poem *Lyudmila,* and by giving him a line that contains the noun "vale" (*dolina*),[7] Gogol seems specifically to be stressing that in this respect at least the tastes of the "masters" and ladies are identical. The choice of poem is significant for two reasons. Based on the poem *Lenore* by the *Sturm und Drang* poet Gottfried August Bürger, it suggests that the "masters" are generally disposed, like Manilov and the postmaster, to turn to products of foreign inspiration for models of "refinement," while the fantastic or mystical character that it shares with the works of Young and Eckartshausen alludes to the fundamental "Manilovan" condition of total detachment from reality. The postmaster's fractured speech, which he is constantly interrupting with his meaningless "auxiliary phrases", in a manner again reminiscent of Manilov himself (157), is merely one manifestation of this common debilitating condition that nearly twenty pages later prompts the following strictures from Chichikov in his tirade against balls:

> One's head [i.e. after a ball] is as empty as after a conversation with a man of the world: he will talk about everything, touch lightly on everything, say everything that he has culled from books in a colorful, eloquent style, but one's head retains none of it, and you see afterwards that even a conversation with a simple merchant who knows only his business, but knows it thoroughly and from experience, is better than all this claptrap. (175)

It need hardly be said, however, that Chichikov's attitude here toward one of the principal symptoms of "superficial femininity" is by no means typical of him. Indeed, his own "Manilovan" attributes are clearly in evidence in the chapter. Not only does he devote more time to preparing himself for the ball than any man "since the creation of the world";[8] he even executes a number of practice bows before the mirror "accompanied by vague sounds which bore a partial resemblance to French, though Chichikov had no knowledge of French at all"

(161). Equally in evidence, at least according to the ladies, are
his "Nozdryovian" and "Sobakevichan" attributes, for both
his "martial and military" expression and his portly frame, as
we have seen, excite their admiration. Between these symbolic
indications, however, of the state of the hero's soul and his
verbal assault on balls and those who frequent them, Gogol
interposes his significant second encounter with the governor's
daughter, and there can be little doubt that his subsequent
critical comments should be related as much to the enlighten-
ing effects of this experience as to the souring effects of Nozdryov's revelations. From beginning to end his criticisms are
leveled against that same "Manilovan" aspect of balls to which
his state of mind before the meeting had been so perfectly
attuned. He exclaims:

> . . . balls are simply rubbish! They're not in the Russian
> spirit, the Russian character. . . . It's all caused by aping,
> by aping other poeple! Because a Frenchman at the age of
> forty is as much a child as he was at the age of fifteen, we
> must be the same. No, truly . . . after every ball one feels
> as if one has committed some sin. . . . What can you
> squeeze out of it, out of a ball like this? Let us suppose that
> some writer took it into his head to describe the entire
> scene, just as it is. Why, it would be just as senseless in a
> book as it is in real life. What is it—moral or immoral? The
> devil only knows what it is! You would spit and then close
> the book. (174–175)

This abrupt intrusion of such words as "sin" and "moral"
into Chichikov's vocabulary can only be related to the young
"Madonna's" effect on him. Every detail supports the conclusion that his second meeting with her is another confrontation
with the human soul in all its "feminine" purity, beside which
the imperfections of his admirers are starkly exposed to his eye.
His first sight of her renders him incapable, we read, of "ut-
tering a single sensible word" (166) and instantly deprives him
of the capacity for replying any longer in kind to the ladies' "refined" questions and vacuous chatter. Rivetted to the

spot, his agile legs similarly lose the capacity to perform the "antics" that a few moments before had so favorably impressed the ladies—the "mincing steps," the "short tail," and the "comma" (165)[9] When he finally approaches the girl and her mother, the narrator notes: ". . . he did not mince in such a lively, foppish manner; he even stumbled slightly, and there was a certain awkwardness in all his movements" (169). Thus the shell of verbal and physical "refinement" suddenly crumbles.

His state of mind is compared to that of a man who, on setting out for a walk, seems to have everything, but is suddenly halted by the feeling that he has forgotten something. "And in confusion and dismay," the narrator continues, "he looks at the moving crowd before him, at the carriages flying past, at the shakos and rifles of a passing regiment, at a shop sign, and he sees nothing clearly" (167). Perhaps in the "carriages" (*ekipazhi*), shakos and rifles we may detect anticipatory allusions to the "strange carriage" (*strannyy ekipazh*) that is soon to bear Korobochka into the town and to the imminent apparition of Nozdryov, but what is clear is that the sight of the girl has the immediate effect of disengaging him spiritually from his perverted environment. When he reflects on this episode later, it seems to him "that the entire ball with all its chatter and noise had for several minutes withdrawn somewhere into the distance; the violins and trumpets were screeching somewhere beyond the mountains" (169). Once more the vocabulary triggers echoes of motifs and phrases used in earlier chapters. The "screeching" of the violins and trumpets recalls the high-pitched sounds that have from the beginning punctuated both the portrait of the "masters" and that of Chichikov himself—the blaring of his nose to which his name alludes,[10] the trumpeting sounds produced by blowing through his fist,[11] the creaking of his bed, and his "thin, nasal whistle"—while the phrase "beyond the mountains" reminds us of the location of Sobakevich's encrusted soul. In the presence of the symbolic "Madonna," the musical symbols of spiritual perversion are appropriately seen to emanate from the same distant abode as that of the perverted soul itself.

Perhaps the most significant phrase, however, in the description of Chichikov at this moment is the remark that he felt "just like a young man, almost a hussar" (169). As Proffer has observed, the statement seems to suggest that a distinct evolution has taken place in Chichikov since his first meeting with the governor's daughter.[12] In chapter five, it will be recalled, Gogol leaves us in no doubt that his hero is "a middle-aged man and of a circumspect, unemotional character" (92–93), and the image of the hussar is evoked to characterize the hypothetical twenty-year-old youth whose reaction to the meeting would allegedly have been quite different. In chapter eight, by contrast, Chichikov is not just momentarily rejuvenated and compared to a hussar himself; his reaction is so unthinkingly emotional that he thoroughly antagonizes the ladies, thereby ensuring that his scheme will fail. In this new context he is no longer prompted to contemplate the possibility of a "profitable match." His response in no longer calculating, but genuinely adulatory. Revealing in this connection is the subject that he is about to broach with the girl as Nozdryov alights on the scene—the philosopher Diogenes (171). Here Gogel uses a Greek name to denote the precise opposite of that which such names signify on almost every other occasion in the novel—asceticism, contempt for worldly things, discipline of mind as well as body. In an earlier draft of the chapter the philosopher's name was followed by the words "who very wittily replied to Alexander of Macedon" (803)—an allusion to the probably apocryphal story that the only boon Diogenes asked of Alexander was that he not stand in his light. So Chichikov is anxious, as he violently forges a path through the dense throng of dancers, that no one shield from him the white light which emanates from the girl's ivorylike features.

The implication of Chichikov's differing reactions to his two meetings with the governor's daughter would appear to be that the effect of the first meeting stimulates in him a need of which he becomes fully, if briefly, conscious only on seeing her for a second time. But Gogol provides no explicit information on which to base this conclusion. Indeed, he leaves the precise nature of Chichikov's feelings conspicuously vague. He writes:

> It is impossible to say for sure whether the feeling of love had been wakened in our hero; it is even doubtful whether gentlemen of such a kind, that is, not fat but not thin either, are capable of love; but for all that, there was something strange here, something of that kind which he could not explain to himself. (169)

Clearly, therefore, this is a significantly different Chichikov from the hero to whom we are accustomed—a Chichikov for whom redemption is by no means inconceivable. Gogol is plainly providing us here with our first glimpse of potentialities that were evidently to be progressively realized in the two succeeding volumes of the "epic." Yet Chichikov's ability to elicit from the governor's daughter nothing but yawns makes it equally clear that his road to Paradise lies through a long and arduous Purgatory. Here we perceive another implication of Nozdryov's intervention at this juncture, with whose disclosures the journey commences. The spectacle of the pure, living soul is now abruptly replaced by the exposure of Chichikov's own "inner stench," for it is at this point, as noted in chapter four, above, that the image of the "crooked wheel" reappears to signal the approach of nemesis, and the hero's "beautifully polished boot" is sullied by a "Korobochkan" puddle that metaphorically transforms his "refined" exterior into a mirror of the inner, "Petrushkan" reality. Comparing him, as he struggles to recover from Nozdryov's assault, to "a man tired or utterly exhausted by a long journey [*dal'ney dorogoy*]" (174), Gogol evokes once more the image that prefigures his imminent reversion to the status of "slave," his impending return to the hardships of the road from which, it seems, his soul was ultimately to emerge resurrected and cleansed.

8

Forgeries
of Fact and
Counterfeit Truths

Although Chichikov is physically absent from the whole of chapter nine and from the greater part of chapter ten, he paradoxically assumes from the end of chapter eight onward an increasingly dominant role in the fiction. This development is motivated, of course, by the revelations of Nozdryov and Korobochka, which have the effect of focusing the entire town's attention on the question of the hero's true identity and purpose and on the mystery of his "dead souls." At the same time, although the answers to most of the questions that trouble the townsfolk are well known to the reader, our own curiosity about Chichikov is just as effectively engaged by the hitherto unsuspected complexity of his personality, which is revealed in how he reacts to his second meeting with the governor's daughter. For different reasons, therefore, the personality of the hero now becomes the central concern of both the reader and the characters. The problem for the reader is that he is obliged to derive his insights into the nature of the hero's soul from the judgments pronounced on him by "dead souls" (i.e. by the "masters" and the ladies).

Since the members of both urban groups exist, as we have seen, in body alone, i.e. appearance, it is fitting that appearances should dictate their judgments. Lacking "inner substance" themselves, they are implicitly ascribed with an inability to perceive it in others. As chapter eight has confirmed, they are capable solely of naming and defining on the basis of superficial impressions, of asserting "facts" and "truths" that usually bear little relation to the reality of the phenomena concerned. Such, appropriately, are the "facts" and "truths" they assert about Chichikov—the "forgeries" of fact and "counterfeit" truths of "dead souls." Their suspicion that he is a forger and Korobochka's alleged contention that he made her sign "a forged document" (184) are precisely Gogol's means of conveying to us explicitly this fundamentally "counterfeit" quality of their perceptions in general. Characteristically, however, Gogol does not restrict the development of this theme merely to the characters' speculations about the identity of Chichikov; he expands it into the dominant symbolic theme of chapter nine which, as a result, becomes an eloquent and coherent body of evidence testifying to the elusiveness of truth and the inadequacy of names.

The subject of names—or, to be more precise, that of the mistaken conclusions to which they can give rise—is significantly broached in the opening paragraph, in which the narrator professes his anxiety about the possible consequences of giving names to the two ladies whose conversation begins the chapter. He remarks: "The author is greatly troubled by the problem of how he should name the two ladies in such a way that people will not be angry with him again as they were in the past.[1] To call people by an invented name is dangerous" (179). He declares his intention, therefore, to call them "the lady agreeable in all respects" and "the simply agreeable lady." But no sooner have these names been bestowed than their "counterfeit" nature is immediately exposed by an indication of their inappropriateness. Thus having assured us that "the lady agreeable in all respects" acquired this name "quite legitimately", the narrator adds:

> . . . indeed she spared no effort to be courteous to the greatest possible extent, though, of course, through her courtesy one could detect—oh, such nimble dexterity of the female character!—and though occasionally in every

agreeable word that she uttered one could glimpse—oh,
such a sharp pin![2] And God save us from the feelings that
seethed in her breast against any woman who by some
means or other wormed her way ahead of her. (174)

The name, therefore, masks a nature that unequivocally invali-
dates it. The same kind of contradiction between word and fact
may also be observed in the narrator's statement about his
intentions, for little more than a page after his lengthy argument in favor of giving them descriptive names they are already addressing one another by Christian names and
patronymics—Anna Grigor'yevna ("the lady agreeable in all
respects") and Sof'ya Ivanovna ("the simply agreeable lady").
Thus both the names and the stated intention are blatant
"forgeries" of fact.

In a typically playful apostrophe to the reader, therefore,
Gogol introduces at the very beginning the theme that pervades the entire chapter. Indeed, it first appears in the opening
sentences—in the form of the verbs *vyporkhnut'* and *vsporkhnut'*
(178), which indicate the rapidity of Sof'ya Ivanovna's movements as she prepares to visit Anna Grigor'yevna, whom she
is anxious to tell the news about Chichikov brought by
Korobochka. Meaning literally "to flit out" and "to take
wing," these verbs convey an impression of birdlike grace and
lightness which conflicts as stridently with the physical image
of the ladies evoked in chapter eight as their "kisses," "modesties," and headdresses.[3] Similarly, we may suspect more than a
conventional distortion of fact when Sof'ya Ivanovna expresses her impatience with the length of the journey by remarking as she passes the almshouse: "Curse the building,
there's no end to it!" (178). In the context of chapter nine
seemingly inconsequential statements of this kind acquire
significant meaning.

The context likewise compels us to respond in a different
manner from usual to the numerous French words and phrases
in the conversation of the two ladies—a feature to which the
narrator directs our attention in an "aside" that closely

resembles in length and character his "digression" in the opening paragraph on the subject of names. He comments:

> It might as well be observed that a large number of foreign words and sometimes whole French phrases of considerable length crept into the conversation of the two ladies. But however reverential the author's attitude may be to the salutary benefits which Russia derives from the French language, however reverential his attitude may be to our upper classes' laudable habit of expressing themselves in this language at all hours of the day out of their profound love for their native land, of course, yet for all that he cannot bring himself to introduce a phrase from any foreign language into this Russian epic poem of his. And so let us continue in Russian. (182–183)

Quite apart from the ironic "forgery" contained in the observation that the use of French by the upper classes is motivated by "their profound love for their native land," the final sentence presents another example of a patently "counterfeit" intention. Not only is his implied adherence to Russian thus far contradicted by the "whole French phrase" (*c'est qu'on appelle une histoire*) inserted in Cyrillic script into Sof'ya Ivanovna's announcement, which directly precedes the passage, but his declaration of intent is also exposed as spurious both by Sof'ya Ivanovna's cry a page later: ". . . it was simply *horreur, horreur, horreur!*" (183), in which the French is again clothed in "counterfeit" Cyrillic attire, and similarly by Anna Grigor'yevna's calque almost immediately after the "aside" of the French phrase *faire la cour,* viz. *stroit' kury* (183). Nor does Gogol confine himself in the pages that follow to Gallicising the language of the ladies, for the Cyrillicised words *commérages* and *tête-à-tête* (192) both appear in comments by the narrator.

Contradictions of this kind, however, are only one of several means Gogol uses to express the fundamental notion that words or names are unreliable. The same idea is conveyed by the French words themselves. Certainly we may assume that they retain here their customary associations, but the substitution of these words for their Russian equivalents seems now to carry the additional implication that words are merely inadequate, interchangeable labels. In this respect the role of French lexical and phraseological "aliases" is directly comparable to that of two other procedures which Gogol uses extensively in this chapter (and in this chapter alone)—the duplication of terms and the accumulation of synonyms. Drawing on colloquial resources, for example, he employs consecutively four different expressions for the concept of "nonsense": "*Androny yedut, chepukha, beliberda, sapogi vsmyatku*" (190). Reference is also made to the murder of the assessor Drobyazhkin (alias "the district police" [*zemskaya politsiya*]) by the peasants of "the village of Hogsham (*Borovki*), alias Bullyton (*Zadiraylovo*)" (194) and to the "various names" under which a forger is allegedly hiding in the province (194–195), while a piece of paper filled with tobacco is given the "alias" *hussar* (189). Similarly, a whole series of sardonic "aliases" are applied by the two ladies to Chichikov, e.g. "our charmer" (*nash prelestnik*), "our new arrival" (*priyezzhiy-to nash*), "our humble one" (*nash-to smirennik*). It is inconceivable that the sudden appearance and prominence of these procedures in the text is coincidental. Like the sprinkling of French words, they hint at the inability of words to pierce the façades of phenomena—above all, the façade of the alleged "forger" (alias "brigand") Chichikov. They merely skate ineffectually over the surface, weaving their colorful patterns, which convey no impression of the underlying reality. And in this context it is perhaps to this sustained emphasis on the superficiality of words that we should relate the two ladies' most favored mode of address—*dusha*.

The most obvious allusions to this impotence of language are the various forms of hyperbole that punctuate the conversation of the two ladies—especially exaggerated outbursts of emotion—and the numerous exclamations of Sof'ya Ivanovna that contain variations of the statement "you cannot possibly imagine." They are particularly conspicuous in their opening exchanges on the subject of fashion—a subject, of course, which fits integrally into an exposure of the discord between form and content. Indeed, on one occasion, speaking of a piece of dress material received by a friend's sister Sof'ya Ivanovna finds even her considerable powers of hyperbole unequal to the task. "Words are simply powerless to express its charm," she declares (180). Thus language is raised in the dialogue of the ladies to the highest degree, and the higher it soars, the more it distorts and falsifies despite their constant endeavors to consolidate their "forgeries" by emphatic repetition. A similar effect is obtained by the profusion of diminutive suffixes in their speech, which not only lend a false "agreeableness" to their conversation, but also convey emotional responses grotesquely disproportionate to the objects that inspire them, e.g. *vesyolen'kiy sitets* ("gay little cotton print"), *materiyka* ("the darling material"), *uzen'kiye polosochki* ("little narrow stripes"), *glazki i lapki* ("little spots and sprigs") (180). By such means the gulf between form and content is again significantly widened and the coin of language is comprehensively devalued.

After the description of Anna Grigor'yevna as "a sincere friend of the lady who had just arrived" (179),[4] the "forgeries" follow one another in a remarkable variety of guises. First, the "gay little cotton print" turns out to be covered in brown spots (180).[5] Then the human face is grotesquely "forged" in the image of the knight with the ladderlike nose and square lips, which adorns the cushion stuffed behind Sof'ya Ivanovna's back (180). Then, after insisting that she will never wear the kind of dress described by Sof'ya Ivanovna, Anna Grigor'yevna promptly demands the pattern for it (181). Two pages later we encounter the "perfectly romantic story" (183) of Chichikov's visit to Korobochka recounted by Sof'ya Ivanovna, a "forgery" from beginning to end, a highly charged fictional embellishment of the prosaic events of chapter three inspired by Vulpius's romantic novel *Rinaldo Rinaldini,* the hero of which is appropriately a brigand.[6] And shortly afterwards, disregarding both the evidence of her eyes and the testimony of her "friend," Anna Grigor'yevna is adamant that the governor's daughter "uses rouge shamelessly" (186). At this point the narrator intervenes with a comic attempt to explain her irrationality, asserting that there are "many things in the world which have the quality of appearing to be completely white when one lady looks at them and as red as a whortleberry when another lady looks at them" (186). After a short interval he returns to Anna Grigor'yevna's defense, even citing the parallel of the scholar who erects an entire edifice of "truth" on the basis of one insubstantial hint, but now the irony is more informative. He remarks:

> She did not know how to lie. To make an assumption was a different matter, but even that was possible only when the assumption was based on inner conviction. If she felt an inner conviction, then she knew how to stand up for herself, and if any expert advocate, famed for his gift of overcoming other people's opinions, should try to compete with her in this matter, he would soon see what an inner conviction means. (188)

The irony, of course, is that the "inner convictions" (*vnutrenniye ubezhdeniya*) which determine Anna Grigor'yevna's assessments of truth and fact are the convictions of a "dead soul." They are "dead" like Anna Grigor'yevna herself, the "dead forgeries" of "living" convictions in which her detachment from life or reality is consistently reflected.

Repeated references to death are another distinctive feature of chapter nine, and they were doubtless intended by Gogol to serve as oblique explanatory comments on this comic ineptitude of his characters as they grapple ineffectually with the mystery that confronts them. The phrase "dead souls" is used more frequently in this chapter than in any other, and its two meanings (or "aliases") are now appropriately exploited to the full. On the one hand, there are the numerous references to physical death in the latter part of the chapter, where we learn of the deaths of the Ust'sysol'sk merchants, the assessor Drobyazhkin and the serfs who suffered from the public health inspector's derelictions of duty, and in each case the causes of their deaths are aptly "forged." On the other, there are the ubiquitous instances of metaphorical death, which allude to the death of the soul. The first duly appears in the opening paragraph in the context of the narrator's remarks about the "danger" of invented names: "Whatever name you think of, you're sure to find in some corner of our state, considering how vast it is, someone who bears it, and he is sure to fly into a deathly rage [*rasserditsya ne na zhivot, a na smert'*]" (179).[7] And shortly afterwards Gogol introduces the prominent motif of the "pallor" of death, which produces some of his most telling ironic effects and is chiefly associated with Sof'ya Ivanovna. On being informed, for example, by Anna Grigor'yevna that Chichikov's real objective is the abduction of the governor's daughter, she "froze on the spot," we read, "she turned pale, as pale as death, and became genuinely alarmed" (185). And a few lines later the barrage of "counterfeit" charges they level against the governor's daughter culminates in her remark: "Oh, my dear [*dushen'ka*], she's a statue and as pale as death." Thus ironically and fittingly the translucent whiteness symbolic of spiritual "life" is misconstrued by the "dead soul" of Sof'ya Ivanovna as the pallor of death. But Gogol, as already indicated, appends an additional ironic flourish. Since pallor is clearly esteemed by Anna Grigor'yevna as a highly fashionable attribute that must never be conceded to the girl who has proved a far more potent attraction to Chichikov than the ladies themselves, the truth must yield to an "inner conviction"—to her conviction that the rouge on her face "was as thick as my finger" (186).

As the ladies, and later the "masters," struggle unavailingly to decipher the meaning of the phrase "dead souls," the irony of the situation is progressively intensified. "What could possibly be the meaning of these dead souls?" asks Anna Grigor'yevna. "I confess I'm absolutely mystified by it all" (184). And scrutinizing the enigma through the eyes of the "masters," the narrator asks: "What is the meaning of these dead souls? There is no logic in dead souls" (189). Predictably, the issue is finally settled by more of Anna Grigor'yevna's "convictions." Solemnly announcing to Sof'ya Ivanovna that "it's not a question of dead souls at all" (184) and that they "have merely been invented to cover up something" (185) (i.e. Chichikov's designs, in her submission, on the governor's daughter), she promptly sets off with her "friend" to alert the town, and within a half hour the "dead souls" whose existence she denies are ironically rising from their tombs:

> The town which hitherto had seemed to be slumbering suddenly sprang into activity like a whirlwind. From their burrows crawled all the recluses and lazybones who had been lying idle at home for years in their dressing gowns, lumping the blame on the cobbler for making their boots too narrow, or on their tailor, or their drunken coach-man—all those who had long ago broken off relations with all their friends and associated only, as they say, with the landowners Mr. Fall-into-Bed and Mr. Take-a-Rest (celebrated terms derived from the verbs "to fall into bed" and "to take a rest" which are very much in vogue in Russia, just like the phrase "to call on Mr. Wheeze and Mr. Snore," which means to sleep like the dead on the side or on the back or in any other position with snores, nasal whistles and other accessories); all those who could not be enticed from their homes even by a pressing invitation to devour a fish soup costing five-hundred roubles with five-foot-long sturgeons and all kinds of meat pies which melt in the mouth; in short, it turned out that the town was both populous and large and populated as it should be. (190)

Thus the motifs of the "sedentary life," boots, "nasal whis-tling," and deathlike sleep (*mertvetskiye sny*) are combined with lexical and phraseological "aliases" to create the scene of a parodic or "counterfeit" resurrection. The "counterfeit" truth of the ladies resurrects the "counterfeit" souls of the "masters"—souls that appear not only with such "counterfeit" names as Sysoy Pafnut'yevich and Makdonal'd Karlovich, but also in such "counterfeit" forms as that of the "very long and

lanky man with a bullet hole through his arm who was so tall
that nothing like it had ever been seen before" (190).[8] Now it is
the turn of the "masters" to display their pallor, and the public
health inspector and the president of the court duly oblige
(193).

The leading role of the ladies in the persecution of Chichikov
is prefigured and explained, of course, by the indications in
chapter eight of their affinities with Korobochka, and it is
noticeable that these affinities are indirectly reasserted from the
beginning. Thus while chapter eight ends with the arrival of
Korobochka's carriage, chapter nine begins with the departure
of the carriage of Sof'ya Ivanovna who is the bearer of
Korobochka's tidings, and again the general status of the male
of the species is conveyed by that of a footman—the hapless
Andryushka. Nor does it seem coincidental that after the reference on the preceding page to the "little sheds" (kletukhi) of
Father Kiril's wife Sof'ya Ivanovna should be endowed with a
"smart checked cloak" (178), for the Russian adjective for
"checked" (kletchatyy) is similarly derived from the noun
kletka. It might also be noted that both her own house and that
of Anna Grigor'yevna are made of wood and that the latter is
graced with a fence around the front garden, which contains a
number of "Manilovan" "spindly trees" (tonen'kiye derevtsa), as
well as a "high wooden trellis" in front of the windows (178).
And appropriately visible from the window is a parrot "swing-
ing in a cage [kletke] and grasping a ring with its beak" (179),
clearly evocative of the birds in Korobochka's pictures and
Sobakevich's thrush. Moreover, we learn on the next page that
the "little cotton print" of Sof'ya Ivanovna's dress is also
covered in "checks" (kletochki), which doubtless explains Anna
Grigor'yevna's ecstatic reaction to it and her description of it as
"gay" (180); Sof'ya Ivanovna then launches into a breathless
account of a material with smaller checks in which "little spots
and sprigs" (literally "little eyes and paws" [glazki i lapki]) are
located between "little narrow stripes" (or "bars" [polosochki]).
Thus numerous details in the portrait of the two ladies evoke
the image of Korobochka's prison.

The additional indications of this "Korobochkan" attitude to males (and to Chichikov in particular) are somewhat more elusive. An example is Anna Grigor'yevna's scornful remark about the cousin to whom Sof'ya Ivanovna has promised to give her sister's dress pattern first: "God only knows what kind of a cousin you have there: a cousin by marriage (literally "from the husband's side [*s muzhninoy storony*]")" (182). Equally expressive are the references to Anna Grigor'yevna's French-named pair of lap dogs, which not only reintroduce the "canine" motif but also, it seems, perform a parodic role comparable to that of the two dogs in Gogol's story *The Diary of a Madman (Zapiski sumasshedshego)* (1835), for the conspicuously shaggy coat of the bitch Adèle and the "spindly legs" (180) of the male Potpourri suggest the possibility of an inversion of canine sexual roles corresponding to that which has doubtless transpired in the household on the human level. Finally, we might note the flattened nose of the knight on the cushion that is meaningfully subjected to the burden of Sof'ya Ivanovna's considerable weight. The allusion in this case is evidently to the fate the ladies are planning for Chichikov, for it is significant not only that Chichikov is later described, in Sof'ya Ivanovna's version of Korobochka's narrative, as "armed from head to foot like Rinaldo Rinaldini," i.e. as a knight, but also that Anna Grigor'yevna is particularly critical of his nose. "Rumors have been spread," she declares, "that he is handsome, but he's not at all handsome, not at all, and his nose is . . . a most unpleasant nose" (182). If we may interpret the nose here, without seeming unduly Freudian, as a phallic symbol—a conclusion to which Anna Grigor'yevna's delicate pause perhaps lends plausibility—the image of the knight on the cushion may be construed as a symbolic representation of the "emasculated" Chichikov whom the ladies are manifestly intent on producing.

As in chapter eight, however, the behavior of the ladies is dictated by more than "Korobochkan" impulses. Although their antagonism toward Chichikov continues to be matched by their intense hostility to the principal male contributor to his misfortunes, Nozdryov, whom they now fatuously suspect of being his accomplice in his attempts to abduct the governor's daughter, nevertheless their own "Nozdryovian" urges are still clearly in evidence. Indeed, perhaps their capacity for producing "counterfeit" truths may itself manifest their "Nozdryovism." The impression conveyed, in short, is that having indicated in the portrait of the ladies in chapter eight symptoms of the four types of spiritual affliction personified by the protagonists of chapters two through five, Gogol now stresses their particular affinities with the two landowners who play the decisive role in determining the hero's fate. An early allusion to their "Nozdryovian" hunting instincts is the comparison of Anna Grigor'yevna's words to hawks "ready to set off in pursuit of one another" (182), and a few pages later she remarks in the course of a verbal assault on Nozdryov: "He wanted to sell his own father, you know, or rather to gamble him away at cards" (187)—a remark which ironically echoes Sof'ya Ivanovna's statement about the governor's daughter on the previous page: "Really, you can make me take any oath you like, I'm ready to forfeit this instant my children, my husband, my entire estate, if there's a single drop, even a particle or shadow of rouge on her!" (186). But the most revealing insights into Sof'ya Ivanovna's mind are provided by the extended simile that evokes her state of rapt attention as Anna Grigor'yevna prepares to divulge the "truth." Here we see how allusions to her affinities with both landowners are subtly combined:

Thus a Russian squire, a lover of hounds and daredevil hunter [*okhotnik*], on riding up to a forest out of which a hare roused by the beaters is about to leap at any moment, is transformed, together with his horse and raised whip, in one congealed instant into gunpowder which is about to be ignited. His eyes are fixed on the murky air and he will surely overtake the animal and finish it off, for he is irresistible, however much the whole tempestuous snowy steppe may rise up against him, hurling silvery stars at his lips, his moustache, his eyes, his eyebrows, and his beaver cap. (185)

While the "leaping hare" is doubtless an allusion to the "hopping" Chichikov, the comparison of Sof'ya Ivanovna to a man (moreover, a man with a moustache), the image of the whip, and the intent to "finish it off" are eloquent indicators of her "Korobochkan" attributes. Similarly, of course, her "Nozdryovian" inclinations are signalled by the imagery of the hunt and the detail of "gunpowder."⁹

"Nozdryovian gunpowder" makes two additional appearances in the chapter, and on each occasion it appears under its customary "alias" of tobacco or snuff (*tabak*). Appropriately, the two instances occur in the description of the ladies' assault on the "masters." The first to have his face "tanned" is the public prosecutor, who is thrown into a state of such confusion by the ladies' questions that "even though he continued standing for some time on the same spot, blinked his left eye and flicked his beard with his handkerchief to wipe the snuff from it, he was still quite incapable of understanding anything" (189). Significantly, the rest of the "masters" have similar explosive charges thrust up their noses:

> During the first moment their position was similar to that of a schoolboy whose classmates, who have got up before him, have thrust up his nose while he is asleep a hussar, that is, a piece of paper filled with snuff. Having in his half-sleep breathed in all the snuff with all the vigor of a sleeping person, he wakes up, leaps to his feet, looks around him like a fool with eyes popping [*vypuchiv glaza*] in all directions, and cannot grasp where he is or what has happened to him, and only later [*i potom uzhe*] does he distinguish [*razlichayet*] the walls lit by the oblique rays of the sun, the laughter of his classmates who have hidden in the corners, and the dawning day which is peeping through a window. He can also make out the awakened forest resounding with thousands of bird voices and the brightly lit river disappearing here and there in shining

eddies between slender rushes and strewn with naked boys summoning others to come for a swim, and only then [*i potom uzhe*] does he finally become aware that a hussar has been stuck up his nose. (189)

The first part of the simile requires little commentary. The schoolboy and his classmates "who have got up before him" are respectively the "masters" and the two vindictive ladies whose morning meeting took place, according to the opening sentence of the chapter, "earlier than the set time for visits in the town of N." (178), while the "hussar" is plainly Chichikov—or, more precisely, the "counterfeit" Chichikov created by the ladies—whose reaction to the governor's daughter in chapter eight, it will be recalled, has already prompted the author to compare him to a hussar (169).[10] Moreover, given the ironic association of the "bird motif" with Sof'ya Ivanovna in the opening paragraph, we may perhaps recognize in the "thousands of bird voices" an allusion to the rumors that the ladies are vigorously spreading. The remaining details, however, are much more difficult to interpret. It might, of course, be argued that any attempt to interpret in this case reflects an entirely wrong approach, that there is, in fact, nothing to interpret, for the simple reason that Gogol is merely giving rein to his imagination. No doubt some readers would also respond with this argument to some of the other interpretations that have been offered in this study. Yet enough evidence has surely been presented to confirm that the imagination of Gogol is rarely left unattended by his intellect and that the details in the latter part of this simile, if indeed they do comprise nothing more than a lyrical flight of fantasy, would be virtually unique in the novel. Certainly the weight of evidence is against such a conclusion.

Nevertheless, it must be conceded that the allusions here, if they exist at all, are among the most elusive in the entire work. Perhaps a clue is offered, however, by the two sentences following the simile, in which the effect of the ladies' announcements on the "masters" is described more literally:

Each one of them stopped like a ram with his eyes popping out of his head [*vypuchiv glaza*]. Dead souls, the governor's daughter, and Chichikov were all mixed up and confused in their heads in an unusually strange way, and it was only later [*i potom uzhe*], after the initial stupefaction, that they seemingly began to distinguish [*razlichat'*] and separate them from one another. (189)

The repetitions here of words and phrases used in the simile have been noted by Proffer simply as additional reflections of the manner in which Gogol links his details together,[11] but it hardly needs to be restated that Gogol does not generally establish links of this kind without some deeper, more meaningful purpose. It is true that the repeated words are in themselves of little consequence, but this does not necessarily mean they have no important role to play. It would suggest that the purpose of the repetitions is to draw attention not so much to the words themselves as to the context in which they appear and, more particularly, to the connection between this context and the simile. In other words, the repetitions may conceivably function to signal that the key to the most "difficult" details in the simile is in the sentences wherein the repetitions occur. Since it was not Gogol's custom to assist the reader by directing his attention in this manner, his use of this exceptional procedure here may perhaps be regarded as a tacit acknowledgment of how difficult a task he had set the reader.

If this interpretation is correct, it can point to only one conclusion—that the simile is essentially a figurative representation of the three contributors to the mystery, who are named explicitly in the sentences that follow it—Chichikov, the governor's daughter, and the "dead souls." And in considering this possibility we need to remember the general context in which the simile is set, for it seems natural that in a chapter replete with "aliases" or "forgeries" Gogol should utilize the device of the Homeric simile to add to their number. One example—the figurative representation of Chichikov and Sof'ya Ivanovna in the simile of the hunter—has already been cited, and it is noteworthy that these are the first Homeric similes Gogol has used since chapter six.

The first connection has already been established. That the "hussar" is an "alias" of Chichikov can hardly be doubted. But can we recognize in any of the other details an "alias" of Chichikov's "dead souls"? Appropriately enough, only one possibility suggests itself. Since, as stated, the "classmates" and the "birds" may be most plausibly interpreted as the "aliases" of the ladies, and since it is inconceivable that "dead souls" could be represented as "rushes," the choice inevitably falls on the image of the "naked boys" swimming in the river, for they are the only remaining plurality. Nor is the choice as implausible as it seems, for the dead serfs have already been associated with a river on two separate occasions. Questioning Chichikov, for example, in chapter seven about the lands on which he proposes to resettle them, the president of the court asks: "Is there a river or a pond?" (147), to which Chichikov replies in the affirmative; and the subject is raised again in the first few lines of chapter eight, which inform us that in the opinion of some of the "masters" "there is no river at all" (154). Both statements, of course, are logically motivated by the apparent concern of the speakers to establish whether the lands are fertile and capable of supporting such a large number of immigrants. Yet like so many logical statements in the novel, they have a distinct air of the illogical or incongruous about them. Why, we are moved to ask, should the "masters" be so concerned about this particular point? And why should Gogol raise the question twice? The absence in the text of any explicit answer to either question, and now the repeated mention of a river in the context of the simile, seem to justify the suspicion that perhaps all three references are to the same river and that its import is primarily symbolic. We may conclude, in fact, that the river is the "alias" of the third contributor to the "masters'" perplexity, the governor's daughter.

Again the possibility is not so remote as it might seem, for it is significant that Gogol stresses in his description of the river a feature similarly emphasized in the portrait of the governor's daughter in chapter five—radiance. The "oblique rays of the sun" by which the river with its "shining eddies" is "brightly lit" recall the "rays of the radiant sun" that pierce and suffuse the "fresh, new-laid egg" to which the girl's face is compared. Moreover, it is possible that even in chapter five a parallel is drawn between the governor's daughter and the image of water by means of the simile in which Uncle Mityay is compared to "a crane with which water is drawn from wells." Since his symbolic function, as we have observed, is to "draw" the soul, in the form of the terrified girl, from the territory of his master, it could well be that the simile is a figurative restatement of this role. And there is an obvious logical basis for this connection. As the Biblical emblem of purification, water is clearly an apt symbol for the pure human soul.

The conclusion, therefore, of this unavoidably lengthy analysis is that there is at least some evidence to contend that the second half of the Homeric simile is a symbolic picture of the living souls of Gogol's dead purchases bathing in the light of spiritual purity which emanates from the governor's daughter. It might be argued that having presented us with a graphic portrait of the dead souls of the living, Gogol now interposes a counterbalancing portrait of the living souls of the dead, thereby introducing yet another ironic contradiction between language and content. And finally, we might consider the possible relevance of this interpretation to the contrast between Chichikov's insistence that his lands are crossed by a river and the "masters' " denial of its existence, for it may conceivably allude to the contrast between the "counterfeit master," who has demonstrated by his reaction to the governor's daughter in chapter eight an unconscious susceptibility to the lure of the purifying spiritual light symbolized by the river, and the genuine "masters," who remain throughout immersed in the darkness of ignorance and incomprehension. Perhaps here is another reason for juxtaposing the hero in the simile with both the novel's main symbol of light and the living souls of the "slaves," with whose status his own, as we have noted, has much in common.

It should not be thought, however, that the two Homeric similes are the only examples in the chapter of extended figurative "forgeries," for toward the end Gogol introduces two episodes described in such profuse and bizarre detail that one again suspects their connection with their context is more complex than appearances suggest. The episodes concerned are the conflict between the merchants of Sol'vychegodsk and Ust'sysol'sk[12] and the murder of the assessor Drobyazhkin, the inclusion of which is ostensibly motivated by the fearful suspicion of the "masters" that the victims of the two incidents might be the true referents of the mysterious term "dead souls." It is important to note, however, that the main subject of the paragraph in which they are recounted is the sharp disagreement between the "masters" and the ladies caused by their differing interpretations of Chichikov's reasons for visiting the town. While the ladies are convinced that his real objective is the abduction of the governor's daughter, the "masters" stoutly contend that the "dead souls" hold the key to the mystery. The paragraph begins:

> But however much the men armed themselves and resisted, their party was totally lacking in the kind of order which prevailed in the female party. Everything with them was somehow crude, uncouth, discordant, inept, disorderly, muddle-headed, commotion, confusion, untidy thinking—in short, everything reflected the empty masculine nature, a coarse, ponderous nature incapable of domestic management or heartfelt convictions, lacking in faith, indolent, full of incessant doubts, and everlasting fear. (192)

Devoid of "heartfelt convictions" (*serdechnyye ubezhdeniya*), therefore, the "masters" have solely the weapon of crudity with which to oppose the greater determination and cohesion born of the "inner convictions" of the ladies.

Let us consider the first of the two incidents against this background:

The first incident involved some Sol'vychegodsk merchants who had come to the town for the fair and after the
trading had put on a feast for their friends, the Ust'sysol'sk
merchants, a feast in the true Russian style with German
embellishments: orgeats, punches, balsams, etc. The party
ended, as is the custom, in a fight. The Sol'vychegodsk
merchants exhausted and killed the merchants of
Ust'sysol'sk, but sustained in their turn severe abrasions
to the ribs, the solar plexus, and the stomach, which testifies to the inordinate size of the fists with which the
deceased were endowed. One of the victorious merchants
even had his "snout," as the combatants termed it, chop-
ped right off, that is to say, his nose was so completely
smashed that there was even less than half-a-finger
breadth of it left on his face. At their trial the merchants
confessed their guilt and acknowledged that they had
misbehaved a little; it was rumored that each of them
added a four-thousand-rouble note to his plea of guilty.
But the case was rather obscure. From the inquiries and
investigations that were carried out, it appeared that the
Ust'sysol'sk lads had died from charcoal fumes, and it was
therefore as victims of charcoal fumes that they were
buried. (193–194)

The suspicion that the merchants of Sol'vychegodsk and
Ust'sysol'sk are respectively "aliases" of the triumphant ladies
and the outgunned "masters" is prompted not only by the
positioning of the passage. In the image of the feast, for
example—a feast "in the true Russian style" which, like the
ladies themselves, is adorned with foreign "embellishments"—we may recognize perhaps an allusion to the rich
feast of rumors with which the ladies enticed "all those who
could not be enticed from their homes even by a pressing
invitation to devour a fish soup costing five-hundred roubles
with five-foot-long sturgeons and all kinds of meat pies which
melt in the mouth." Likewise the "inordinate size of the fists"
of the defeated merchants suggests the "masters' " alleged

"crudity." Yet clearly the "crudity," i.e. the "masculine" attributes, of their conquerors is even more awesome and may
consequently be linked with the more pronounced "masculinity" of the ladies to which their portrait in chapter eight so
unequivocally testifies. Significant in this connection is not
only the disclosure in an early draft of the passage that the
merchants of Sol'vychegodsk were impelled to launch their
assault by a "heartfelt pleasure" (*udovol'stviye serdechnoye*)
(823), which can only allude to the "heartfelt convictions" that
are the ladies' most formidable weapon, but also the intrigu-
ingly detailed description by Sof'ya Ivanovna earlier in the
chapter of the new type of dress and underbodice the ladies, she
claims, have taken to wearing:

> It is made with two seams: wide armholes and above
> . . . But it's this that will amaze you and make you say
> that . . . Well, just wonder at it: just imagine, under-
> bodices have become even longer, coming to a point in
> front, and the front bone sticks out more than ever. (181)

The interesting point is the connection that seems to exist
between these curious distortions (or "forgeries") of the
human figure and the injuries sustained by the victorious merchants. Thus just as the abrasions to the ribs may be attributed
to the lack of protection afforded by the wide armholes, so the
"swelling" of the underbodices in front may conceivably allude to the blows' effects on the solar plexus and stomach. And
again we should not ignore the information forthcoming from
the early drafts, which suggest unexpectedly that the longer
underbodices were intended as a further indicator of the ladies'
more potent "masculinity." In one of the drafts, for example,
Sof'ya Ivanovna describes them as follows: "Just imagine,
underbodices are now cut just like those of men and even
longer," while another version reads: "Just imagine, underbodices are now almost longer than men's and come to a point"
(812). The implication of the latter detail (repeated in the final
version) seems unmistakable, particularly when we consider a
reference in the account of the battle between the merchants.

There the nose of one unfortunate victor was apparently reduced to less than half the thickness of the rouge which, according to Anna Grigor'yevna, encrusts the governor's daughter's face. And finally, there is the distinct possibility that the charcoal fumes, the officially determined cause of death, allude to the ladies' tobacco fumes by which the "masters" are rudely awakened from their sleep.

There are clearly some grounds, therefore, for believing that the description of the fight between the two groups of merchants is not only inserted as another pretext for exposing the "masters' " gross maladministration of the town and that its function is directly comparable to that of the two Homeric similes. Revealing once more the vital importance of considering the interrelationships of all the details that fill a given chapter of the novel, it seems to be an extended metaphor or "alias" in which the preceding literal account of the dispute between the "masters" and the ladies is translated into the symbolic language of the overarching allegory. And precisely the same kind of figurative (or "counterfeiting") role seems to be performed by the second of the two incidents, though here, it seems, the reference is not to the mutual hostility of the two sexual groups but to their common hostility to the hero:

> The other incident had happened only recently and was as follows: the crown peasants of the village of Lousy-Swank, having joined forces with the crown peasants of the village of Hogsham, alias Bullyton, were alleged to have swept from the face of the earth the district police in the person of an assessor, a certain Drobyazhkin; it was also alleged that the district police, that is, the assessor Drobyazhkin, had taken to visiting their village too frequently, which in some cases is as bad as an epidemic, and the alleged reason was that the district police, having certain weaknesses of a romantic nature, was paying too much attention to the women and girls of the village. Whether or not this was true, however, is not known, though in their testimony the peasants stated quite frankly

that the district police was as lecherous as a cat and that
they had warned him more than once and on one occasion
had even driven him stark naked out of a cottage which he
had just entered. (194)

The most striking feature of the passage is its number of
apparent allusions to Chichikov's meeting with Korobochka—both to the narrator's description of the meeting in
chapter three and, perhaps, to Korobochka's own description
as recounted by Sof'ya Ivanovna. Their combined effect
suggests that the purpose of the passage, like that of the knight
depicted on Anna Grigor'yevna's cushion, is to represent
metaphorically as accomplished fact the vengeance planned
against the hero by the "Korobochkan" ladies and their reani-
mated male accomplices for his improper attentions to the
governor's daughter. It will be recalled, for example, that
Chichikov finally prevails over Korobochka's obstinacy in
chapter three by posing as an assessor—we are reminded of this
by Korobochka's disclosures to the "masters" toward the end
of chapter nine (195)—and also that the term "assessor" in that
context alludes to an aspect of the hero's split personality, viz.
the "Petrushkan" aspect.[13] Considered from this angle, therefore, the name "Drobyazhkin" seems a wholly fitting "alias"
for Chichikov, for it is derived from the verb *drobit'*, which
means "to split up." Moreover, it will also be recalled that the
term "hog" (*borov*) in the same context alludes to Chichikov's
affinity with the "emasculated" Ivan Petrovich. Thus just as
the name "Lousy-Swank" (*Vshivaya-spes'*) may plausibly be
interpreted as an allusion to the airs and graces of the "refined"
ladies, whose "alias" duly appears first, so the "crown peasants" of the village of "Hogsham" (*Borovka*) are conceivably
the "alias" of their "emasculated" spouses, and it is possible
that the term "crown peasants" (*kazyonnyye krest'yane*) is
meant to reaffirm the point, for, like the "masters," such
peasants were employees of the state. Finally, it may be noted
in relation to the last sentence of the passage that Sof'ya
Ivanovna's account of Korobochka's narrative prompts Anna

Grigor'yevna to assume that Chichikov visited the latter's estate for romantic reasons (183), and also that chapter three is the only one wherein Chichikov appears naked.

While the account of the first incident, therefore, possibly alludes to the triumph of the ladies over the "masters," the description of the second seems to refer to their joint triumph (in which the ladies, of course, play the leading role) over the unfortunate hero, who is ultimately "swept from the face" of the town. Having "killed" the souls of their own menfolk, the ladies are duly impelled by the same "Korobochkan" urge to "kill" their recently acclaimed visitor's soul, which at the ball, in the presence of the governor's daughter, had displayed such disconcerting signs of "life." Clearly neither interpretation is beyond dispute, and it is plainly fitting that the accounts of both incidents should contain the statement: "But the case was rather obscure." Nevertheless, the obvious logical connections between the two episodes and their context that the interpretations suggest, and more generally the particular character of the context in which they appear, add considerably to the plausibility of these readings. Indeed, the context all but impels the reader to look for ulterior meanings, for the reality beneath the "aliases," and the search does not seem futile. As metaphorical commentaries on the events, the two episodes may be regarded as two of the most elaborate "forgeries" of fact that Gogol contrives in this highly distinctive chapter. The "forgeries" of the two ladies mark the chapter's beginning; the "forgeries" of the landowners, to whom the "masters" turn vainly for information about the hero, mark its end.[14] And between these terminal points, as we have seen, the impulse to "forge," characteristically mimicked throughout by the narrator, continues unabated, expressing itself in the Homeric similes and the two interpolated episodes merely in its most extravagant and challenging forms.

9

The "Paternal" Theme

Having alerted the town to the danger the hero represents, the ladies now withdraw, leaving their alarmed menfolk to reflect further on the precise nature of the danger. Their deliberations form the main content of chapter ten, giving birth to the conjectures that Chichikov is an official of the governor-general's office, a forger, Captain Kopeykin, Napoleon, and even Antichrist. Characteristically, however, the chapter's central theme is revealed less explicitly. Once more Gogol introduces it in the opening sentence, in the part that echoes the final sentence of chapter nine. The latter sentence informs us that to establish Chichikov's true identity "it was proposed" by the "masters" "to hold a special meeting at the house of the chief of police, the father and benefactor of the town who is already well known to the reader" (196). In the opening sentence of chapter ten the appositional clause is repeated verbatim: "When they gathered at the house of the chief of police, the father and benefactor of the town who is already well known to the reader, the officials . . ." (197). The repetition cannot be simply passed off as crude stitching. Like all Gogol's repetitions, it is meaningful. It highlights the fundamental symbolic theme of the entire chapter—the theme of "fathers," a term used here not only in the sense of natural or biological fathers, but also with the extended meaning of protectors, benefactors, advisers, or comforters. More precisely, Gogol is chiefly concerned in this chapter with the portrayal and exposure of "false fathers," "fathers" who are found wanting and whose allegiance is solely to the ultimate "false father," the devil. Such are the "paternal" chief of police, the prophet, the Tsar and his minister in "The Story of Captain Kopeykin," and Nozdryov, to whom the despairing "masters" are finally impelled to turn in their futile search for enlightenment. Opposed to them is solely the ultimate "true father," God, who has only one "earthly" representative in the person of the unfortunate Kopeykin. Examined from this standpoint, the interpolated "story," which is the novel's longest "digression", appears as an integral part of the chapter.

A feature of the novel as yet not discussed is the remarkable abundance of statements, usually voiced by the author himself, that include variations of the words "God knows," "the devil knows," "the devil take it." Examples can be found in every chapter, but two from chapter one will suffice:

> ... who makes them for bachelors I truly cannot say—God only knows—I have never worn such scarves myself. (10)

> ... they did not wear their hair either in quiffs or in curls or in "the devil take me" manner, as the French say. (15)

So numerous, in fact, are statements of this kind that in retrospect God and the devil may almost be considered two of the principal characters. They alone seem to attend, in the inconspicuous forms Gogol devises for them, each stage of Chichikov's adventures, leading us to conclude that there is much more to these repeated statements than individual instances suggest. By keeping perpetually before our gaze the two rivals for possession of the ambivalent hero's soul, Gogol subtly reminds us that this soul's fate is the main subject of the fiction.

What distinguishes chapter ten in this respect is that it contains considerably more statements of this type than any other chapter. There are eleven references to God and twelve to the devil (to which we may add the two references to Antichrist). This increase in their number can only be attributed to their connection with the chapter's fundamental theme, and as if to confirm this point, the first reference to the only "true father" occurs in the chapter's second sentence, i.e. immediately after the reference in the opening sentence to the "false father," the chief of police: "Indeed, the appointment of a new governor-general, and these papers of such a serious nature which had been received, and these *God only knows*[1] what rumors—all these things left visible marks on their faces . . ." (197). Thus the first two sentences introduce the basic contrast of the chapter and disclose obliquely its moral implications. The implicit contrast between the chief of police and God alludes to the link between the chapter's "false fathers" and the devil. Indirectly, it identifies them with the "father" of dead souls and thus explains both their inability to offer genuine comfort and their "unfatherly" insensitivity to the lot of their "children." Like the suspicion that Chichikov may be a forger, the belief that he may be Antichrist is most informative about those who express it.

The whole of the chapter's first part, i.e. that which precedes "The Story of Captain Kopeykin," is another illuminating example of the typically "devious" way Gogol develops his symbolic themes. Particularly noteworthy are the replies of the "masters" to the postmaster, who alone seems to be totally unaffected by their "troubles and worries." Significantly, among the factors to which they ascribe his continuing peace of mind are his undemanding paternal responsibilities. "You, of course, have nothing to worry about," they say to him, "for you've got only one son, while God has endowed my Praskov'ya Fyodorovna with such fertility that every year she presents me with a Praskushka or a Petrusha" (198). In this elusive manner the transition is effected from the idea of the individual father of the body to that of the universal father of the soul. Still more significant, however, is that this sentence is between sentences dominated by the universal father of dead souls. It is preceded by the statement: "But what if the devil were to make a habit of turning up at your elbow every day, so that even though you don't want to take anything, he keeps thrusting it at you?" (197–198). The sentence following reads: "This is what the officials said, but whether or not it is really possible to resist the devil is not a matter for the author to judge" (198). Thus God is implicitly contrasted on this occasion not with the "father and benefactor of the town" but with the "father" of the "father and benefactor of the town," and the sequence of the statements seems itself to confirm that the devil is in control.

After quoting these extracts from the "masters' " deliberations, the narrator is prompted by the futility of their meeting to deliver a few general remarks on the tendency of all such gatherings in Russia—representative assemblies, learned committees, charitable, philanthropic, and "goodness only knows what other societies"—to produce confusion and nonsense, "unless they have a single person at their head who can control everything" (198). As usual, the digressive appearance masks a point of fundamental relevance. The "council" of the "masters" does have a single controlling figure at its head—the "father and benefactor" who in chapter seven is credited with the powers of a "miracle-worker." Similarly the commission to which Captain Kopeykin addresses his appeal has a single powerful figure at its head—the ministerial representative of the national "father." Yet the result in the first case is chaos, and in the second gross insensitivity. Again the explanation is provided obliquely. Stressing the vital importance for the "masters" of reaching some firm decision, the narrator comments: ". . . and so willy-nilly there should have been more unanimity and unity here, but for all that *the devil only knows what* emerged" (198). It is thus implied that in the person of the town's "false father" the universal "false father" is actually in charge of the proceedings. And in a similar manner Gogol indicates his control over the "father" of the "charitable" commission. Having, in effect, rejected Kopeykin's plea and thereby provoked a "rather rude" riposte, the minister reflects with some annoyance that while important affairs of state urgently demand his attention, "here *some importunate devil* was pestering him" (204). Superficially, of course, the word "devil" refers to Kopeykin; in reality, it alludes to the minister's prompter, explaining the "soul-destroying gaze" with which he rounds on the defiant supplicant. Kopeykin's true identity is revealed a few lines later in the postmaster's phrase "the servant of God" (204), in which capacity he is appropriately dumped in a cart and unceremoniously expelled from the devil's realm.

The character of this realm and of the philanthropy it dispenses is most eloquently conveyed by the "Sobakevichan" attributes of the porter at the minister's residence and of the courier charged with escorting Kopeykin to his distant abode. While the former, like his master, is endowed with the appearance of a "generalissimo" and a face resembling that of "a fat, overfed pug-dog" (201), the courier is portrayed as "a seven-foot giant of a man [*tryokharshinnyy muzhichina*] with huge hands fashioned by Nature herself for dealing with coachmen—in short, a veritable dentist" (204). Thus the two main character traits of the novel's principal misanthropist are combined once more—the selfish, tenacious, "canine" aspect of his personality and the physically daunting, "ursine" aspect. Like Sobakevich, the courier is a product of nature, and in chapter eleven he duly reappears to disclose his "paternity" while venting his wrath on the hapless Chichikov and Selifan: " 'I'll give you a taste of my sabre!' shouted a courier who was galloping towards them with moustaches more than two feet long [*s usami v arshin*]. 'Can't you see, a wood goblin flay your soul, that it's an official carriage?' " (221). Having already caricatured the paternalistic Russian Emperor in the figure of Sobakevich, Gogol now repeats the caricature, identifying the paternalism of the Tsar's representative—and, by association, the Tsar himself—with the whip of a mythical creation of the pagan Slavonic Fantasy, adding a few pages later: ". . . there are still many relics of paganism in the Slavonic nature" (229).[2]

The subjection of both Kopeykin and Chichikov to dispiriting encounters with the courier is merely one of the hints provided by Gogol that their "stories" are closely linked with one another. The other hints generally take the characteristic form of unobtrusive details. Preparing himself for his first meeting with the minister, Kopeykin, in the postmaster's words, "got up early and scraped his beard with his left hand, for to pay a barber would mean, in a certain sense, running up a bill" (200–201). Eleven pages later Chichikov likewise feels the need for a shave before visiting the "masters" after his three-day confinement with a cold: ". . . feeling his beard with his hand and glancing into the mirror, he exclaimed: 'Oh, what a forest!' " (211). The two heroes, therefore, prepare themselves in a similar manner for the same experience—the experience of rejection. Kopeykin is rejected both by his natural father (200) and by the national "father" (in the person of his representa-tive), while Chichikov is rejected by the "fathers" of the town, who either refuse to see him or lapse in his presence into acute embarrassment and incoherence. When Kopeykin presents himself at the minister's residence for the fourth time, "the porter," we read, "was loath even to look at him" (203). Similarly Chichikov, on presenting himself at the governor's residence, is disrespectfully informed by the porter that the doors are closed to him (212).

Perhaps an additional indicator of the link between the two heroes is Kopeykin's name, evidently derived from the name of a Volga brigand whose exploits had been recorded in a cycle of folk songs.[3] Although, however, the derivation seems beyond dispute, the reason for Gogol's choice has not been determined. The clue is perhaps found in chapter eleven—in the com-mandments dinned into the young Chichikov's ears by his authoritarian father: "Do not treat or entertain anyone, but rather conduct yourself in such a way that others will treat you and, above all, take care of and save your copecks [kopi kopeyku]" (225). It is this paternal advice which, in effect, converts Chichikov into a criminal, indirectly inspiring his dream of acquiring "copecks" by becoming, in the phrase used by the postmaster in chapter eight, "a kind of father" (156) to a brood of nonexistent peasants. Likewise Kopeykin, on address-ing himself to the authoritarian representative of the national

"father," is rewarded with similar precepts ("Try to help yourself . . ., look for some means yourself" [203]), which produces a similar effect: Kopeykin also becomes a criminal to
whom the postmaster ascribes a similar "paternal" role—that
of "ataman" (probably derived from the Turkic *ata,* "father")
of a band of brigands. Thus both heroes are sent forth armed by
their respective "fathers" with the "canine" philosophy associated with the devil. Both are enjoined to make "copecks"
their goal, and they both turn logically to crime.

But although these details and similarities indeed suggest
that Gogol was intent on establishing a certain parallel between
the "stories" of the two heroes, there are, too, fundamental
differences between them which inevitably lead us to believe
the parallel is yet another Gogolian mask. It seems that in the
revised version of "The Story of Captain Kopeykin" Gogol set
out to create a genuine parallel by making Kopeykin mainly
responsible, like Chichikov, for his own predicament,[4] but the
relation of the definitive version to the "story" of Chichikov is
certainly one of contrast, and this probably explains, in part, its
isolation in the text. Describing the misfortunes of a genuine
"servant of the devil" (Chichikov) in the realm of the devil,
Gogol contrasts with them the misfortunes of a "servant of
God" (Kopeykin), screening the contrast with a network of
similarities. While Chichikov is rejected by the devil's "servants" for employing the devil's methods, Kopeykin is rejected for invoking the "divine" principle of justice. Although
the crime of Chichikov is merely a logical extension of the
devil's precepts as voiced by his father and is motivated solely
by the aspiration to join the company of the devil's elect, the
crime of Kopeykin is an act of protest against the injustice that
is born of these precepts. In the pursuit of justice he converts
the devil's precepts, as voiced by the minister, into a weapon
against the devil's realm. Thus although the postmaster's conjecture that Chichikov may be Captain Kopeykin is not so
ludicrous as it might appear, it displays the superficiality that is
the hallmark of all the "masters' " reasoning, and we may

conclude that the contradiction between the parallel and the contrast was created for the specific purpose of exposing once more this fundamental deficiency.

In the context of Gogol's indictment of "false fathers," superficiality is now represented as the dominant characteristic of the devil's realm in its entirety—both of the town of N. (in the "story" of Chichikov) and of St. Petersburg (in the "story" of Captain Kopeykin). Hence the reappearance of the motif of "cleanliness," which hinges, as usual, on the contrasting relation of body to soul, implying that the "cleanliness" of the former is inversely proportionate to the "cleanliness" of the latter. The "servants" of the Unclean One are ironically obsessed with external cleanliness, and we might note again in this regard the shaving of Kopeykin and Chichikov before they embark on their visits; besides establishing a superficial link between the two heroes they also disclose the contrasting conditions of their souls. While a "scrape" with the left hand suffices for the captain, Chichikov's act of feeling his beard is a mere prelude to an elaborate ritual: "Without further delay he at once set about his toilet, opened his box, poured some hot water into a glass, took out his shaving brush and soap, and took up his shaving position" (211), and the ritual duly ends with a sprinkle of eau de Cologne.

The minister's dedication to cleansing of the body merely confirms that his links with Chichikov are considerably more significant than Kopeykin's. Indeed, Kopeykin is obliged to wait for some four hours while the ritual is performed. The postmaster explains: ". . . as you can imagine, he had arrived at a time when the general, so to speak, had barely risen from his bed and the valet had perhaps just brought him a silver basin for his various ablutions, you understand" (201). And while Kopeykin waits, his senses are bombarded by the additional evidence of the minister's fastidiousness, especially by the gleam of the doorknob which, in the postmaster's words, was "of such a kind that first you would have to dash into a grocer's shop, buy half-a-copeck's worth of soap and rub your hands with it for some two hours in advance, and only then could you bring yourself to take hold of it—in short, the polish on every-thing was such that, in a manner of speaking, it took your breath away" (201).

The residence of the minister, however, is simply a micro-cosm of the magnificent capital, which is described by the postmaster in terms that call to mind the opening section of Gogol's story *The Nevsky Prospect (Nevsky Prospekt)* (1835). Attempting to convey the effect on Kopeykin of this resplen-dent spectacle, he declares:

> Suddenly a whole world lies before him, so to speak, a certain arena of life, a fairytale Scheherazade. . . . The bridges, if you can imagine it, are hanging there *by some devilish power* [*etakim chertom*], that is to say, without touching anything—in a word, a Semiramis, my dear sir, and that's that! . . . Curtains, blinds, *every devilish thing* [*chertovstvo takoye*], you understand, carpets—a veritable Persia! (200)

As significant here as the oblique association of the city with the devil are the references to the Assyrian queen who con-quered Persia, and the resourceful Arabian queen who con-trived to subdue her husband for 1001 nights. The implication seems clear: St. Petersburg, like the town of N., is subject to female rule, and the juxtaposition of the two names with the two references to the devil was evidently intended as a com-ment on the nature of this rule.

It is equally significant, of course, that the postmaster in-vokes the names of two foreign queens, thereby reinforcing the allusion to the "rulers" of the town of N., whose addiction to foreign tastes and fashions is so evident in chapters eight and nine. The St. Petersburg that greets the hero of the postmaster's tale is an emphatically non-Russian city. Confident that a pen-sion will duly be awarded him, he treats himself to cutlets and chicken at the "London restaurant"; shortly afterward he notices "a slender Englishwoman" walking along the pave-ment "like a swan" (202); and "he'd be walking past some restaurant," the postmaster continues, "and the chef there, as you can imagine, would be a foreigner, a Frenchman with a friendly face, wearing fine Dutch linen [*gollandskoye bel'yo*][5] and an apron as white as snow,[6] and working away at some 'finez herbz' or other and cutlets with truffles—in short, some delectable delicacy that would give you such an appetite that you would feel like devouring yourself, so to speak" (203). Again the Gallic influence predominates; it should be noted in the references in the "story" to the absence of the Tsar and the Russian army in Paris and the "masters' " contention that Chichikov might be Napoleon in disguise. The implication is not only that the national "father" is insensitive to the needs of such deserving "children" as Kopeykin, but that he even prefers to spend his time at the source of the Gallic influence, which these "children" have helped to combat at the cost of severe mutilation. The main point, however, is that in his absence the Gallic "conquest" of St. Petersburg continues apace. The Tsar, in effect, has abandoned his capital to the enemy he has defeated, and Gogol is ironically alluding to this point when the narrator offers the following explanatory comment on the "masters' " conjectures about Napoleon: ". . . it must be remembered that all this took place soon after the glorious expulsion of the French" (206). "The Story of Captain Kopeykin" confirms that far from having been expelled, the French have taken control of the Russian capital, and we may now appreciate the ironic force of the narrator's later remark that "at that time" the journal *Syn otechestva (Son of the Fatherland)* was read "most avidly" (*nemiloserdo*) (206). Apprehensively the "masters" refer to a cartoon in the newspapers "in which a Russian is depicted talking to an Englishman. The Englishman stands there holding behind him a dog on a rope, and the dog is meant to be Napoleon. 'Take care,' he says, 'if things are not to my liking, I'll set this dog on you right now!' " (205). Again the postmaster's story reveals the irony, confirming that the Englishman's threat has already become reality. Not only has the French dog been released; as the London restaurant and the slender Englishwoman testify, the English have also participated in the conquest.

Though defeated, therefore, in military conflict, Napoleon—or, more precisely, French influence—has won a conclusive victory, and with the aid of the cartoon, Gogol indicates its moral overtones. The representation of Napoleon as a dog identifies the Gallicized life of the Russian capital with the "canine" attributes of the devil and thus explains the later announcement of the prophet that Napoleon is Antichrist (206). In the absence of the Russian national "father" and in the guise of the Gallic influence signified by the French national "father," the supreme "false father" has taken possession of the Russian national soul. Clearly the suspicion that Chichikov may himself be Napoleon or Antichrist implies that his soul has suffered a similar fate. With their Gallic veneer, their "cleanliness," and their strict adherence to "canine" principles, Chichikov[7] and St. Petersburg alike bear the brand of the devil's paternity.

The same brand is unmistakably inscribed on the brow of the last "false father" to be named in the chapter, Nozdryov—the landowner whose two children, according to chapter four, were "completely unnecessary to him" (70) and for whom a friendly or paternal gesture could only represent a tactic. Evidence of Nozdryov's susceptibility to two of the three symptoms of "diabolical" inspiration has already been presented by his weakness for Gallicisms and his "fatherly" devotion to his hounds. His susceptibility to the third—an obsession with "cleanliness"—is now appropriately represented as an offshoot of this devotion: "Porfiriy," we read, "had to clean the mastiff puppy's navel with a special brush and wash it with soap three times a day" (208). Moreover, it may be noted that the motif of "cleanliness" is similarly combined with the first reference in the chapter to "Nozdryovian gunpowder," which is met in the postmaster's preparations for recounting his tale, i.e. nine pages before Nozdryov appears in person:

> . . . he only half-opened his snuffbox, fearing that someone standing nearby might thrust into it fingers in whose cleanliness he had little confidence, and he even had the

habit of saying: "We know very well, old chap, that you
could have been poking your fingers in the most unlikely
places, and snuff is a thing that requires cleanliness." (199)

Perhaps the image of snuff (*tabak*) here is meant to herald the
fact that for the "masters" "The Story of Captain Kopeykin" is
indirectly to be a "Nozdryovian" slap in the face. However
that may be, there can be little dispute about the implications of
the motif fourteen pages later in the description of Nozdryov's
visit to Chichikov. The scene opens with a quintessential
"Nozdryovian" contradiction. Presenting himself as a friend
and counselor[8] and addressing Chichikov as "brother" (*brat*)
—a term which, like his claim in his statement to the "masters"
that he knew Chichikov's father, doubtless hints at the "Nozdryovian" element in Chichikov's personality—he immediately requests the services of Petrushka to fill his pipe, i.e.
to load his rifle.[9] He then relates a seemingly pointless tale
about some "false benefactress" who had quarreled with her
son and accordingly bequeathed all her property to her
nephew, which also presumably alludes to the falsity of his
own beneficent pose. Rather more significant, however, is the
self-revelation contained in his statement: "But, *the devil knows
me,* I'm quite incapable of being angry" (214)—a statement
echoed shortly afterward when he finishes telling how the
"masters" were affected by the "yarn" (literally "bullet"
[*pulyu*]) about Chichikov that he has "spun" (literally
"moulded" [*slil*]) for their benefit:[10] "*The devil only knows* how
mad they've gone from fear" (214). In the person, therefore, of
the mockingly solicitous, houndlike "hunter," the Unclean
One makes yet another appearance in the chapter, presenting
unequivocal evidence, in the form of Nozdryov's offer to assist
Chichikov in his abduction of the governor's daughter, of his
relentless pursuit of the "clean human soul.[11]

Unlike Chichikov, who is an involuntary recipient of
Nozdryov's "asistance," the "masters" actually request his
help, and it is noteworthy that the responsibility for soliciting
his aid is assumed by the "father and benefactor of the town,"

who appropriately uses as his messenger a policeman "with engagingly rosy cheeks" (207) like Nozdryov himself. Here the position of the "masters" in relation to the "hunter" is directly comparable to that of Kopeykin in relation to the minister. They seek from him the resolution of their fears, just as Kopeykin seeks from the minister the resolution of his financial problems. Indirectly compared on three occasions to children (209–210), they also turn for help to a "servant of the devil," and the result is predictably the same. The difference, of course, is that the "masters," like the "benefactor" to whom they appeal, are themselves in the devil's service. Their souls are similarly dead. They likewise exist in body alone and are remembered solely for their physical idiosyncrasies, like the public prosecutor with his thick, black eyebrows and winking left eye, or for their physical adornments, like the official Semyon Ivanovich mentioned in the opening paragraph of the chapter whose sole claim to attention is the ring on his first finger (197). It is entirely fitting, therefore, that their response to the crisis now confronting them should be expressed physically: "Everything collapsed," we read. "The president had grown thinner, the inspector of the public health authority had grown thinner, and the public prosecutor had grown thinner" (197).[12] And in the end the poor prosecutor simply expires, thereby prompting the thought that he must have had a soul after all, "though because of his modesty he had never shown it" (210).

Commenting on the "masters' " appeal to Nozdryov, the narrator observes:

> . . . they knew very well that Nozdryov was a liar, that it was impossible to believe a single word he said, even if it concerned the most unimportant matter, and yet it was precisely to him that they turned. What can you do with man? *He doesn't believe in God,* but he believes that if the bridge of his nose itches he will die without fail. (207)

These words mark the first of a series of generalizations about "man" or "humanity" in the latter half of the chapter, which

seem to pave the way for the more famous "lyrical digressions" in chapter eleven, and it is generally considered that they
reflect in a particularly vivid form the more overt moral or
didactic emphasis which allegedly characterizes the concluding
sections of the novel. Yet although this view seems entirely
reasonable, it should not be thought that these passages are less
closely related to their contexts than are the narrator's personal
statements in the preceding chapters. The tendency to consider
them in isolation has not only obscured the fact that, as in the
passage quoted above, the terms "man" and "humanity" usually refer to a quite specific character or group of characters; it
has also precluded a proper appreciation of their often concealed irony.

The following statement will suffice to illustrate the point:

> What tortuous, remote, narrow, impassable, and indirect
> paths humanity has chosen in its striving to attain to
> eternal truth, while before it the straight road lay open,
> like the road leading to a magnificent mansion destined to
> become a palace for the Tsar. (210)

Our response to the statement, of course, is wholly dictated by
the simile and, in particular, by the final word. The few references to the Tsar before chapter ten have a single function—to
highlight some particular feature of a character—and two
examples have been quoted: the reference to him in the description of Manilov's daydreams at the end of chapter two (39), and
Sobakevich's declaration in chapter seven that his coach-
builder Mikheyev is worthy of being in the Tsar's employ
(147). But in "The Story of Captain Kopeykin" the Tsar,
though absent in Paris, suddenly acquires an independent identity as an object of implicit censure. It is scarcely conceivable,
therefore, that Gogol would have used the term *Tsar* again only
five pages after the conclusion of the "story," and in the context of the same chapter, if the "negative" associations of the
term established in the "story" were not to be implied. The
early drafts are again informative here, for in one of them the
road to which the "straight road" is compared leads to a

"magnificent Tsar's palace," which is described as "a mansion of shining cleanliness" (833). The recurrence of the familiar motif would seem to confirm that the road which leads humanity to "eternal truth" is simply an ironic allusion to the road which leads Kopeykin to the minister's resplendent office. We may perhaps conclude that, having for obvious reasons avoided direct censure of the Tsar even in the original, definitive version of the postmaster's story, and having substituted the minister as the butt of the indictment, Gogol was now intent on using the simile to identify the Tsar with his representative. The "eternal truth," in other words, at the end of the "straight road" that lies before "humanity" is the "truth" apprehended by Kopeykin—the "truth" of the devil as proclaimed by the minister on behalf of the "father" of the Russian nation.

10

Chichikov and Russia

By the end of chapter ten the mystery of Chichikov's personality has been largely dispelled. Most of the essential information about him has already been imparted, and the condition of his soul has been thoroughly illuminated from a variety of angles and by a variety of methods. The ease with which he affects the attitudes, manners, and speech modes of the diverse "dead souls" who cross his path, his relations with his servants, the symbolic motifs that pervade his portrait, his reactions to the governor's daughter, the development of the "paternal" theme—all combine to project the image of a soul corrupt but not beyond redemption. Why, then, we may ask, is the final chapter chiefly devoted to a biography of the hero, from which we learn nothing that prompts us to change our judgment? The definitive term *priobretatel'* ("acquirer," "moneymaker") that Gogol applies to him in this chapter (242) merely confirms what has been apparent almost from the outset—that the single goal of his endeavor is to acquire the wealth and property which will elevate him to the status of "master." Is it really important for us to know that since childhood his commitment to this goal has been unwavering, that his methods have been consistently ruthless and usually fraudulent, and that his efforts, like those described in the novel, have invariably ended in failure?

Perhaps the most obvious reason why the answer must be affirmative is that the evidence the biography presents of Chichikov's seemingly inexhaustible capacity for surmounting obstacles and recovering from disappointments illustrates far more vividly than the foregoing narrative the presence in his character of certain qualities—resilience, patience, determination, inner strength—which seem in some measure to have portended for the author his eventual moral rebirth. But this is only one of the biography's four distinct functions, which are all of considerable importance. It is far more than simply a culminating "prop"[1] for the character of Chichikov.

Particularly important is its hitherto unnoticed structural role, the means with which it provides Gogol of tying together the most prominent strands of the novel. Incorporating all the symbolic motifs that signal the corruption of the soul in chapters one through ten, it forms a concluding "knot" which corresponds directly to the opening "knot" of chapter one. Clearly, however, it is not coincidental that Gogol chooses the biography of his hero for this purpose. We may assume that the structural scheme was not dictated by aesthetic considerations alone, and that it was also designed to tell us something about Chichikov. More specifically, by implicitly suggesting that Chichikov and the town are essentially one and the same,[2] it seems to confirm the truth that has become progressively more apparent in the course of the novel's development—that with the exception of the governor's daughter, who has spent most of her sixteen years away from the town, every character in the work is really a splintered facet of the hero's personality. And if we may interpret the town and its rural environs as a microcosm of Russia in all its "indigenous" and "nonindigenous" aspects, then Chichikov may accordingly be viewed as Gogol's judgment incarnate on the Russian nation. Hence the question that the narrator addresses to the Russian public: "Which of you, full of Christian humility, not publicly but in peaceful solitude, in moments of solitary discourse with himself, will look into his own soul and ask himself this painful question: 'Is there not some part of Chichikov in me also?' " (245).

The final aspect of the biography that needs to be emphasized is its obvious relevance to the "paternal" theme—to the theme which expresses most clearly the moral implications

of the allegory. Not only does the battle of God and the devil
for the hero's soul continue to be signified in the customary
indirect manner, but as an account of the progressive mortification of his soul the biography also records the "fathering" of
the perverted soul of Russia. And in order to stress this particular aspect of the biography and insure that his public would
recognize its relevance to themselves, Gogol appends to it an
explanatory parable—the parable of Kifa Mokiyevich and
Mokiy Kifovich.

The figure of Mokiy Kifovich, as the Greek Christian name
suggests, is a culminating embodiment of the "indigenous"
Russian attributes that are primarily associated with
Sobakevich. As in the portrait of Sobakevich, the term *bogatyr'*
is again employed to convey the "ursine" qualities of physical
might, crudity, and violence (244)—the qualities so vividly
demonstrated in the early part of the chapter by the ferocious
courier—while the lament "the town . . . will call him a cur
[*sobakoy*]" (244) highlights the complementary "canine" streak
in his nature. The difference is that the attributes of Mokiy
Kifovich, like those of Chichikov, are explained. They are
explained by the accompanying portrait of his contrasting
father, just as those of Themistoclus and Alcides are explained
by the portrait of the contrasting Manilov. Like Manilov, Kifa
Mokiyevich, who is significantly introduced as "the father of a
family" (243), is given to "solitary meditation," and his intellectual preoccupations, while markedly different, reflect a similar unfamiliarity with the notion of a soul. He ponders:

> Take, for example, a wild animal [*zver'*]. . . . A wild ani-
> mal is born naked. Why naked? Why isn't he born like a
> bird? Why isn't he hatched from an egg? Goodness me,
> truly—er—you can't understand nature, however deep
> you may go into it! (244)

The irony, of course, is that Kifa Mokiyevich, as an unrepen-
tant materialist, seeks from nature the answer to questions
which relate metaphorically to the existence of the soul. The
name "Kifa" is derived from the Aramaic *kēfā*, "rock," and

doubtless alludes to the soul of its bearer. It implies petrifica-
tion, impenetrability, ignorance of the truth disclosed by the
symbolic portrait of the governor's daughter that man *is* "born
like a bird," that he *is* "hatched from an egg," and that the shell
of the living soul is not rocklike but fragile and translucent.
Man is conceivable to Kifa Mokiyevich only as a creation of
nature, i.e. in the form of a Sobakevich. Hence the concentra-
tion of his thought on the birth of a "wild animal"—a term that
denotes here the materialist's conception of man; in the person
of his son Mokiy, whose name is traceable to the Greek *mōkos*
("a scoffer"), this conception is ironically brought to life. The
offspring of the "rock" is an "elephant"—the elephant that
prompts him to speculate: ". . . if an elephant were born in an
egg, the shell would probably be extremely thick. You
wouldn't be able to pierce it with a cannon. Some new kind of
gun would have to be invented" (244–245). Such is the shell
that encases the soul of "indigenous" Russia, symbolized by
the philosopher's son, of this personified indictment of the
materialist who loudly proclaims:

> Because I am busy with philosophy and occasionally have
> no time, does this mean that I'm not a father? Not at all! I
> am a father—a father, the devil take them, a father! Mokiy
> Kifovich sits right here in my heart![3] (244)

The purpose of the parable, therefore, is directly comparable
to that of Chichikov's biography. Tracing the disease of the son
to the influence of the father, it pinpoints the source of Russia's
spiritual malaise. Significantly, however, the parallel goes
further than this, for the portrait of Mokiy Kifovich, like that of
Chichikov, is not entirely pessimistic. It endows him with
certain attributes which, like the indicated character traits of
Chichikov, may be regarded as signals of his possible salvation—above all, the attribute of youth. He is not simply young;
he is specifically twenty years of age—an age which, as we have
seen, has a particular resonance in the novel and invariably
"positive" connotations. It implies that the soul of the
"elephant," like that of the "bear," is not unalterably

foredoomed. Indeed, the narrator even refers to him as a "kind soul" (244), ascribing his violence more to ebullience and uncontrollable vitality than to malevolence. The implicit question is whether the soul can reassert its authority over this vitality and convert it into a power for good, and this same implicit question, expressed in different form—the question marking the culmination of the "paternal" theme—two pages later ends the novel.

Although, however, the question may be taken as an allusion to the optimistic denouement of the "epic," it must be stressed that in chapter eleven the optimism, if it exists at all, is extremely muted. Gogol may be pointing here toward the exit from the Inferno, but to the end the action is unequivocally played out in the realm of the wood goblin, the "elephant," and the "bear"—the "pagan" realm of the devil or nature. Although Chichikov abandons the town, which is the symbol of his vices, and returns to the hardships and uncertainties of the "road," the stimulus is rational necessity rather than instinctive inclination. Hence the opposition to the idea of the instinctive, irrational Selifan, whose hostility to the dictates of reason is translated at the end of chapter ten into the eloquent gesture of scratching his head (215)—a gesture that foreshadows the sharp conflict between reason and instinct which is dramatized in the opening pages of chapter eleven.

The nature of the conflict is indirectly disclosed by Chichikov's failure to wake up the next morning for the early departure, on which he had insisted after Nozdryov told him about the rumors circulating in the town. The error alludes both to the inactivity of reason during sleep and to his "instinctive" recalcitrance in the face of his reason's demands. Immediately afterward this recalcitrance assumes the animate form of Selifan, who is duly charged by Chichikov (for his failure to prepare the carriage) with planning to cut his throat "on the highway" (*na bol'shoy doroge*" (217), i.e. with seeking to inflict on him the fate that he unwittingly foresaw for himself in his daydreams in chapter seven. In response, Selifan refers in his defense to the necessity of tightening the symbolic crooked wheel, and also appropriately resumes his vendetta against his "rational" master's equine symbol, the dapple-gray. He declares:

> . . . as for the dapple-gray, if only we could sell him, for he's a proper villain [*podlets*], Pavel Ivanovich. . . . Really and truly, Pavel Ivanovich, he only looks impressive; in reality, he's a very cunning horse. You won't find another such horse anywhere. (217)

Particularly striking here is the term Selifan uses for "villain," for it is the one he himself has already been branded with a few lines earlier by Chichikov (216). The term is applied, in other words, to both the rational and the instinctive aspects of Chichikov's personality, and it is therefore fitting that Gogol, alluding once more to the tripartite equine symbol of his hero, should later begin his biography with the words: "And so let us harness the villain [*podletsa*]" (223).

The term "villain," however, also merits attention for another reason: it is yet another lexical emblem of Sobakevich. In this respect it resembles another word repeatedly applied to Chichikov in the course of his biography—the past tense of the verb "to swindle" (*nadul*). "Here again Sobakevich, the villain [*podlets*], has swindled [*nadul*] me!" exclaims Chichikov in chapter seven (137) on discovering in his lists the name "Yelizavet Vorobey," thus combining in a single reference to the "bear" the two lexical emblems that are now applied to himself. It is noteworthy that on calling Selifan "villain," he demonstrates again a penchant for "Sobakevichan strong words," and even the same "Sobakevichan" violence that is later displayed by the courier and Mokiy Kifovich. "I'll, I'll . . . bend you into a horn," he cries, "and tie you in a knot! . . . If everything is not ready in two hours' time, I'll give you such a hiding that you won't be able to see your head on your shoulders" (217).[4] The term *podlets,* therefore, may be seen as an additional allusion to the affinity between Chichikov and the novel's main symbol of "indigenous" Russia. Implicitly branding Russia as a country of "villains," the repetitions of the term further indicate the relationship between Chichikov and Russia that is the basis of the novel's last chapter. "Oh, you villain [*podlets*]!" thundered Chichikov in an earlier draft, addressing his "instinctive" self in the form of Selifan. "What monster brought such a fool as you into the world?" (837). The implied answer is: the "fatherland" of "villains," Russia.

The pairing of the term "villains" (*podletsy*) with Sobakevich's "strongest" word "rascals" (*moshenniki*) in Chichikov's tirade against the blacksmiths (217) (who duly capitalize on his anxiety to leave the town, just as he himself, we learn later, used to capitalize as a schoolboy on the hunger of his classmates [226]) brings to a temporary halt this expressive motif, which prepares the way for the hero's biography. The eventual rectification of the fault in the wheel enables Chichikov at last to effect his escape from the town—an escape that on one level is an evasion of the law and on another a momentary liberation from the power of his own corrupt instincts. Now the carriage, which "had been standing so long in the town" (218), can bear him on his way to the open "road," the symbol at once of hardship, freedom, and new possibilities, and "God only knew," the narrator comments as he passes the familiar urban sights, "whether he was ever fated to see them again in his life" (219). Three times in the chapter Gogol reminds us that it is the kind of carriage "in which bachelors ride" (218, 237, 241), and Chichikov's continuing attachment to the town is indicated both by the "indeterminate feeling" (219) with which he takes his leave and perhaps by the "bouncing and rocking" caused by the town's cobbled streets (219), which slow down his progress. But there can be little doubt that his cry "Glory to Thee, O Lord!" (218) as he emerges from the gates of the inn is meant to convey more than his sense of relief at eluding retribution. Denoting his temporary release from materialistic values, from the demands of the body,[5] from the realm that now receives its concluding emblem in the form of the soulless corpse of the public prosecutor, his departure from the town clearly represents something more to him than self-preservation. It is a prospect that he relishes, a prospect congenial to the same aspect of his personality that revealed itself in chapter seven in his envious reflections on the freedom of Abakum Fyrov.[6] His responsiveness to the "road," in short, offers further evidence that his capacity for rebirth is not exhausted. As the last traces of the town disappear from view, "he devoted his attention," we read, "to the road alone [*odnoy dorogoyu*] and kept looking only to the right and to the left, and it seemed as if the town of N. had been blotted from his memory, as if he had traveled through it a long time ago, in his childhood" (222). Thus while the "road" points to the future, the evil of the town is linked with the hero's past, and it is to this past that the author now turns in an attempt to identify both the sources of evil and the grounds for hope.

The biography begins with the narrator's acknowledgment that his hero will win few admirers. Particularly hostile, he suggests, will be the reaction of his female readers, whom he credits with a craving for perfection and an acute distaste for the slightest stain on body or soul. Indirectly, of course, Gogol is associating them with the "Korobochkan" ladies of his provincial town, and since the "Korobochkan" female's hostility to the male, as the ladies' attitude to Nozdryov attests, is directly proportionate to the degree of his "masculinity," their anticipated negative response to the ensuing narrative in effect foretells its character.[7] It is to be a record of the comprehensive "masculinization" of the hero's soul—a record that the narrator feels obliged to preface with a few explanatory comments.

Listing his reasons for rejecting the custom of choosing a "virtuous" hero, he remarks:

> . . . I have not taken a virtuous man for my hero, and I can even tell you why: because it is finally time to give the poor virtuous man a rest; because the words "virtuous man" fall idly from the lips; because the virtuous man has been transformed into a horse, and there isn't a writer who does not ride him, goading him on with a whip or with anything else that lies at hand; because the virtuous man

has been exhausted to such an extent that there isn't a trace
of virtue in him, and instead of a body there is only skin
and bone left; because appeals to the virtuous man are
hypocrisy; because the virtuous man is not respected. No,
it is finally time to harness even the villain [*podletsa*]. (223)

The main reason, in short, is simply that the "virtuous man" no
longer exists in Russia, that a character like Chichikov is the
only true mirror of the times. But it is essential to appreciate the
underlying contention that the "virtuous man" who did once
exist was also Chichikov—the Chichikov who was born, in the
words of the proverb the narrator quotes a few lines later,
"neither like his mother nor like his father, but like a fine,
handsome stranger" (224). The "virtuous man" has not been
replaced; he has been transformed—transformed into the "villainous" dapple-gray. The equine metaphor points forward
rather than backward—forward to the biography, to the combination of equine and ornithological symbols that conveys the
success of Chichikov's father in destroying the virtue of his
son while enjoining him to "carry virtue in his heart." The relevant passage significantly describes the journey that rewards
Chichikov with his first experience of a town:

> . . . one day, when the early spring sun was shining and
> the streams had burst their banks, the father took his son
> and set off in a small cart drawn by a bay skewbald nag of
> the kind known among horse-dealers as "magpies"; it was
> driven by a little hunchback, the father of the only serf
> family that belonged to Chichikov's father, who occupied
> almost every post of responsibility in the house. They
> trailed along with the "magpie" for just over a day and a
> half . . . and reached the town early on the morning of the
> third day. The streets of the town shone before the boy's
> eyes with unexpected splendor and made him gape for
> several minutes. Then the "magpie" together with the cart
> fell plop into a hole at the entrance to a narrow lane which
> ran steeply downhill and was a sea of mud; for a long time
> there the "magpie" strove might and main and worked

away with her legs, urged on by the hunchback and by the
master himself, and finally she dragged them into a small
yard standing on the slope. (224–225)

The passage portrays symbolically a crucial stage in the
hero's "transformation." In the image of the skewbald (i.e.
brown and white[8]) "magpie" we detect the precursor of the
dapple-gray, the emblem of the young Chichikov, whose soul
still merits comparison to a bird, but now only to a thieving
bird, an ornithological "villain." The image conveys the effects
not only of his father's precepts but, more generally, of his
prolonged exposure to the "pagan" influence of a household in
which "almost every post of responsibility" is allegedly oc-
cupied by a creature whose grotesque physical shape identifies
him with the wood goblin (leshiy) invoked by the courier. But
the time has now come for the "magpie" to be propelled into a
new stage of "villainy," to translate precept into practice in the
appropriate setting of the town. The struggles of the horse with
the glutinous mud express the difficulty of the transition for the
still inexperienced soul, but the whips of the hunchback and
"the master himself" finally break its resistance.

After Chichikov has crossed the urban boundary and begun
his formal schooling, the evidence of his "transformation" is
rapidly accumulated. Though academically undistinguished,
he soon makes his mark by a predictable concern for his physical appearance and a corresponding aptitude for affairs of a
practical, i.e. "nonspiritual," nature. In an evident caricature of
the parable of the talents the narrator describes his ingenious
methods of adding to the fifty copecks donated by his father—
including the skillful molding of a bullfinch in wax and the
assiduous training of an unfortunate mouse in a "little wooden
cage," both of which are sold at an impressive profit. The
allusions are self-evident. While the inanimate bullfinch, which
doubtless alludes to the fate of the "magpie," i.e. to the state of
its maker's soul, reminds us once more of the inanimate birds
on Korobochka's walls, the "wooden cage" again evokes the
image of the wooden pens in her garden, and as if to insure that

the point will not be missed, the narrator also informs us that when the boy had saved up five roubles, "he sewed them up in a little bag [*meshochek*] and then began to save in another" (226). These allusions to Korobochka provide an early glimpse of the biography's indicated summatory character, a preliminary insight into Gogol's intention of presenting in his hero's concluding portrait a complex synthesis of the diverse motifs that evoke the memory of the novel's principal "dead souls."

Given the numerous affinities between Korobochka and Sobakevich, it seems suitable that the allusions to the former should be followed in the same paragraph by allusions to the latter. The image of the "bear" is evoked repeatedly in the narrator's description of Chichikov's first schoolmaster, for whom, we learn, the faintest glimmer of individuality in his charges, even the twitching of an eyebrow, is a pretext for brutal reprisals. His substitution of "good conduct" for intellectual attainment as the only worthy ideal and his profound contempt for Krylov, who had the temerity to declare: "In my opinion, a drunkard who knows his business is better than a sober man who doesn't" (226), remind us at once of the similar regard for "good conduct" and sobriety reflected in Sobakevich's testimonials for his serfs; and a suspected allusion is confirmed when Chichikov's graduation and his invariable ability to keep his eyebrows as still as those of the dead public prosecutor are marked by the award of a similar testimonial inscribed with the familiar words: "For exemplary diligence and reliable conduct" (227). And if any doubts still remain, they are effectively banished by the master's words: "If I see a bad spirit or a mocking attitude in anyone, I'll give him naught even if he can outdo Solon!" (226). Although the name of the Athenian statesman is used ironically, i.e. to indicate nonphysical distinction, it reveals a familiarity with the Greeks from which only one conclusion can be drawn. Similarly we cannot mistake the implication of the schoolmaster's cry: "He has swindled me . . ." (228) when, having taken to drink on being expelled from the school, he receives generous assistance from all his former victims with the conspicuous exception of the one who most expertly curried his favor. The verb "swindled" (*nadul*) identifies the young Pavlusha as a fully qualified Sobakevich.

Despite his "commendable testimonials," he must accept for his first job the post of a menial clerk in the local courts of justice allegedly because "even in the most out-of-the-way places one needs patronage" (228), i.e. a corrupt "father." The job provides Gogol an opportunity to bring within the orbit of his hero's education the influence of the same kind of dispiriting environment as that which is entered by Chichikov and Manilov in chapter seven. Again the administrators of justice are comically pilloried with the aid of mythological imagery and the motif of "cleanliness" (228–229), and again the scene is darkened by the shadow of the "bear." Its source in this case is Chichikov's next "father," the head of the department in which he works, "who was a model," we read, "of stony insensitivity and callousness." The portrait continues:

> His callous, marblelike face, which was devoid of striking irregularities, displayed no hint of a resemblance to anything; his features were arranged in strict proportion to one another. Only the many pockmarks and holes with which they were riddled[9] placed his face in the category of those on which, according to the popular saying, the devil came at night to thresh peas. (230)

Thus in combination with the image of the supreme "false father" the imagery of "natural produce" is employed once more to denote the atrophy of a human soul—the image of "peas," which the bear Misha in chapter five is so adept at stealing. The face of the head clerk, it is clearly implied, mirrors his ravaged soul, and again the metaphorical *exposé* is complemented by a personified indictment in the form of the subject's female offspring—a girl with a face, we are told, "which also looked as if peas were threshed on it at night" (230). At the same time the references to his "quills" (*per'yev*— literally "feathers") and the traces of snuff (*tabak*) on his desk signal that in his personality "Korobochkan" and "Nozdryo-

vian" elements coexist with his fundamentally "Sobakevichan" characteristics. Yet significantly it is in the description
of Chichikov's actions here that "Nozdryovian" motifs tend to
be most prominent. The statement that in his search for a way
to get the better of the head clerk he "at last smelled out
[*pronyukhal*] his domestic, family life" (230) indicates that to his
other attributes Chichikov can now add the nose of a "hunter,"
and having "smelled out" the existence of the clerk's daughter,
"he took it into his head," we read, "to launch an assault
[*pristup*] precisely from that side" (230)—an image that recalls
Nozdryov's "assault" (*pristup*) on Chichikov's "impregnable
[*nepristupnuyu*] fortress" in the Homeric simile at the end of
chapter four (86–87). The "assault" is brilliantly executed. By
skillful courting he wins the clerk's approval as his dauther's
fiancé and secures with his prospective father-in-law's aid a
position of equal standing in the service, whereupon he instantly severs his ties with the family, leaving his "benefactor"
to reflect: "He has swindled me, swindled me [*nadul, nadul*], the
son of the devil!" (230). The curse implies that, as the son of this
"diabolical father" whom he had even affected to address as
"Papa," the hero has nothing further to learn.

After this notable success, Chichikov marches swiftly from
one triumph to another, even turning a government campaign
against bribery and corruption to his personal advantage.
Then, as one of the most active members of a commission
appointed to administer the construction of an important government building he receives his fair share of the proceeds from
the ensuing swindle.[10] Now at last the bonds of iron self-
discipline can be slightly loosened, and for the first time his
body feels the caress of "fine shirts of Dutch linen", eau de
Cologne, and "very expensive soap" (232). But the respite is
brief, for soon afterwards a new chief is appointed to eradicate
the corruption and—"God alone knows why," the narrator
remarks (232)—he conceives an instant dislike for Chichikov's
face. As a result, while the other officials are permitted to
persecute injustice "as a fisherman pursues some meaty sturgeon with a harpoon" (i.e. with Sobakevich's dedication in

pursuing the chief of police's "product of nature" in chapter seven) and perform their task "with such success that in a short time each one of them found himself in possession of several thousand roubles" (233), Chichikov is compelled to "arm himself with patience once more" and begin his career anew.

Once more, however, adversity is rapidly overcome. After several job changes he finally obtains a post in the department to which he had always secretly aspired, the Customs and Excise—a post that offers him unlimited access to his cherished "linen shirts" and to "a special kind of French soap that imparted an unusual whiteness to the skin and freshness to the cheeks" (234). Here his "Nozdryovian" "canine scent" (235) proves an invaluable asset, and within a very short time his superiors are referring to him approvingly as "a devil rather than a man" (235). Promotion follows quickly, and invested with his new authority he prepares to capitalize on the confidence his efforts have inspired. Aided by an accomplice, he concludes an arrangement with a group of smugglers that soon yields the anticipated rewards. But just when the fulfilment of his dreams seems assured, "some evil power [literally 'wild animal' (zver')]", we read, "intervened to ruin everything. The devil confused the two officials: to put it bluntly, they went mad[11] and quarreled for no reason" (236–237). Perhaps the reference here to the devil as a "wild animal" was intended to influence our response to the term zver' when it is later applied to Mokiy Kifovich, but the allusion is more probably, and ironically, to the very attributes of the hero and his accomplice that ensured their initial success—their "Nozdryovism" and the incapacity for harmonious relationships it implies.

The narrator's explanation of the quarrel is that it was instigated by use of the term "son of a priest" (popovich), which the conspirators allegedly hurled at one another during a heated exchange—a term to which, as "sons of the devil," they naturally reacted with acute distaste and which casts a revealing light, as we have seen, on the implications of Chichikov's daydream about Popov in chapter seven. Equally revealing,

however, is the second explanation, which the narrator attributes to rumor:

> . . . it is said that they had had a quarrel over some wench
> who was as fresh and firm as a juicy turnip [*yadryonaya
> repa*], to use the expression of the customs officials; that
> men had even been bribed to beat up our hero in a dark
> lane toward evening, but that she had made fools of the
> two officials and that in the end some Major Shamsharyov
> had taken his pleasure of her. (237)

Here the imagery clearly reaffirms the status of the hero and his
accomplice as "sons of the devil," for whom the human soul is
indistinguishable not from just any vegetable, but from the
same one Chichikov's own soul is aptly compared to by
Sobakevich in chapter five. At the same time the violence of the
quarrel, the detail of the "beating up," and the introduction of
the "military motif" in the form of the successful rival are
proof that the entire account of this episode in Chichikov's
career was conceived as a culminating revelation of his fully
matured "Nozdryovian" instincts. The narrator's postscript
merely confirms the point: "Let the reader who wishes to [or
alternatively 'the reader who is a hunter (*chitatel'-okhotnik*)')
give the tale his own ending" (237).

The result of the quarrel is that Chichikov is betrayed by his
accomplice and from a hunter is transformed into a quarry.
Prosecution is avoided with his customary skill, but only at the
cost of his newly acquired riches: ". . . he lost all his capital and
his various foreign articles; it turned out that there were others
who wanted them all [*na vsyo eto nashlis' drugiye okhotniki*]"
(237). Yet again, therefore, his efforts prove futile. But even
this disaster does not break his resolve. Gritting his teeth and
cursing his fate, he turns reluctantly to the profession of
solicitor—a profession, comments the narrator, "which has
not yet achieved general recognition among us" (239). The
implied disrespect of Russians for the law is duly demonstrated
by the hero himself, who loses little time in devising the
swindle that forms the novel's plot. "Crossing himself," we

read, "in the Russian fashion, he got down to the business of carrying it out" (240), and the biography ends with a description of his methodical preparations.

Although many significant allusions are inevitably omitted from this summary, it is sufficiently detailed to show that the biography is a cacophony of echoes. Masked as a digression, it is a compilation of the allegory's most expressive ingredients and, as such, it forms a fitting conclusion. The less obvious point, however, is that evidence of a similar function is also perceptible in the equally famous "digressions" that flank the biography, i.e. in the long passages of personal comment and celebrated apostrophes usually ascribed to the author himself. In reality, it is soon apparent that these apostrophes and observations, like all the other passages of personal comment in the novel, are expressed by his distanced narrator and accordingly are as much a part of the allegory as the latter's descriptions of scene and character. Here again familiar notes are struck repeatedly, disclosing the irony beneath the mask of candor.

Passing final judgment on the hero, the narrator observes:

> That he is not a hero filled with all kinds of perfection and virtue is evident. What is he then? A villain [*podlets*]? Why a villain? Why be so hard on others? These days we don't have villains; we have well-intentioned, agreeable people. (241)

This is not the first time the narrator makes claims here on the hero's behalf that are implicitly contradicted by his choice of words—not only by the term *podlets,* with which Chichikov has already been branded in both his human and equine forms, but also by the adjective "well-intentioned" (*blagonamerennyy*), one of the more conspicuous epithets applied to him by the "masters" in chapter nine (195), i.e. one of the epithets applied by "villains" to a fellow "villain." The statement "these days we don't have villains" is of the same order as the narrator's remark that precedes his description of Chichikov's involvement in the affairs of the building commission: ". . . these days there are no bribe-takers" (231). But it is also different in the sense that the negation is exposed as an ironic assertion not only by the events that follow, but also, as noted, by the already established associations of its lexical content. In this respect it may be compared with a number of statements in the narrator's first apostrophe to Russia, e.g.:

> You are a poor, straggling, and inhospitable land. No bold wonders of nature crowned with bold wonders of art will gladden or startle the eye—no cities with tall, many-windowed palaces built upon rocks, no picturesque trees, no expanses of ivy covering houses in the roar and ever-lasting spray of waterfalls; . . . no distant gleam will be visible through dark arches piled one on top of another and entangled in vines, ivy, and countless millions of wild roses, no distant gleam will be visible through them of everlasting lines of shining mountains rising into clear, silvery skies. (220)

Just as the label "villain" is removed from Chichikov after it has repeatedly been "stuck" on him, so Russia is now declared void of certain features she previously had. For Russia not only has "bold wonders of nature" in the form of Sobakevich and the sturgeon he consumes; she also displays the kind of harmony between nature and art that startled the eyes of the traveling hero when he surveyed the garden of Plyushkin—a garden over which "picturesque [kartinnyye] trees,"[12] ivy (plyushch), and tangled vines had assumed total control. Gogol is not compiling here, as Smirnova-Chikina asserts, a list of the regrettably non-Russian features of the Italian city in which he was writing;[13] through his narrator he is reminding us in his habitual ironic manner of his allegorical Russia's distinctive features—a "naturalized" Russia whose "wonders of nature" are testimony to the death of her soul. When he composed this part of the chapter, the imagery of chapter six was firmly lodged in Gogol's mind, additional evidence of which is supplied on the following page by the narrator's lyrical medita-tion on the significance of another familiar image—the word "road" (doroga)—in which "dark houses made of logs" are again contrasted with "white brick houses" in the description of a moonlit Russian landscape, which ends with the unambiguous words: ". . . not a soul anywhere—everything is asleep" (221).

However, the vein of irony that runs through the "lyrical digressions" is produced as much by the echoing of details within their own chapter-context as by the repetition of details that have acquired specific associations in the context of earlier chapters. The first apostrophe to Russia, for example, poses the question: "Is it not here that a *bogatyr'* will arise, where there is room for him to spread himself [*razvernut'sya*] and roam at will?" (221). Once more, of course, the noun *bogatyr'* evokes the image of the "bear," and surely Gogol would not have inserted it here without this association in mind. But the combination of the noun with the verb *razvernut'sya* suggests that in this case the allusion yet again points forward rather than backward—to the parallel figure of the "wild animal" Mokiy Kifovich, in whose portrait the combination recurs: "He was what is called in Russia a *bogatyr'*, and while his father was busy studying the birth of the wild animal, his twenty-year-old, broad-shouldered nature was bursting to spread itself [*razvernut'sya*]" (244). The question in the apostrophe, therefore, is another example of a statement in which the apparent meaning of the whole and the associations of individual words conflict with one another. It provides a vivid indication that even when appearing to express through his narrator his most cherished thoughts about Russia's potentialities, Gogol does not lose sight of the violent, soulless land that has "fathered" his characters, of the "inhospitable" (*nepriyutno*) land (220) in which life from the beginning "gazed in a sour, inhospitable manner [*kislo-nepriyutno*]" (224) on the young Chichikov, preparing him for "transformation."

Nor should we be deceived by the following questions that appear earlier in the same "digression": ". . . what incomprehensible, mysterious force draws me to you? Why do I hear incessantly ringing in my ears your melancholy song which is borne over your entire length and breadth from sea to sea?"

(220). At first it seems scarcely credible that the allusion here could be to Selifan, but on the evidence accumulated in this study we must assume it is not fortuitous that when the images of the sea and the song are used in this chapter on other occasions they are associated with the hero's willful servant. While the phrase "from sea to sea" directs our attention to the curious term of abuse "sea monster," which Chichikov hurls at Selifan in the opening scene (217), the image of the song anticipates the later appearance of Selifan as the driver of the speeding troika—the tripartite personality of the hero in its equine guise, which ultimately merges with the image of Russia:

> The driver is not wearing German jackboots; he has a beard and mittens, and the devil only knows what he's sitting on; but as soon as he half-rises, cracks his whip, and strikes up a song, the horses are away like a whirlwind. (247)

Not only is the "melancholy song" that of a "sea monster," but the monster is also armed with a whip and inspired by the devil, and embodies the perverted instincts of the novel's hero. The "mysterious force" of Russia detectable in the song is the "force" of corruption, a "force" equated by the epithet "incomprehensible" (*nepostizhimaya*) with the "force" of nature, which is equally "incomprehensible" to Kifa Mokiyevich,[14] and the circle closes logically when this latter "force" is itself equated with Russia in the corrupted animate form of the destructive Mokiy Kifovich.

Other examples of the same irony are encountered in the well-known section of the "preface" to the biography in which the narrator suddenly interrupts his remarks on the female reader's predictable reaction to Chichikov and looks ahead to the later development of the "epic":

> . . . perhaps in this very tale different chords will be heard which hitherto have not been struck; perhaps the incalculable riches of the Russian spirit will manifest themselves, and a man will pass by endowed with divine

valor, or a marvelous Russian girl of a kind which cannot be found anywhere else in the world with all the wondrous beauty of the feminine soul, full of generous aspirations and selflessness. And compared with them all the virtuous people of other races will seem dead, just as a book is dead compared with the living word! And Russian impulses will stir . . . and men will see how deeply that which has merely skimmed over the nature of other peoples has sunk into the Slavonic nature [*gluboko zaronilos' v slavyanskuyu prirodu*]. (223)

Although the passage seems to offer a perfectly genuine foretaste of projected developments in volumes two and three, it is as firmly anchored to its context as every other "digression" in the novel, for Gogol, as we have seen, does not wait until volumes two and three to tell us what *has* "sunk deeply into the Slavonic nature"; six pages later the narrator announces: ". . . there are still many relics of paganism in the Slavonic nature [*v slavyanskoy prirode*]" (229), and less than two pages elaspe before Chichikov, Gogol's all-embracing symbol of the "Slavonic nature," takes leave of his "pagan" father, whose "words and instructions had sunk deeply into his soul [*zaronilis' gluboko yemu v dushu*]" (225). Again the lexical echoes have the effect of qualifying the reference to Russia's potentialities with allusions to her present malaise, to the subservience of the Russian soul to the "pagan force" of nature, and when Gogol ends the passage with the narrator's question: "but why speak of what lies ahead?" (223), he could well be referring not only to volumes two and three, but equally to the evidence of this subservience provided by the biography and also, perhaps, to the portrait of Mokiy Kifovich which so graphically displays the "ursine" symptoms of the malaise. Is it coincidental that the narrator "strikes" again at this point the "chord" of belligerent chauvinism so redolent of chapter five? Do we not detect here Sobakevich's pervasive "presence"? And is it not fitting that Gogol should evoke this "presence" in the "preface" to the biography of his hero in which the same "presence," as our summary has shown, is almost palpable? Just as the long line of Chichikov's "fathers" are cast in the image of Sobakevich, so the fatherland of them all evinces the same unmistakable bearlike features. And appropriately, when hero and country finally merge in the image of the speeding troika, the violent chauvinism of the "bear" is evoked once more. The novel ends with a picture of the troika forging its path into the future with the same ruthlessness as that displayed by the violent courier:

> . . . the air thunders, it is torn into shreds and becomes wind; everything that exists on earth flies past, and, looking askance [kosyas'], other nations and states step aside and make way for her. (247)

Even the optimistic prophecies, therefor, about Russia's future are not allowed to obscure the image of Russia created by the allegory. They do not "deny," as Erlich has claimed, the novel's "subject."[15] The troika is still the kind of carriage "in which bachelors ride," and in light of the allusions that have been noted it does not seem coincidental that its construction, as described in the penultimate paragraph of the novel, strongly calls to mind the creation of Sobakevich by the "diabolical" or "pagan force" of nature. It "is not clamped together," we read, "with an iron screw," but has rather been "quickly fitted up and assembled in a rough-and-ready manner with only an axe and a chisel by a smart Yaroslav peasant" (246–247).[16] It is a troika, the narrator affirms, that "could only have been born among a lively [boykogo] people" (246), i.e. a people characterized by one of the most distinctive attributes of the destructive "hunter." Just as other nations will "look askance" at this people as it hurtles on its violent course, so the reader, he claims, will "look askance [glyadet' koso]" at his hero "if he is made the hero of a drama or epic poem" (242). It is "still a mystery," he adds, "why this figure has appeared in the epic poem which is now being presented to the world" (242), thereby implying that neither the hero nor the country he personifies is yet fit for this role.

The resolution of the mystery, however, is clearly predicted. As the conversation between the two peasants on the opening page of the novel preannounces, the troika and its passenger are not foredoomed to reach Kazan', a name derived from the noun *kazan,* "cauldron," doubtless alluding to the infernal flames. The passions, observes the narrator, that feed like a "terrible worm"[17] on the "vital sap" of man are not part of his essential being (242); they are merely accretions born of the "paternal" influence or, in the narrator's phrase, "directed by the higher will" (242) to which man, as the hero's biography illustrates, is subject from birth. The shell that encloses the soul, Gogol implies, must not be confused with the soul itself, just as the gray of the dapple-gray and the brown of Sobakevich's thrush must not be confused with the speckles of white. Even in the "cold existence" of Chichikov, we are assured, "there is that which will later make man fall on his knees in the dust before the wisdom of the heavens" (242). Like the soul of Sobakevich, the sould of Chichikov lies "somewhere beyond the mountains," but the biography bears witness to certain innate powers in him which offer hope that the "road" will ultimately lead him to that distant destination. Although the "strong words" of Chichikov are still needed to rouse Selifan from his torpor, the gathering momentum of the troika alludes not only to the negative attributes of the hero and his country already noted, but also to the strength of character and immense vitality that augur the possibility of their redemption. Hence the narrator's reference to it, as it flies along "inspired by God" (247), as "a birdlike troika" (246). To the very end the ambivalence remains, but the intended issue cannot be doubted.

Conclusion

The main object of this study has been to show that although the first volume of *Dead Souls,* as a moral allegory, is of unequivocally serious and didactic intent, it is above all else a work of art, in which a vision of moral decline is translated into an autonomous, coherent fictional reality governed by its own unique system of laws and relationships. Our principal tasks have been to determine the nature of these laws and relationships, to interpret their meaning, and to consider the structure of the novel in light of the conclusions. It simply remains for the reader to decide whether the conclusions have been convincingly substantiated.

Briefly summarized, the view of the novel offered in the study is that it is an allegory of the perversion of the "Russian soul" and a prediction of its eventual rebirth—an allegory that hinges on the portrayal of spiritual perversion as a divergence from the symbolic ideal of "pure femininity." Distinguishing between five main types of perversion, Gogol first introduces them individually in chapters two through six, associating each with a specific range of psychological attributes conveyed by recurrent symbolic motifs; then, as in the introductory opening chapter, he integrates the symbolic indicators of the various types in chapters seven through ten in his portrayal of the town and its inhabitants. At the same time indicators of all five types are also woven into the portrait of Chichikov, whose meetings with the landowners and then with the dignitaries and their ladies may accordingly be viewed as a journey through a hall of mirrors in which he is unwittingly confronted with manifestations of his own corruption. Twice, however, the journey also confronts him with evidence of an unconscious yearning for

purity, which at once insures his downfall in the kingdom of
the devil and portends his rebirth in the kingdom of God. Such
is the fate predicted for the "Russian soul" by the allegorical
journey of Gogol's "villainous" hero.

Of course, not every important question relating to the
novel's meaning and structure is treated in the study, nor is any
attempt made to consider the connections between volume one
and the four surviving chapters of volume two. But this does
not mean that the conclusions herein are irrelevant to this
question. A searching examination of these chapters has inevitably been precluded by the approach to the novel that has been
adopted, for a study of coherence must obviously concern itself
only with that which is complete, and we have seen that the
first volume is just as complete and self-sufficient in aesthetic
terms as the individual *cantiche* of Dante's "comedy." Even so,
it is possible to deduce from the four extant chapters that Gogol
intended to make the connections between the three volumes
of his "epic" much closer than those that bind the three *cantiche*
and that the story of Chichikov was not to be the sole unifying
element, for they confirm beyond doubt that the principal
elements of the allegory in volume one were to be retained. In
volume two, for example, we encounter once more the motifs
of sweetness and sugar,[1] boots (29, 79) and birds (73, 78, 87),[2]
the "military motif" (22, 26), and the imagery of "natural
produce," especially turnips (20, 32), and God and the devil
continue to intervene in the usual manner (20–21). Moreover,
the reference to Tentetnikov as "a man who was still un-
married" (9), his relationship with Ulin'ka, and the abusive
exchanges between his domestic serf Grigoriy and his housekeeper Perfil'yevna (10) suggest that the symbolic theme of the
relationship between the sexes was again to play a major role.
Still more revealing, however, are the links between the main
character-portraits in the two volumes. The affinities, of
course, between Manilov and the feckless Tentetnikov are
immediately apparent, but only an awareness of the pivotal
role of symbolic motifs in volume one enables us to posit a
similar relationship, for example, between Sobakevich and
Kostanzhoglo, whose name and "swarthy complexion," al-

legedly reflecting his "passionate southern origin" (61), are merely the most obvious indications that he embodies the Greek virtues so highly esteemed by the "bear." Like Sobakevich, he rules his vast territories with the authority of an autocrat, even erecting a skylight on top of his house for surveillance, which is merely a more sophisticated version of Sobakevich's "dark store-room," while at dinner he is wont to unburden himself of "ursine" tirades, interspersing laments on the degeneration of the "Russian character" with contemptuous jibes at the French (67–68). "One fool sits on another and drives him on with another fool," he comments on political economists (69), thus repeating almost verbatim the celebrated comment of Sobakevich on the officials of the town of N., merely substituting the word "fool" (*durak*) for Sobakevich's "scoundrel" (*moshennik*).

Likewise are links forged between the two Platonov brothers and Nozdryov. The most striking signals of the relationship are the constant canine companions of the brothers, Yarb (51) and the "English hound with long thin legs" (90); Platon's reluctance to tie himself to any settled mode of existence; the pipe with an amber mouthpiece that he smokes after dinner at Kostanzhoglo's (74); and Vasiliy's impressive array of kvasses (92), which recalls the "hunter's" array of wines. The description of Khlobuyev and his estate is similarly peppered with allusions to Plyushkin, e.g. his disheveled appearance (79); the motif of "old age" (80); the reference to the "ramshackle, unfenced cottages" on the estate (79); the high mortality-rate of his serfs, many of whom have preferred to flee (85); and the lexical signal "gaps" (*prorekhi*), which is inserted into one of his interior monologues (87). Finally, the reference to the four hundred canaries of Khlobuyev's aunt Khanasarova (87) suggests that Gogol may have intended to relate her in a similar way to Korobochka.

In volume two, therefore, not only Chichikov, whose most familiar idiosyncrasies are still evident, but also the other principal characters of volume one continue to make their presence felt. It is true, of course, that in this new fictional setting, which

Gogol evidently conceived as an intermediary stage or Purgatory between the Inferno of volume one and the Paradise of volume three, they not only reappear with different names, but also display significant differences of character and make a much more favorable impression on the reader. But the important point is the indication in seemingly insignificant details that the principle of direct continuity was to form the basis of the triptych. Considered in relation to volume one, the surviving chapters of volume two merely strengthen the contention of Andrey Belyy: "To analyze the plot of *Dead Souls* means to ignore the fiction of the fable and to grasp the small details which have absorbed both the fable and the plot. . . . There is no plot in *Dead Souls* apart from the details; it must be squeezed from them."[3] It is hoped that this study has served to demonstrate the truth of these words.

Notes

PREFACE

1. N. V. Gogol', *Polnoye sobraniye sochineniy* (Moscow, 1937–1952).

INTRODUCTION

1. From a letter of Gogol to Zhukovsky of 10 January 1848 (N.S.) (*PSS,* vol. xiv, p. 37).

2. Vladimir Nabokov, *Nikolai Gogol* (New York, 1961), p. 149.

3. Erlich, *Gogol* (New Haven and London, 1969), p. 136.

4. *PSS,* vol. viii, pp. 440–441.

5. Cf. his remark in a letter of 28 February 1843 to the critic Shevyryov: ". . . those who rise up against me have read my book only once. . . . See how proudly and contemptuously they look upon my characters. It took a long time to write the book, and they should take the trouble to give it a long and careful scrutiny" (*PSS,* vol. xii, p. 144).

6. Belyy, *Masterstvo Gogolya* (Moscow, 1934), hereafter *Masterstvo.*

7. Proffer, *The Simile and Gogol's "Dead Souls"* (The Hague and Paris, 1967), hereafter *Simile.*

8. Belyy, *Masterstvo,* p. 94.

9. Proffer, *Simile,* p. 91.

10. *Ibid.,* p. 88.

11. Erlich, *Gogol,* p. 138.

12. *PSS,* vol. viii, p. 447.

13. Cf., for example, his letter of 15 May 1836 to Pogodin (*PSS,* vol. xi, p. 45).

14. *PSS,* vol. viii, p. 442.

15. Letter to Pushkin of 7 October 1835 (*PSS,* vol. x, p. 375).

16. Cf. Nabokov, *Nikolai Gogol,* p. 44.

17. Nabokov is alluding to Chekhov's famous remark that if in the first act of a play a shotgun hangs on the wall, it must go off in the last act.

18. Richard Freeborn, *The Rise of the Russian Novel* (Cambridge, 1973), p. 104, hereafter *Russian Novel.*

CHAPTER 1

1. *PSS,* vol. viii, p. 288.

2. "Sobakevich," we read, "... rarely spoke favorably of anyone ..." (18).

3. Cf. V. G. Belinsky, *Polnoye sobraniye sochineniy,* 13 vols. (Moscow, 1953–1959), vi, p. 222.

4. These "strong words" of Chichikov make it difficult to agree that in this chapter "he is no longer a chameleon" and that "his style and manner are now his own" (Freeborn, *Russian Novel,* p. 108).

5. It may be noted that in earlier drafts of the chapter the connection between Sobakevich and Chichikov's display of Russian verbal resourcefulness was further reinforced by the hero's use, in reference to Nozdryov, of the term "brigand [*razboynik*]" (739)—the word that makes so strong an impression on him later in the chapter when Sobakevich "sticks" it onto the governor (97).

6. "... going up to the table where the snacks lay, the host and his guest quaffed a glass of vodka each and sampled the snacks as they are sampled throughout the length and breadth of Russia in both towns and villages ..." (97).

7. "For some reason Chichikov began very remotely. He touched upon the whole Russian state in general, referred with effusive praise to its huge expanse, and remarked that even the

ancient Roman empire itself was not so large and that foreigners were justly astonished . . ." (100).

8. Cf. the repetition of the "canine motif" in the portrait of
Korobochka (54).

9. Proffer, *Simile,* p. 95.

10. The name originally devised for Yeremey Sorokoplyokhin was Minay Protrukhin (750). While the surname
suggests "rottenness," the Christian name, a diminutive of
Mikhail, carries the same force as the name Mikheyev. The
change was evidently prompted by a wish to place greater
stress on the violence with which Sobakevich imposes his
authority.

11. Equally ironic is Chichikov's imaginative reconstruction
of the life of Maksim Telyatnikov in chapter seven, in which
the emphasis is placed on his sufferings not at the hands of
Sobakevich, but at those of the taskmasters to whom
Sobakevich himself would readily have apportioned the
guilt—his German employers and commerical competitors in
Moscow (137).

12. Proffer, *Simile,* p. 102.

13. Gogol does not make it explicitly clear that the villagers
who try to separate the carriages are serfs of Sobakevich, just as
he refrains from identifying the location of the collision. In
both cases the information is conveyed obliquely.

14. Cf. the similarities between the portrait of Uncle Minyay
and that of the red-faced shopkeeper in chapter one. Uncle
Minyay is described as "a broad-shouldered peasant with a
beard as black as coal and a belly that resembled the kind of
gigantic samovar in which spiced honey drinks are brewed for
the whole frozen market-place . . ." (91). In chapter one we
read: "In the corner shop, or rather in its window, a seller of
spiced honey drinks was ensconced with a red copper samovar
and a face as red as the samovar, so that from a distance one
might think that there were two samovars standing in the
window, if it were not for the fact that one of them had a
jet-black beard" (8). Since Uncle Minyay, as stated, is simply
an extension of Sobakevich's personality, the portrait of the

strikingly similar shopkeeper may be regarded as an indication of the "Sobakevichism" that forms part of the composite "personality" of the town. It may be compared in this respect to the label "scoundrel [*moshennik*]" which the waiter in chapter one, responding to Chichikov's inquiries, "sticks" on the proprietor of the hotel (10).

15. Cf. M. N. Chernyshevsky, *Ocherki gogolevskogo perioda russkoy literatury* (St. Petersburg, 1892), p. 144.

16. Proffer, *Simile,* p. 99.

17. In earlier drafts St. Petersburg was explicitly identified; Bobelina was described as being "of such gigantic size and height that all those gentlemen who walk down the Nevsky Prospect in narrow frock coats and with walking sticks would seemingly have been incapable of coping with her finger" (744).

18. In reference to this contradiction cf. A. Yefimenko, "Natsional'naya dvoystvennost' v tvorchestve Gogolya," *Vestnik Yevropy,* 1902, no. 7, pp. 243–244.

19. Cf. an earlier version of this sentence: "She entered in an unusually grave and dignified manner and held her head completely erect, as though afraid of lowering it" (744).

20. The similarity to a portrait was specifically indicated in an earlier version of the sentence: "Sitting down on the divan, she very cleverly draped her large merino shawl with its multicolored hem about her in the manner depicted in portraits, and sat the whole time without moving an eye, an eyebrow or her nose" (745).

21. Cf., for example, F. F. Seeley, "Gogol's *Dead Souls,*" *Forum for Modern Language Studies,* 1968, no. 1, p. 37.

22. Cf. the famous passage: "It is well known that there are many faces in the world over the finish of which nature has taken few pains, having used no small tools, such as files, gimlets, etc., and having simply hacked away straight from the shoulder: one stroke of the axe, and there's the nose; another stroke, and there are the lips; with a large drill she gouged out the eyes, and without scraping it smooth she sent it forth into the world, saying: 'It lives!' " (94–95).

23. Proffer, *Simile,* p. 98.

24. A possible additional implication of this simile is considered in the analysis of chapter nine.

25. V. Setchkarev, *Gogol. His Life and Works* (New York, 1965), p. 197, hereafter *Gogol Life.*

26. Nabokov, *Nikolai Gogol,* p. 97.

27. Apparently forgetting the thirty-six pounds (*tselyy pud*) that Chichikov contrives to put on during the meal (100), Smirnova-Chikina ascribes the substitution simply to the host's thrift (Ye. S. Smirnova-Chikina, *Poema N. V. Gogolya "Myortvyye dushi." Literaturnyy kommentariy* (Moscow, 1964), p. 85), hereafter *Poema.*

28. Cf., for example, N. M. Kolb-Seletski, "Gastronomy, Gogol, and His Fiction," *The Slavic Review,* 1970, no. 1, p. 50.

29. Cf. Proffer, *Simile,* pp. 85–86.

30. *Ibid.,* p. 85.

31. *Ibid.*

32. *Ibid.*

33. The meaning of the image of the fly both in the simile and in the novel as a whole is considered in chapter four.

34. Cf. the abruptness with which he first greets Chichikov: "When he saw his guest, he said curtly: 'Please!' and led him into the inner rooms" (94). In an earlier draft the sentence read: "When he saw his guest, Sobakevich did not bother with questions about his health but merely said: 'Please!' " (743).

35. Sobakevich replies: "I have no need to know anything about your relationships. I do not interfere in family matters. That's your business" (104).

36. Nikolai Gogol, *Dead Souls,* translated with an introduction by David Magarshack, 7th edn. (London, 1972), p. 108.

37. The final clause means literally "as the soul demands."

38. Cf. Virgil, *Aeneid,* I, 177.

39. *Dead Souls,* Magarshack, p. 111.

40. *Ibid.,* p. 113.

41. Cf. Chichikov's reference to Nozdryov in the opening paragraph of the chapter: "Эк какую баню задал!" (89), which means literally: "Oh, what a bath he gave me!"

42. It is true that in chapter one Chichikov is described as "neither too fat nor too thin" (7), but Gogol never allows us to forget that his hero is a gentleman of considerable corpulence. Cf., for example, the description of him boarding his carriage in chapter three: ". . . Chichikov placed his foot on the step, and tilting the carriage to the right, for he was rather heavy, he finally settled himself . . ." (59). It should be remarked, however, that the narrator's comments on fat men in chapter one are also explicitly related to those who, "like Chichikov, were not too fat and yet not thin" (14).

43. Proffer, *Simile,* p. 93.

44. Setchkarev, *Gogol,* p. 190.

45. *PSS,* vol. VIII, p. 427.

46. *Ibid.,* vol. V, p. 142.

CHAPTER 2

1. Freeborn, *Russian Novel,* p. 105.

2. Cf. the more detailed earlier version of this remark: "If he discovered that a friend of his was getting married, he would talk so much nonsense to the bride's relatives on the day before the wedding about the bridegroom's weaknesses and about various imaginary affairs that they would slam the door in the face of the astonished suitor, who would be left without any idea of the reason for such a sudden change" (729).

3. Proffer, *Simile,* p. 95.

4. Cf., for example, Setchkarev, *Gogol Life,* p. 195.

5. Cf. the narrator's remark: "He was incapable of staying at home for more than a day" (70).

6. Cf. the reference to his disruptions of weddings (71).

7. Freeborn, *Russian Novel,* p. 104.

8. Erlich, *Gogol,* p. 122, and Nabokov, *Nikolai Gogol,* p. 72.

9. Gogol apparently liked to use the phrase in normal discourse. Cf. his remark in a letter of 10 January 1840 to M. A. Maksimovich: "Pogodin has told a lie [*slil pulyu*] in informing you that I have written a great deal" (*PSS,* vol. XI, p. 249).

10. V. Dal', *Tolkovyy slovar' zhivogo velikorusskogo yazyka,* 4 vols. (Moscow, 1956), VI, p. 611.

11. Cf. the comparison of Nozdryov to "a desperate lieutenant" as he assaults the "fortress" of Chichikov in the famous Homeric simile at the end of the chapter (86).

12. Initially Nozdryov was given a roan (*chalaya*) instead of a chestnut (*kauraya*) (731), while his dapple-grey was simply grey (*seraya*) (713 and 723).

13. The Russification of this latter phrase (*subditel'noy syuper-flyu*) should presumably be regarded as yet another indication of Nozdryov's inexhaustible transformative powers.

14. Belyy, *Masterstvo,* p. 82.

CHAPTER 3

1. Belyy, *Masterstvo,* p. 100.

2. *Ibid.,* p. 96.

3. Cf. the similar implications of the proverb that Gogol employs to denote his lack of character: ". . . he was neither Bogdan in the town nor Selifan in the village" (24).

4. The adverb *zamanchivo,* derived from *manit',* was a substitution for the earlier *priyatno* ("pleasantly") (705).

5. Italics mine—J.B.W.

6. Cf. the description of Chichikov's preparations for the journey: ". . . he washed himself and rubbed himself down from head to foot with a wet sponge, which he did only on Sundays, and that day happened to be Sunday . . ." (21).

7. Cf. Manilov's request as Chichikov prepares to leave: "Do stay, Pavel Ivanovich! . . . Just look at those clouds!" (38).

8. Cf. Gogol's use of the same image of the "pecked cock" in an early draft of chapter eleven to denote another instance of defeated "masculinity"—the failure of Chichikov and his accomplice in a customs swindle: "Their colleagues, the other customs officials, helped to relieve them on all sides of their various burdens, so that they fled from the court looking like those cocks which, goaded on by romantic passion, intended to

visit other henhouses, but were assailed by the beaks of other cocks which were so powerful that they escaped with only their feathers and, accompanied by the laughter of the hens, made off by the shortest possible route" (870).

9. Cf., for example, the "sweetening" of the "Temple of Solitary Meditation" with a "flat, green dome" and "light blue wooden columns" (22).

10. Cf. Proffer, *Simile,* pp. 105–106.

11. Gogol's original choices were Menelaus and Alcibiades (707, 712).

CHAPTER 4

1. Cf. the author's ironic reference to her, when Chichikov first meets her, as "one of those dear old ladies (*matushek*), small landowners, who complain about bad harvests" (45).

2. Cf. the description of her as "one of those dear old ladies, small landowners, who . . . hold their heads on one side" (45).

3. The significance of the "blue paper" is revealed by the reference in chapter six to the "blue sugar paper" Plyushkin sticks on one of his windows (112).

4. Cf. the name "Korobkin" given to one of the retired officials in *The Inspector General (Revizor).*

5. This exclamation was deleted by the censor and consequently omitted from the first edition of the novel of 1842 (714).

6. Belyy, *Masterstvo,* p. 100.

7. A. de Jonge, "Gogol'," in J. Fennell (ed.), *Nineteenth-Century Russian Literature* (London, 1973), p. 126, hereafter *Russian Literature.*

8. The adjective is formed from the noun *koleso* ("wheel").

9. Proffer, *Simile,* p. 133.

10. The absence of the "human" Petrushka and the play with the word "assessor" would seem to invalidate conclusively Belyy's unexplained suggestion that Selifan be identified with

the bay and Petrushka with the light chestnut (Belyy, *Masterstvo*, p. 100).

11. Smirnova-Chikina's suggestion that her fortune-telling can be attributed to a sense of remorse or guilt (Smirnova-Chikina, *Poema*, p. 68) is irreconcilable with the rest of her portrait.

CHAPTER 5

1. D. Tamarchenko, " 'Myortvyye dushi' N. V. Gogolya," *Russkaya literatura*, 1959, no. 2, pp. 18–19.

2. Freeborn, *Russian Novel*, p. 91.

3. *PSS*, vol. VIII, p. 293.

4. Cf. P. V. Annenkov, *Literaturnyye vospominaniya* (Moscow, 1960), p. 87.

5. The adjectives *zhivopisnyy* and *kartinyy* are essentially synonymous and would normally both be rendered as "picturesque."

6. Cf., for example, Smirnova-Chikina, *Poema*, p. 93.

7. Cf. the image of the "broken pot" in chapter three (*supra*, pp. 80–81).

8. For example: ". . . as the carriage changed direction, first to the right and then to the left . . ." (112).

9. Another "tendril" may perhaps be discerned in the article tied around Plyushkin's neck, which is reminiscent of Korobochka's "piece of flannel." Describing it, the narrator comments: ". . . it was impossible to determine whether it was a stocking, a garter, or an abdominal band, but it was certainly not a tie" (116).

10. Cf. the repetition of the irony later in Plyushkin's remark that he is not "a great lover of tea" now that "the price of sugar has gone up cruelly" (129).

11. Cf. the "very long" inn in chapter one (8).

12. Cf. Proffer, *Simile*, pp. 110–111.

13. Cf. the reference to the "blackened chandelier" of the inn in chapter one (9).

14. Cf. the variation of the device in the chapter's second paragraph, in which a similar comment on Plyushkin is masked as a comment by the narrator on his own old age.

15. Cf. his remark about life on the estate at this time: "Everything was done in a brisk [literally "living" (*zhivo*)] manner . . ." (118).

16. Cf. the statement that while his wife was alive, "all the windows in the house were open" (118).

17. Cf. once more the death of Nozdryov's wife.

18. Cf. Gogol's statement in the second of the two letters to the poet Yazykov that he published under the title *Subjects for a Lyric Poet at the Present Time (Predmety dlya liricheskogo poeta v nyneshneye vremya)* (1844) that compared to old age "iron is merciful" (*PSS,* vol. VIII, p. 280).

19. Cf. the contrast between these "cupolas" of foliage and the "sparse, fine-leaved tops" (22) of the trees in Manilov's garden.

20. Cf. the "asymmetrical" house of Sobakevich (94).

21. Cf. the blackened body of Korobochka's blacksmith.

22. Cf. Chichikov's muted comment on Korobochka in chapter three: "Good heavens, what a blockhead she is [*dubinnogolovaya kakaya*]!" (52).

23. The phrase "Moscow timber market" was a later substitution for "the extensive part of Moscow from Plyushchikha to the Smolensk market" (763). Here the name of the suburb Plyushchikha, in which the affricate "shch" of the noun *plyushch* ("ivy") is retained, was conceivably inserted as an allusion to the source of the name "Plyushkin," in which the affricate is replaced by a fricative. Again, however, Gogol evidently decided that he was being too helpful.

24. Cf. the reference to Plyushkin's young daughters as "both fair [*belokuryye*] and as fresh as roses" (118).

25. It may be noted that the use of the parallel verb-forms *raskhodilis'* and *razoydutsya* was a later addition. Instead of

waiting "for the orchards . . . to part", in earlier versions the narrator waited simply for the house "to emerge (*vyglyanet*)" or "to appear" (*predstanet*) (757).

26. Cf. the upper story of the inn in the town of N., which is described in chapter one as "painted in the everlasting shade of yellow" (8) and also the "yellow paint" of the town's stone houses (11).

27. Cf. the "marble column" to which the birch tree in the garden is compared.

28. Cf. the use of the adjective "menacing" (*grozna*) in relation to old age (127).

29. Cf. the "natural" sunlight, to which the white, transparent egg is exposed by the housekeeper with the dark-skinned hands in the simile that characterizes the face of the governor's daughter. In an earlier draft of the passage the "unnatural" light that illuminates the spendthrift's garden was significantly linked with the motif of youth: "A crowd of people strolling can be glimpsed rejoicing with the joy of a child on seeing that the dark night has been so magically banished . . ." (765).

30. The verb "refreshed" (*osvezhal*) in this description was a later substitution for "enlivened" (*ozhivlyal*) (759). Perhaps Gogol concluded that with the earlier verb he was going too far.

31. The allusion is presumably to Plyushkin's failure to shave at all—to the "wire currycomb" on his jutting chin.

32. Significantly, his prey in both cases is the female of the species (*tetyorek ili utok*).

33. Instead of the "infantry officer," an earlier version of the opening paragraph contained another conspicuous lexical component of the "military motif"—"shop-assistants playing checkers [*shashki*]" (756).

34. The Russian means literally "burning life right through [*prozhigayushchiy naskvoz' zhizn'*]."

35. The Russian noun *pero* means both "quill" or "pen" and "feather."

36. The effect of this play with homonyms, of course, is to equate the whole "manor" with a "giant lock" (cf. Proffer, *Simile,* p. 110).

37. Cf. Plyushkin's words to Mavra: "Stop! You'll get hold of a tallow candle, and tallow is a thing that melts. It will burn up and there'll be nothing left of it, nothing but loss. Just bring me a thin splinter of wood" (127).

CHAPTER 6

1. Cf. Smirnova-Chikina, *Poema,* p. 273.

2. See the comparison to an eagle of Ivan Petrovich (in chapter three) in his capacity as head of department.

3. Cf. Chichikov's remark to the governor in chapter one that "entering his province was like entering paradise" (13).

4. Perhaps a link is intended between the verb "to creak" here—*skrypela*—and the "violin" (*skripka*) in the reference to Manilov.

5. The *skomorokh* was a popular entertainer, a wandering minstrel-cum-clown.

6. The allusion here is probably to Chichikov's meeting with the governor's daughter in chapter eight rather than to the meeting in chapter five.

7. Cf. the motif of "Promethean" fire in chapters three and six.

8. Cf. the analogy of the "slaves" in the government offices to "industrious bees scattered over their honeycombs" (145) and also the accompanying allusion to the image of the bird in the reference to the "hen's feather" on the back of the "new Virgil" who leads Chichikov and Manilov to the president's office (144).

9. On the meaning of the term *zertsalo,* cf. *supra,* p. 14.

10. Erlich, *Gogol,* p. 126. Cf. A. de Jonge, "Gogol'," in Fennell, *Russian Literature,* p. 123.

11. Appropriately in this "military" context Gogol's term for "lover" is *okhotnik* ("hunter").

12. Cf. the reference to the repacking of the boot trees at the end of chapter ten (215).

13. The fate of Maksim (and Popov) is implicitly contrasted in the same way with the idyllic existence on his fraudulently seized estate of the landowner on whom an official report is being copied by the clerk in the "light-gray jacket" as Chichikov and Manilov enter the government offices (141).

14. Note that when the chief of police invites his guests to examine the sturgeon, he refers to it as "this product of nature" (150)—a phrase that recalls the description in chapter five of nature's creation of Sobakevich, and also refers literally to Sobakevich himself, for by this time the sturgeon is no longer on the table, but in his stomach. It is also noteworthy that the sturgeon's weight is given as "nine poods" (149), exactly the same as the loads hooked on their backs by the Volga stevedores, among whom Chichikov's imagination places Abakum Fyrov (139). It seems to be implied that these loads are the food which ultimately finds its way to shops in the town of N. and thence to the table of the chief of police.

15. It may be recalled in this connection that the "slaves" in the government offices are threatened by the "majestic voice" with the removal not only of their boots but also of their food (142).

16. Cf. the desciption of the two servants' departure from the tavern: ". . . they came out arm-in-arm, maintaining complete silence, showing great attention to one another and warning each other about every corner" (153).

17. "The friends ran rather than walked up the stairs, because Chichikov, trying to avoid Manilov's attempts to support him by the arm, quickened his pace, while Manilov, for his part, shot ahead in an attempt to prevent Chichikov from tiring, and as a result they were both panting hard when they entered the dark corridor" (141). Cf. the ironically contrasting manner in which the inebriated Petrushka and Selifan ascend the stairs of the inn: "Arm-in-arm, without letting go of each other, they spent a whole quarter of an hour climbing the stairs, but at last they mastered them and reached the top" (153).

18. Cf. the bizarre positions that the servants take up on Petrushka's bed after their return from the tavern (153).

19. Cf., for example, V. G. Belinsky, *Sobraniye sochineniy v tryokh tomakh*, II (Moscow, 1948), p. 337; Smirnova-Chikina, *Poema*, p. 110; Setchkarev, *Gogol Life*, pp. 202–203.

20. Quoted from Smirnova-Chikina, *Poema*, p. 121.

21. *Ibid.*

CHAPTER 7

1. The suspicion that the reference to Chichikov's insomnia alludes to Korobochka is strengthened on the following page, where we see that she has not been able to sleep for three nights because of her worries that Chichikov may have duped her (177).

2. It is referred to simply as "the house of the archpriest's wife" (177). That the archpriest is Father Kiril is confirmed in chapter nine (183).

3. In the Russian three iambic trimeters are followed by an anapaestic trimeter, which is presumably a final comment on the writer's "refinement".

4. *Key to the Mysteries of Nature (Schlüssel zu den Hieroglyphen der Natur)* is really the subtitle of Eckartshausen's *Zahlenlehre der Natur, oder die Natur zählt und spricht* (1794). A possible explanation of Gogol's preference for the subtitle is suggested later.

5. The reference is to the educational system of the English Quaker educator Joseph Lancaster (1778–1838).

6. Cf. Manilov's complete dependence on his estate manager for knowledge of what is happening on his estate.

7. "The pine forest sleeps, the vale slumbers" (156).

8. Cf. his preparation for the governor's party in chapter one (13).

9. Cf. his "bowing and scraping" and the *entrechat* he performs while preparing himself for the ball (161–162)—an "antic" which is foreshadowed by the entrechat of the two billiard

players in the shop-sign in chapter one (11). The motif is also apparent in the following description of the dancers at the ball: "And already on one side four couples were performing a mazurka; their heels were hammering the floor, and a staff-captain in the army was working with body and soul, arms and legs, as he executed such steps as no one had even dreamed of executing" (168). Finally, we might note the following remarks from Chichikov's attack on balls: ". . . a grown man, an adult, will suddenly leap out, all in black, with well-plucked whiskers and his waist pulled tight, just like a little devil, and off he goes working away with his legs. Some dancers, while standing with their partners, will even discuss an important matter with someone else, and at the same time they will be moving their legs unsteadily, like a kid, to the right and the left . . ." (174–175).

10. The name is seemingly derived from the verb *chikhnut'* ("to sneeze"). Cf. the comment on him in chapter one: ". . . he blew his nose extemely loudly. No one knows how he did it, but his nose sounded like a trumpet" (10).

11. Cf. his high spirits during the journey from Plyushkin's estate to the town: "He was unusually cheerful the whole way; he whistled and, putting his fist to his mouth, made noises with his lips as if he were playing a trumpet . . ." (130).

12. Proffer, *Simile*, pp. 127–129.

CHAPTER 8

1. The reference, as an early version of the sentence confirms (807), is to the "angry" accusations of some contemporaries that he had based the characters of his play *The Inspector General (Revizor)* on living prototypes.

2. Cf. the later comment on the two ladies: ". . . during their conversation there arose in them spontaneously a small desire to taunt [literally "to prick" (*kol'nut'*)] one another" (187).

3. Cf. the later description of Sof'ya Ivanovna as she waits

impatiently for Anna Grigor'yevna to reveal Chichikov's "true" objective: ". . . although she was rather heavily built, she suddenly became thinner and began to resemble a light piece of down which a puff of wind might carry away into the air" (184).

4. Cf. the later exposure of the "forgery"—the reference to their "small desire" to taunt one another (187).

5. Initially, it seems, Gogol had no intention of treating the epithet "gay" as a "forgery," for in earlier drafts the spots were not brown but lilac (810).

6. Cf. the narrator's remark in the opening paragraph: "Nowadays in Russia people of all ranks and classes are so irritated that everything in a printed book seems to them to refer to someone" (179).

7. Cf. the "masters' " later reflection on the new governor-general's possible reaction to the rumors circulating in the town: ". . . for this reason alone he might fly into a deathly rage [*vskipyatit' ne na zhizn', a na samuyu smert'*]" (193).

8. Cf. the "long figure" of the waiter "in a long cotton frock coat" in chapter one (8).

9. In an earlier draft the "silvery stars" were described as "sharp" and "prickly" (*kolyuchiye*), which suggests a connection with Anna Grigor'yevna's "Nozdryovian" habit of "pricking" people. Perhaps it is implied that Sof'ya Ivanovna is so preoccupied with her "friend's" imminent revelation that even the latter's pinpricks could not divert her attention.

10. Ironically, the "masters" later reject the claim that Chichikov intends to abduct the governor's daughter on the grounds that it "was the kind of thing a hussar and not a civilian would do" (192).

11. Proffer, *Simile*, pp. 87–88.

12. Under its new name, *Syktyvkara*, Ust'sysol'sk is now the capital of the Komi Autonomous Soviet Socialist Republic.

13. Perhaps it is in relation to this allusion that we should consider the reappearance of Petrushka and Selifan at the end of the chapter.

14. Cf., for example, Sobakevich's contention that he had

sold to Chichikov "peasants of the most excellent quality who were alive in every respect" (196).

CHAPTER 9

1. Italics mine. All subsequent statements of this kind quoted in this chapter will be similarly italicized.

2. In the revised version of "The Story of Captain Kopeykin" demanded by the censorship, Gogol was obliged to omit the Tsar completely. The role of the Tsar was performed by the minister and that of the minister by a "head of department (*nachal'nik*)".

3. Cf. Smirnova-Chikina, *Poema*, pp. 153–154.

4. Cf. Gogol's letter of 10 April 1842 to the censor A. V. Nikitenko in *PSS*, vol. xii, p. 55.

5. Cf. the "fine shirts of Dutch linen [*tonkiye gollandskiye rubashki*]" which Chichikov, according to his biography in chapter eleven, took to wearing on surmounting one of the major obstacles to his self-advancement (232), and also the taste for "Dutch linen" (*gollandskogo kholsta*) reflected in Nozdryov's lists of purchases (72).

6. Cf. the motif of "cleanliness."

7. Cf. the manner in which Gogol, having informed us earlier (161) that Chichikov could not speak a word of French, now reminds us of his Gallic tastes by referring to the "volume of *La Duchesse de la Vallière*," which he allegedly reads during his three-day confinement (211).

8. Cf. his quotation of the proverb: "For a friend seven versts is no detour!" (213).

9. In an early draft Gogol prepared the way for the reintroduction of this detail by comparing the hotel tea that Chichikov is drinking at the time of Nozdryov's arrival to tobacco (836). He presumably considered it more fitting that the first reference to it should come from Nozdryov.

10. Cf. Nozdryov's use of this phrase in chapter four of the novel.

11. Cf. the additional allusion to the theme of "false fathers" introduced by Nozdryov's reference to the priest Father Sidor whom he had allegedly coerced into agreeing to officiate at the wedding of Chichikov and the governor's daughter "by promising to inform on him for having married the corn-chandler Mikhaylo to a fellow-godparent" (209).

12. Cf. the "collapse" of Chichikov during his three-day confinement with his cold (". . . he gargled incessantly with milk and figs, which he afterwards ate, and wore tied to his cheek a little pad soaked in camomile and camphor" [211]) and that of Nozdryov during his four-day confinement with his cards (". . . he had even grown thinner and turned green" [208]).

CHAPTER 10

1. Freeborn, *Russian Novel*, p. 113.

2. The identity, of course, is suggested from the outset by the ease with which he adapts himself to his new surroundings in chapter one. Cf. the statement that his arrival in the town "created no stir at all and was accompanied by nothing unusual" (7).

3. Cf. the ironic echo here of the commandment addressed to Chichikov by his father: ". . . carry virtue in your heart" (224).

4. Cf. his "execution" of a fly with his finger "from annoyance" as he waits for the blacksmiths to repair the wheel (218)—a detail that recalls the "execution" of the "beast" by the policeman's nail at the end of chapter eight (cf. *supra*, p. 173).

5. Cf. the "two hot loaves" (218) that the Chichikov who is wont to dream of "carriages, a well constructed house, and good dinners" (228) is content to equip himself with for the journey.

6. It may be noted that in the same version of the novel in which Gogol also introduced for the first time the "lyrical

digressions" of chapter eleven, Abakum Fyrov was added to the list of peasants who inspire Chichikov's dreams.

7. Cf. the narrator's prediction that they will particularly dislike his "plumpness" and "middle age" (223).

8. Cf. the image of Sobakevich's thrush.

9. Cf. the "pockmarked" faces of the "fat men" in chapter one (15).

10. Noting that in an earlier draft the commission is described as "a commission for the construction of a church of God" (561), Smirnova-Chikina conjectures that Gogol may have had in mind here a real-life swindle connected with the construction of the Church of Christ the Savior in Moscow in 1826 (Smirnova-Chikina, *Poema*, pp. 173–174).

11. The verb here for "to go mad" is *perebesit'sya*, which is derived from the noun *bes*, "devil."

12. Cf. Gogol's ironic use of epithets meaning "picturesque" in chapter six (*supra*, pp. 109–110).

13. Cf. Smirnova-Chikina, *Poema*, p. 159.

14. As indicated above, Kifa Mokiyevich's reflections on the birth of the "wild animal" end in the definitive version of the chapter with the exclamation: "Goodness me, truly—er—you can't understand nature, however deep you may go into it!" The corresponding statement in earlier drafts is: "How truly incomprehensible [*nepostizhimo*]!" (853, 876).

15. Erlich, *Gogol*, p. 130.

16. Cf. the description of the "creation" of Sobakevich in chapter five of the novel.

17. Cf. the allusion both to the description of Plyushkin's chandelier (115) and to Chichikov's exclamation after the collapse of the customs swindle: "Why do others prosper, and why must I perish like a worm?" (238). The image of the "worm" is first introduced in chapter one in the narrator's remark that in Chichikov's conversation with the town dignitaries his speech "assumed somewhat bookish turns of phrase—for example, his observation that he was an insignificant worm in this world" (13). Shortly afterward it reappears in the ironic description of the "fat men" playing cards—

in the exclamation "Hearts!" (16), the Russian name for which (*chervi*) is homonymous with the word for "worms."

CONCLUSION

1. Cf. *PSS,* vol. vii, pp. 10, 17, 69, 73. All references to volume two are to this edition and are included hereafter in the text.

2. Cf. the reappearance of the image of the cock in the name Petukh (which means "cock").

3. Belyy, *Masterstvo,* p. 103.

LIBRARY OF CONGRESS CATALOGING
IN PUBLICATION DATA

Woodward, James B.
  Gogol's Dead souls.

  1.   Gogol', Nikolai Vasil'evich, 1809–1852.   Mertvye
dushi.   1. Title.
PG3332.M43W6   891.7'3'3   77-85573
ISBN 0-691-06360-5